Baseball's Western Front

ALSO BY DONALD R. WELLS
AND FROM MCFARLAND

The Federal Reserve System: A History (2004)

*The Race for the Governor's Cup: The Pacific Coast
League Playoffs, 1936–1954* (2000)

Baseball's Western Front

The Pacific Coast League During World War II

Donald R. Wells

McFarland & Company, Inc., Publishers
Jefferson, North Carolina, and London

LIBRARY OF CONGRESS CATALOGUING-IN-PUBLICATION DATA

Wells, Donald R., 1932–
   Baseball's western front : the Pacific Coast League during World War II / Donald R. Wells.
       p.   cm.
   Includes index.

   ISBN 0-7864-1998-9 (softcover : 50# alkaline paper) ∞

   1. Pacific Coast League — History — 20th century.
   2. Baseball — Pacific States — History — 20th century.   I. Title.
GV875.P33W43   2004
796.357'64'0979 — dc22   2004016413

British Library cataloguing data are available

©2004 Donald R. Wells. All rights reserved

No part of this book may be reproduced or transmitted in any form or by any means, electronic or mechanical, including photocopying or recording, or by any information storage and retrieval system, without permission in writing from the publisher.

On the cover: Oakland Oaks player Bill Rigney, Seals Stadium, 1942 *(Oakland Museum of California; photograph by Tommy McDonough; collection of Doug McWilliams*

Manufactured in the United States of America

McFarland & Company, Inc., Publishers
   Box 611, Jefferson, North Carolina 28640
       www.mcfarlandpub.com

To the memory of my two favorite
Los Angeles Angels players of the 1940s,
Ray Prim and Johnny Moore

Table of Contents

Preface	1
Introduction	5
1 — The 1942 Season	9
2 — The 1943 Season	37
3 — The 1944 Season	67
4 — The 1945 Season	129
Appendix A: Records of Individual Players	185
Appendix B: Won-Loss Records of Wartime Pacific Coast League Teams	217
Index	219

PREFACE

My interest in the Pacific Coast League during World War II is from personal memory. I was nine years old when the war started and my two older brothers soon had to leave for the navy, leaving me at home with the radio and the newspapers to keep up on the pennant races. I saw very few games in person with my brothers gone because my father, although a fan, did not like to go because he associated going to games with my mother, who had died in 1935. So I listened to as many of the Los Angeles and Hollywood games as I could on the radio, with Frank Bull doing the broadcasts in 1942 and Fred Haney doing them from 1943 through 1948. I also read the *Los Angeles Times* sports page with Al Wolf writing up the local games. On Sundays, we would also get the *Los Angeles Examiner* and each weekday evening my father would bring home the *Los Angeles Herald Express*, with John B. Old, among others, writing about baseball. I read the box scores each day, especially for my team, the Los Angeles Angels.

After I retired as an economics professor at the University of Memphis, I wrote a book on the Pacific Coast League playoffs, which were controversial because they often lost money. Afterwards, I got interested in the Portland Beavers, a team that finished last four years in a row from 1939 through 1942, but then improved to fourth place in 1943, to second place in 1944 and finally to first in 1945. Intending at first to write only about that team's wartime seasons, I soon concluded that there was too little material for a book, and that by expanding the scope to include all PCL teams from that time, the research I generated might be useful to a greater number of people. The book now attempts to measure the effects of World War II on the PCL and on each of its teams, beginning in 1942 and ending in 1945. This involved getting newspapers from each Pacific Coast League city for that four-year period.

It is arranged by year, the chapters discussing each club, in order of finish that season. Players often had to leave in midseason for military service or to report to their draft board, which could have been in another part of the country. Even if he was turned down for military service, the player might be gone from his club for a month. In 1944 and 1945, some players returned from the service if discharged for medical reasons.

Another wartime feature was the part-time player who had to hold down a job in a war plant to avoid military service. These players usually could play for their team only when it was at home or in a nearby city, unless they took their two-week vacation during the season. Tommy Seats, a San Francisco pitcher, had a war job in Los Angeles and would try to get a flight to where the Seals were playing to pitch for them on Sunday. Sometimes he was bumped off the plane and the team had to get along without him.

The war also caused teams to use very young or very old players. Los Angeles had to obtain a work permit to sign 15-year-old Bill Sarni, a catcher, who returned to high school when the season ended. There were several teams using 17- and 18-year-old pitchers. At the opposite end of the spectrum, there were many players in their early to mid 40s, the oldest being Herman Pillette of Sacramento, who was born in 1895. The Seattle Rainiers, who finished second in 1945, had four pitchers over the age of 40, three of whom were regular starters. In addition, some players had been out of baseball for a year or two and were enticed to return to the game when teams lost players to the service. Lefty O'Doul, manager of San Francisco, was able to convince first baseman Gus Suhr and outfielder Harry Rosenberg to come out of retirement and play for the Seals.

There are limited but immensely useful resources for PCL research. The newspapers I relied on included: the *Seattle Post Intelligence; Portland Oregonian; Sacramento Union; San Francisco Chronicle; Los Angeles Times;* and *The Sporting News.*

Notable among the books used were: *The Pacific Coast League: A Statistical History, 1903–1957* by Dennis Snelling; *The Angels: Los Angeles in the Pacific Coast League, 1919–1957* and *The Hollywood Stars: Baseball in Movieland, 1926–1957,* both by Dick Beverage; *The Seattle Rainiers: The*

Preface

Glory Years, 1938–1942 by Gary Waddingham; *Sacramento Senators and Solons: Baseball in California's Capital, 1886–1976* by John E. Spalding; and the three-volume *Coast League Cyclopedia, 1903–1957* by Carlos Bauer, which was used to compile the individual records of each player in Appendix A.

Photographs were provided through the courtesy of Dick Beverage, Douglas McWilliams and Dave Eskenazi.

INTRODUCTION

The Pacific Coast League had emerged from the Depression of the 1930s in fairly good condition. There were four new ball parks constructed in the 1930s; Seals Stadium in San Francisco in 1931; Lane Field in San Diego in 1936; Sick's Stadium in Seattle in 1938; and Gilmore Field in Hollywood in 1939. Attendance was very good in Seattle but low in Sacramento and somewhat in between in the other cities. At the end of the 1941 season, the owners decided to expand the playing rosters to 25 players for 1942 to give managers more room to maneuver than they had with the reduced rosters, which were an economy move. But after the attack on Pearl Harbor, there was some doubt that baseball would be allowed to operate during the war.

Commissioner Kenesaw Mountan Landis asked President Franklin D. Roosevelt if baseball should continue and the president sent the commissioner a "green light" letter stating that baseball would be good for public morale but that players would receive no special deferments from the military draft. This question came up because President Woodrow Wilson in 1918 issued a "work or fight" order that shut baseball down in the late summer of 1918. But even though baseball was allowed to continue, there was a shortage of players which caused many lower minor league teams to cease operations. The Pacific Coast League owners rescinded their approval to go to 25-man rosters and cut this to 20 players, but no distinction was to be made between veterans and rookies as in the past.

There was alarm and uncertainty on the West Coast about possible

Japanese attacks so it was somewhat surprising that the Coast League teams were allowed to play night ball when the 1942 season began. The Rose Bowl game in January 1942 was shifted from Pasadena to Durham, N.C., the home field of Duke University, and the Rose Parade was cancelled for the duration. Blackouts were declared all up and down the West Coast during the first several months of 1942 and stadium ushers were instructed how to evacuate the fans in the dark if this became necessary. Announcers were not allowed to mention anything about the weather on the radio, but it was obvious why games were called or postponed because of "unplayable conditions." The team announcers were also taken off the air midgame if radio stations had to broadcast alerts to the public. By June, the Los Angeles announcer, Frank Bull, was taken off the air three times for special bulletins.

The military authorities reversed themselves in August 1942 by forbidding night ball in any of the eight Coast League parks. The last night game was on August 20. This restriction lasted all of the 1943 season, but with the war going better, night ball returned with no restrictions in 1944 and the league set a new attendance record, which it did for four straight years through 1947. Because many sportswriters could recall the late 1920s before any night ball was played, many of them predicted the public would get used to day ball during the week as was the case about 15 years earlier, but by the early 1940s, new fans that were used to night ball had emerged and thus attendance suffered during the week.

Another problem was rail travel. The Coast League traditionally played week-long series beginning on Tuesday and ending with a doubleheader on Sunday afternoon. Monday was the normal travel day and before the war, teams could make the trip between Southern California and the Pacific Northwest in time for a Tuesday night game. Occasionally the second game of the Sunday double-header had to be cut short to allow a club to catch a train. But with military trains taking priority, very often during the war years teams could not get to a city in time to start a series until Wednesday, necessitating a double-header sometime during that week. In addition, rail fares were increased and no separate Pullman cars were set aside for teams, so each player had to carry his own bag and find a berth wherever he could. Travel got worse at the very end of the war in July 1945 when the War Department declared that no civilian could use a sleeper on a train trip of less than 450 miles. This meant that all travel within the state of California had to be in coaches, but Pullmans were permitted for trips to Portland and Seattle.

Another annoyance to players was the fact that meal money on road

Introduction

trips was kept at $2 a day. It had been $3 a day until the early 1930s and had yet to be restored. This did not occur until 1945 but, by then, players complained that even $3 was inadequate for the Bay Area.

On a sad note, many Japanese living in the United States, whether citizens of the U.S. or not, were rounded up and sent to relocation centers. Many of them were avid baseball fans and the teams missed their support.

1—The 1942 Season

Final Standings

	W	L	PCT	G.B.	MANAGER
1. Sacramento	105	73	.590	—	Pepper Martin
2. Los Angeles	104	74	.584	1	Jigger Statz
3. Seattle	96	82	.539	9	Bill Skiff
4. San Diego	91	87	.511	14	Cedric Durst
5. San Francisco	88	90	.494	17	Lefty O'Doul
6. Oakland	85	92	.480	19.5	Johnny Vergez
7. Hollywood	75	103	.421	30	Oscar Vitt
8. Portland	67	110	.379	37.5	Frank Brazill

While the war was not going very well for the United States in most of 1942, the full impact of wartime restrictions had not yet been felt by the general public. Railroads were still advertising for vacation travel, and most ballplayers were still able to return to their teams. Rationing of various consumer goods was just beginning but with employment picking up, many fans had the money to spend on baseball tickets. Each Coast League team agreed to play one game for army and navy relief, as did each major league team. Other minor leagues probably did this too as a patriotic gesture.

But one wartime restriction that the Coast League teams had to endure was the 20-player limit. This meant that teams either carried eight pitchers and 12 position players or nine pitchers and only 11 position players. During the season, pitchers would have to bat when their team was trailing late in a game because there was no available pinch hitter or had to stay on the mound and take a pounding because other pitchers were in need of rest. The quality of play thus suffered and led to some attempts to evade the restriction. San Francisco manager Lefty O'Doul accused the Portland manager, Frank Brazill, of suspending a pitcher after he pitched a game and then reinstating him when it was his turn to pitch again. The limit was enforced more carefully after O'Doul's protest.

The 1942 season had a race for the pennant that was not settled until the very last game and a race for fourth place, which determined a playoff spot, that also was not settled until the last day.

The opening ceremonies for each team had a patriotic theme; the national anthem was played, which had not been the case before the war. In Los Angeles, there was a "Remember Pearl Harbor" subject with the mayor and a military color guard present. Seattle, Sacramento and Hollywood opened at night to allow war workers to attend. The Veterans of Foreign Wars were honored in Sacramento. During the battle of Midway on Friday night, June 5, all radio stations were taken off the air from 9 P.M. to 5:30 A.M., Pacific War Time. Obviously, baseball fans that night had to wait until the morning paper to see how their team made out.

Another wartime measure the league had to take was to reduce their umpiring staff. Instead of three umpires at each game, there were now only two, which meant the league had only eight umpires under contract instead of 12. This made the job harder for the men in blue and caused many arguments because some calls had to be made from a greater distance than before.

Even though the war had not reached full mobilization in 1942, quite a few Pacific Coast League players were called into the military before the season ended. The team that could least afford losing players, the last-place Portland Beavers, lost outfielders Danny Escobar and Herman Reich just before the season started. Then in August, their double-play combination, shortstop Lindsey Brown and second baseman Al Wright, went into the navy. The hapless Beavers finished the season with just 16 players on their roster. When Seattle suffered injuries to a couple of their outfielders, they had to play a pitcher and a catcher in the outfield. They resolved part of the problem by talking retired outfielder Bill Lawrence into leaving his job as city playground commissioner for the summer months and returning to the Rainier outfield. But before Lawrence could play, a rule had to be waived that required a retired player to wait 60 days before becoming eligible to play. The Seattle general manager, Bill Mulligan, appealed to William G. Branham, chief of

1—The 1942 Season

Patriotic raising of Old Glory before Seattle and Sacramento open the first wartime season at Sacramento's Cardinal Field in April 1942. Courtesy of Dave Eskenazi.

the minor leagues, to allow Lawrence to play sooner because of the shortage of players and permission was granted.

As mentioned, the 1942 pennant race was not decided until the very last game of the season when Sacramento beat Los Angeles and the battle for first division (fourth place and higher) was not decided until the last day when San Diego won the opening game of the Sunday double-header from San Francisco.

1. Sacramento. The Solons had not won a pennant before 1942, but in 1937 they did finish in first place, four games ahead of San Francisco. The pennant that year was decided by the Shaughnessy playoff system and Sacramento was eliminated in four straight games by third-place San Diego, which went on to win the playoffs, and hence, the pennant. But in 1941, Sacramento, under manager Pepper Martin, built a 15-game lead over the second-place Seattle club by June by winning 50 and losing only 19; but the team slumped from then on and won only 51 while losing 56 and fell to second place behind the Rainiers.

Therefore, Martin was very anxious to make up for the failure to hold the big lead the previous season. The 1942 Solons were a solid club with Ray Mueller behind the plate, an iron man who hit .297 and hit 16 homers. The infield of Jack Sturdy at first, Gene Handley at second, Eddie Lake at short and former Padre Steve Mesner at third was almost as good as the Los Angeles infield. In the outfield, the Solons had the former National League batting champion, Deb Garms, and Buster Adams and Averett Thompson. Martin filled in just about everywhere when needed. But the pitching was very good with lefty Tony Freitas winning 24 games and Blix Donnelly winning 16. Other pitchers were Clarence Beers, Bill Schmidt and Hershel Lyons.

The Solons played in the league's smallest market and attendance was not very good. They had a lot of rain in April, which hurt them a great deal, but they also went into a slump that month, losing five of seven to the Seals and then had a total collapse in Los Angeles, losing six of seven to fall into last place. Right after leaving Los Angeles, the Solons broke out of their slump by winning 15 of the next 20 games, but the fans were not turning out. They drew only 6,000 fans for a week's series against lowly Portland, with only 343 on Saturday.

By the third week of May, Sacramento was back in first division. They received the good news that pitcher Blix Donnelly was declared 4-F and was able to stay with the team. They had to play a 10-game series with Seattle at home in late May because of all the rainouts when Seattle opened the season at Cardinal Field, the Solons' ballpark. It was at this time that catcher Ray Mueller was establishing his reputation as an iron man as he caught all 10 games of the Seattle series, of which the Solons won six. He also caught all seven games the next week against the Angels, a week the Solons regained first place by taking five of seven from Los Angeles. LA won the first two games and then lost the last five, which was a forerunner of things to come, that was to make the Solons league champions.

On Friday night, June 12, the Solons announced that all receipts from that game against the Angels would be turned over to the army so it could build a swimming pool at Mather Field for the airmen. A total of 8,111 tickets were sold, raising $4,500, but only 6,575 came out to see their Sacs take over first place that night by beating the Angels.

The Solons then went up to Portland and Seattle and won nine and lost four with some rainouts. Ray Mueller again caught every game, but back-up catcher Charlie Marshall had to fill in at second base because Gene Handley broke his hand.

The Solons continued their winning ways when they returned home to take five of eight from Oakland and six of seven from San Diego. By mid–July, it became apparent that this was going to be a two-team race, with the Angels in close pursuit while third-place Seattle was already nine games off the pace.

Two unusual events occurred during the Oakland series. Forty-six-year-old coach Ken Penner pitched a couple of innings. He had not pitched for Sacramento since 1923 and last pitched in the Coast League in 1925 for Vernon. He was to appear in a few other games for the Solons in 1942 and to manage the team in 1943, through its nightmare of a season. The other event was unfortunate. A big argument occurred during the Wednesday night game with Oakland and three players were ejected. The small crowd of 1,689 became unruly and a bottle shower erupted from the right field stands. This caused the team to serve all drinks in paper cups thereafter to prevent serious injury.

Just as the Solons were to make their last visit to Los Angeles, they received some sad news. One of their former catchers, Jim Grilk, was killed in a car wreck. He had been on the team in 1936, 1939, 1940 and briefly in 1941, and then became the civilian athletic director for the Sacramento Air Depot. He was only 28 years old.

The Solons were fortunate that this series in LA was only three games. They went in with a two and a half game lead and came out a half game behind as the Angels swept them. LA won nine of the 10 games played with Sacramento at Wrigley Field, but it was a different story in Sacramento. The Wednesday night game was the Angels' turn to donate the receipts to the Army-Navy bat and ball fund. A crowd of 7,000 turned out that evening but 10,000 seats were sold. A total of 33,000 saw the three games, giving Sacramento a bigger check than it had received for any seven-game series in 1942.

The setback in Los Angeles caused the Solons to go into a slump. They lost the next three series to the Seals, San Diego and to last-place Portland. Attendance was hurt by the slump and the extreme heat in the Sacramento summer as three double-headers drew a total of only 7,955 with a low of 989 on a Saturday.

On August 5, the whole league got an announcement that none of them wanted to hear. No more night ball was to be permitted after August 20 for the duration, and all outdoor signs had to be turned off. Some pessimists predicted the league would not operate in 1943. Sacramento was an inland city and the officials felt the prevention of night ball was unnecessary and would hurt the team more than others because Sacramento had the hottest summers of the other Coast League cities.

The 1942 Sacramento Solons, managed by Pepper Martin, who won the franchise's only Pacific Coast League pennant in dramatic fashion by winning the last five games of the season from Los Angeles to overcome a four-game Angel lead. Courtesy of Dave Eskenazi.

On August 18, the Solons began a seven-game series at home against San Diego during which the last two night games were played. Only 2,857 saw the last night game, which was a double-header. Sportswriters urged the team to play twilight ball so the teams took Thursday off and played a Friday game that began at 5:30. But only 507 paid to see that game. Even the Sunday double-header drew only 2,595, which was the smallest Sunday crowd of the season.

When Hollywood followed San Diego into Cardinal Field, the Solons kept playing at 5:30 but just a few hundred fans showed up each evening. Even a double-header on Saturday drew only 1,429 even though the Solons were now winning and were close on the heels of first-place Los Angeles.

As the Solons embarked on their final road trip of the season to Portland and Seattle, they got some good news that was to be a decisive factor in their winning the pennant. The parent Cardinals were sending them slugging third baseman Gene Lillard, a former Angel, who could also pitch. He hit 56 homers for the Angels in 1935 and won 14 games for the Seals in 1937 and 16 for the Angels in 1938. He was to hit .340 and three homers for the Sacs during the final three weeks of the season. The Solons won five of nine games from Portland and four of the first six from Seattle to tie the Angels for first place at the end of play on Saturday, September 12. But on Sunday the 13, the Angels won a double-header and the Solons lost their double-header at Seattle.

So the final series of the season pitted Los Angeles at Sacramento for seven games. The Solons played very poorly in Los Angeles but much better against the Angels at home. Because of the poor attendance at twilight games, the Solons decided to start all weekday games at 3 P.M., but this also failed to draw many fans, possibly because school had started. But this was to be the most crucial series in all Sacramento history. The Angels, just as they had on their earlier trip in June, won the first two games to increase their lead to four games with five to play. Only 1,287 and 1,472 saw those two games. But after that, attendance dropped below 1,000 as fans assumed the Solons had no chance to catch the Angels. But on Thursday, the Solons eked out a 5–4 win with three in the eighth and one in the ninth. They won easily on Friday, 10–2, to cut the Angel lead to two games. On Saturday, the Angels took a 5–4 lead in the top of the 11th inning, only to have Gene Lillard hit a game winning two-run homer to bring Sacramento to within a game of the lead. Finally, on Sunday the 20th, the largest crowd of the year, 11,663, turned out to see what they had hoped to see. The Angels blew a five-run lead in the opener, losing 7–5, and then Tony Freitas won the nightcap 5–1 to clinch Sacramento's only pennant.

After Sacramento won the first game of the opening round of the playoffs against third-place Seattle, the sportswriters were saying that the Solons did not know how to lose. But they learned quickly, as the Rainiers took the next four in a row to eliminate the Sacs. This put somewhat of a damper on their pennant celebration.

2. Los Angeles. After a very poor seventh-place finish in 1941, the parent Chicago Cubs sent some good ballplayers to the Angels for the 1942 season. The Angels were managed by Arnold "Jigger" Statz, who was in his third year as manager after playing 18 years with the team as its best center fielder. He had been with the club continuously since 1929 and had some great years. But in 1942, Statz was 45 years old although he remained on the active roster. To assist him, the Angels hired

Wrigley Field, Los Angeles, the largest park in the league. It was called a "homer haven" because the power alleys were only 345 feet from home plate. The league headquarters was in the tower, where the clock had the letters "W R I G L E Y   F I E L D" instead of numbers. Courtesy of Dave Eskenazi.

Bill Sweeney, deposed manager of Hollywood, as their coach and Sweeney too remained on the playing roster despite his 37 years. With rosters restricted to only 20 players, this was to hurt the team in the stretch drive.

The popular radio announcer for both Los Angeles and Hollywood, Mike Franckovich, went into the service and was replaced by Frank Bull, who had been a football announcer for the two local universities, UCLA and USC.

The Angel club looked like a winner with the best infield in the league: Eddie Waitkus at first, Roy Hughes at second, Bill Schuster at short and Eddie Mayo at third. The outfield began the season with Fern Bell, Barney Olsen and Johnny Moore. Catching was a bit weak with 34-year-old Gilly Campbell, who was over the hill, and 40-year-old Al Todd, a former National League catcher with the Phillies, Pirates and Cubs. But the pitching looked good with ace Ray Prim, Jesse Flores, Red Lynn, Ken Raffensberger, Paul Gehrman, Ray "Peaches" Davis, Pete Mallory and Jess Dobernic. But the bench was weak. Besides Statz and Sweeney, LA had infielder Jack Hanson, who later was replaced by Glenn Stewart.

Bell was released when the Angels got Harry "Peanuts" Lowrey back from the Cubs.

The 1942 Angels won the season series from each of their seven opponents. But many of them were close, such as 16–14 over Oakland, 12–10 over San Francisco and 13–11 over Sacramento. Most troublesome were their nine losses against 15 wins over last-place Portland, because some of those losses were in games that the Angels let get away.

Attendance was very good at Wrigley Field because the club was vastly improved over the 1941 aggregation. A big series took place during the second week of May when Seattle came to LA. The Rainiers had won three straight pennants and many predicted them to repeat, but the Angels won five of six from the visitors, with one 15-inning tie. Over 15,000 came out for the Sunday double-header, which was the largest crowd at Wrigley Field since 1932. As often happened during the war, the second game Sunday was cut short to allow the teams to catch a train for the Northwest.

The Angels won nine and lost five from Portland and Seattle up north, but were forced to play an exhibition game on Monday night, May 25th, for army and navy athletic equipment. A combined team of Angels and Seals defeated a combined team from Seattle and Portland. Again, with train travel having to make way for the military, the Angels could not get home in time to play Oakland on Tuesday and had to open on Wednesday night with a double-header scheduled for Friday night. The Oaks were the only team to win a series from the Angels in Los Angeles in 1942 and the Oaks won both of them by four games to three.

In mid–June, the Angels got a preview of bad things to come when they went up to Sacramento. They won the first two games of the series to extend their league lead but then lost five in a row to lose that lead. During this series, the Angels got Peanuts Lowrey from the Cubs and released Fern Bell. Originally Lowrey went to left and Olsen remained in center, but later they switched positions.

After the loss in Sacramento, the Angels played much better ball, beating Hollywood, San Diego and pounding Oakland up in Emeryville six out of seven games. But the Solons were also winning so the Angels could not overtake them.

But things were about to change. On July 14, 15 and 16, the Solons went to Wrigley Field for their final visit. The Sacs were lucky it was only a three-game series because they lost them all to the Angels and the lead as well. But with crowds of 9,000, 10,000 and 14,500, the Solons were better rewarded financially than in any series of seven games in 1942.

The Angels then went on a 14-game winning streak, beating San Diego and Hollywood. By Monday, July 27, it was apparent that it was going to be a two-team race for the pennant because the Sacs trailed by only three games, but third-place Seattle was nine back.

In another split week, the Angels won three of four from the Seals and three of five from Seattle, which finished the Rainiers as a serious challenger. But then the Oaks went to Wrigley Field and won four of seven as they had done earlier. One game in particular was galling to the Angels. On Thursday night, August 6th, LA had a 7–1 lead going into the eighth inning and the Oaks came up with seven runs to win 8–7.

After that disappointing loss to Oakland, there was only one more night game at Wrigley Field until 1944. The military announced that no night ball could be played after August 20, but the Angels would be on the road then, so on Friday night, August 7, during the seventh inning stretch, the lights were turned way down and the fans held up matches. Taps was played and the national anthem was sung. Night ball began in the Coast League in 1930 and the fans were used to it. Attendance was to drop sharply for day games during the week.

The Angels then made their last trip to the Northwest, but it was a split week with four games in Portland and in Seattle. The Angels split evenly with each team, but the two losses to lowly Portland, along with that 8–7 loss to Oakland, would haunt the Angels over the winter.

The Angels then lost a nine-game series at San Francisco five games to four before returning home to play Portland. Even though they won five of the eight games from the Beavers, it was not very satisfying because Portland won two extra-inning games and a 2–1 game from the Angels, who were still leading the league. Glenn "Gabby" Stewart had to fill in at first base in San Francisco for the injured Eddie Waitkus and at third base against Portland when Eddie Mayo was hurt.

Rosters were allowed to be expanded after Labor Day and the Cubs did not help the Angels the way the Cardinals helped Sacramento. The Angels called up outfielder Clarence Maddern but he played very little. They also called up a catcher who had been with them in 1940 and 1941, Billy Holm, but he too saw little service. Pitcher Red Adams, who had been with the team briefly at the start of the season, was not recalled. They probably could have used him the final week.

In any case, the Angels won five of seven at home against Hollywood to take a two-game lead over the Solons going into the final week at Sacramento. Ray Prim and Red Lynn won the first two games to extend the lead to four games with just five remaining. Barney Olsen played the first two games but then had to go into the hospital with an infected foot. Jigger Statz went into the outfield, but this was no 1934 Jigger Statz. He could neither hit nor get to many balls in the field. Clarence Maddern made no appearance in this series. The Angels lost the last five to lose the pennant and Statz lost his job.

The Angels did manage to beat San Diego in the first round of the playoffs, winning two of three in San Diego and then splitting two double-headers in Los Angeles. But the final round was against Seattle, with all games played in Wrigley Field because of travel restrictions. The Angels lost the first three to Seattle in midweek afternoon games played before very few fans, but then won the Saturday game and the first game of the Sunday double-header before losing the nightcap, and the series, four games to two. That was Seattle's third straight year to win the playoffs.

3. Seattle. The Rainiers were coming off three straight pennant-winning seasons, the last two of which also saw Seattle win the post-season playoffs. Seattle sportswriters were optimistic that this team could win its fourth straight pennant in 1942 and they referred to their club as the champs, even when they were nine games out of the lead. Manager Bill Skiff was back for his second year after taking over after the death of the very successful Jack Lellivelt, who had managed the team since 1938.

Seattle had a good infield back from 1941 with Les Scarsella at first, Al Niemiec at second, Ned Stickle at short and "Tricky" Dick Gyselman at third. The outfield consisted of Jo Jo White, Lynn King, Bill Matheson and 42-year-old Spencer Harris. Bob Collins was back at catcher, assisted by Bill Beard. A new rookie, 18-year-old Earl Torgeson, could play first or outfield. He was farmed out in May and recalled in June when Scarsella was sold to Oakland. Seattle had the two best pitchers in the league, "Kewpie" Dick Barrett and the Oregon farmer, Hal Turpin. By mid–June, these two aces were a combined 23–7 compared to 11–31 for the rest of the staff. Other pitchers were Ira Scribner, Carl Fischer, Mike Budnick, Dewey Soriano, Bill Bevens and Al Libke. In June, the Rainiers added Ed Carnett and Larry Guay to their pitching staff and released Scribner and Bevens.

Seattle began the season in Sacramento and won the only game played because of "unplayable conditions." They then went to San Diego and won five of six there, including Hal Turpin's no-hitter on Sunday, April 12. It was the first no-hitter by a Seattle pitcher since 1906.

The 1942 Seattle Rainiers, who failed to win their fourth straight pennant, but did win the postseason playoffs for the third year in a row. Courtesy of Dave Eskenazi.

Very often, either Seattle or the visiting club could not get to Sick's Stadium in time to start a series on Tuesday. The home opener against Oakland was held on the night of April 22nd, a Wednesday. This was the first time Seattle opened at night but it was done so war workers could attend. A big pre-game celebration was held, raising the 1941 pennant flag and the players from that championship team were honored. Seattle won the Oakland series and the following home series against Hollywood each by 5 to 2 margins, to give the team a record of 19–9 and a half-game lead over the second-place Angels. Seattle sportswriters predicted a two-team race with the Angels and Seattle, omitting the Solons. At this point in the season, Barrett and Turpin were a combined 12–1, winning over 60 percent of Seattle's games.

The Rainiers then lost a series at Oakland and then went to LA. The first game went 15 innings and was called a 1–1 tie with Hal Turpin going all the way. The next night, Ray Prim beat Barrett, which was the first time LA had beaten Barrett since the 1939 playoffs, and Prim beat him that night also. In any case, the Rainiers lost the series to the Angels 5 games to 1, and lost the league lead, which they never regained.

When the Rainiers returned home in late May, they took on the Seals and then the Angels. Seattle lost both series, 4 to 2 to the Seals and 5 to 3 to the Angels. But during the first game of the Sunday doubleheader against Los Angeles a very unusual fight took place. Angel shortstop and ex–Rainier Bill Schuster stepped on Ned Stickle's foot, but the latter's case was taken up by Al Niemiec. The other fighter was not

1—The 1942 Season

"Kewpie" Dick Barrett posing with a spring training sign which told of Seattle's success in beating the Los Angeles Angels. Courtesy of Dave Eskenazi.

Schuster but another ex–Rainier, catcher Gilly Campbell. The former teammates, Niemiec and Campbell punched each other for several minutes and the umpires, players and even a park policeman stood in a circle and let them exhaust themselves. When order was restored, neither player was kicked out of the game.

When Seattle embarked on a road trip to Sacramento and San Francisco, the team got word that Al Niemiec, a graduate of Holy Cross, passed his test to become a navy ensign. However, he was not called until the end of the season. The Rainiers lost six of the 10 games played at Sacramento; the extra games were make-ups from the opening week rainouts. The Seals then beat Seattle five games to two, pushing the Rainiers into the second division for the first time since August 1938.

When the Rainiers returned home in early June, they appealed to the city playground commission to let former centerfielder Bill Lawrence play for the team and return to his job when the season was over. It took some doing, but permission was granted and Lawrence rejoined his old team. He was able to hit .310 after being off since the end of the 1941 season.

The 20-man roster limit hurt all clubs but with Seattle there were several injuries. When second baseman Al Niemiec cut his hand, right fielder Bill Matheson came in to play second with catcher Bill Beard going to right. Then when shortstop Ned Stickle had an ankle problem, Matheson played shortstop in both games of a double-header. Pitcher Ed Carnett also played some outfield.

After beating Hollywood in a series that covered the fourth of July six games to two, Seattle was still 11 games out of first place. They were just now going to play Portland for the first time all season. The Beavers shocked the Rainiers by winning four of the six games that could be played, sending them 14½ games off the lead. After a split week with Hollywood and Oakland, the Rainiers got to play Portland in Seattle and this time they swept all seven games from the tailenders. But catcher Bob Collins broke a finger which necessitated young Bill Beard catching all the games. Manager Bill Skiff was able to contact the Yankees and get Ed Kearse to be sent to Seattle. Kearse, who was at Newark, was the backup catcher on Seattle's great team of 1940. This sweep of Portland extended Seattle's winning streak to 10 games and put them comfortably ahead of the Seals and Padres in third place, but still 10 games out of the lead.

At the beginning of August, Seattle went to San Diego and to Los Angeles for a split week. They split the four games at San Diego and lost three of five at LA, which put them 11 games behind the Angels, who were leading the league then. That was their last real chance to gain on the two leaders, but they probably now realized that third place was as high as they could go in 1942.

On Monday night, August 3, the Pacific Coast League all-star game was held at Gilmore Field in Hollywood. The South stars, consisting of the Seals, Angels, Stars and Padres, beat the North stars 1–0. This game delayed many players from joining their teams in time for Tuesday night games, so double-headers had to be held later that week. Seattle had to go to Portland for an eight-game series, which the Rainiers won five games to three. Ed Kearse was doing a lot of catching now and young Bill Beard got word that he would be called into the military, but he could remain with the team a little while longer. The next week was a split week at home for Seattle against the Seals and Angels. Seattle won three of four from the Seals but split the four with the Angels. Bob Collins returned to catch on Sunday, August 17.

1—The 1942 Season

On Monday night, the 18th, a team of navy fliers beat the tired Rainiers in an exhibition game the team would rather not have played, but they felt it was their patriotic duty. Portland now went to Seattle for its fourth series in six weeks with the Rainiers. This was the week that night ball ended, so the Rainiers tried a 6 P.M. start on Thursday evening, the 21st, which went fine, but on Friday night the teams played to a 7–7 tie as darkness set in. So the tired clubs with short rosters had to play double-headers on both Saturday and Sunday afternoons, which the visiting Beavers won, to take the series from Seattle, four games to three. Attendance dropped for twilight games compared to what it had been at night.

After losing a series at San Francisco, the Rainiers returned home to play their final two home series of the year. They had to play San Diego nine games and Sacramento ten because of previous rainouts, and a Labor Day double-header. Because it was getting dark earlier, the weekday single games started at 4:30. Four double-headers were played with San Diego because the Padres could not get there by Tuesday and it rained on Wednesday. Saturday was the only single game so the weekday double-headers were started at 2:30. The Rainiers won eight of nine from the Padres, clinching third place, but Sacramento came in and eliminated Seattle from the pennant race. The teams had to play five double-headers, with the Solons taking six of the 10 games played.

Before Seattle left to go to Oakland for its final series, the team was informed that all playoff games would have to be played in California because of wartime travel restrictions. The Coast League was given special priorities during the regular season by the railroads, but this did not extend to the postseason. This last series did not mean anything to either club; the Oaks won four of seven but Hal Turpin and Dick Barrett ended up winning 50 of their team's 96 victories.

Seattle was at the Oakland depot the Sunday night the season ended when they got word that Sacramento had beaten LA for the pennant. So instead of going to LA, the Rainiers went back to their Oakland hotel and went up to Sacramento the next day. The Rainiers finished nine games behind Sacramento but walked off with the most prize money by winning their third straight playoff series. After losing the first game at Sacramento, the Rainiers won four in a row and then went to LA and won that series in six games. The weekday games in LA were very poorly attended with school back in session and the World Series being broadcast. Seattle was not given the privilege of batting last in any of these postseason games.

4. San Diego. The San Diego Padres, still managed by Cedric Durst, finished in the first division for the third year in a row in 1942, but it would be 1949 before the Padres were able to finish that high again. This Padre team had a lot of players return from their 1941 team that finished in a tie for second place. George McDonald was back at first, George Detore and Bill Salkeld were still catching and the outfield of John "Swede" Jensen, Hal Patchett and Mel Mazzera was still there. Mel Skelley was now at second, Jack Calvey at short and Johnny Hill at third. Art Garibaldi was still available at third or in the outfield but newcomers Frank Stinson and Jack Whipple were now reserves. The pitching staff included Wally Hebert, Al Olsen, Frankie Dasso, Norm Brown, Cletus "Boots" Poffenberger, Rex Dilbeck, Bill Thomas and Ed Vitalich, who was picked up late in the season.

San Diego was a navy town and many sailors attended Padre games. But the Coast League players were not always happy playing in the border city because some of the navy men resented players who were not in the military. Even though it was the southernmost city in the league, the weather was often cool and sometimes foggy because the ballpark, Lane Field, was right on the waterfront.

This 1942 San Diego team did not start out like a first-division club, losing three of five to the lowly Portland Beavers and five of six to defending champion Seattle, all at home. They were victims of Hal Turpin's no-hitter on Sunday, April 12. Their third series, also at home, went a little better, as they beat Los Angeles four of six games.

At no time in 1942 did San Diego threaten to take the lead. In fact, the Padres were only second briefly in mid–June and then fell back into third place. They were very successful against second-division clubs,

Pitcher "Kewpie" Dick Barrett, ace of the Seattle pitching staff, who won 234 games in the Pacific Coast League from 1935 to 1950. He won 20 or more games seven times with Seattle and played on three pennant winners and three playoff winners with the Rainiers. Courtesy of Dave Eskenazi.

Lane Field, home of the San Diego Padres from 1936 to 1957. It was the closest park to the Pacific Ocean and the one in the most need of blacking out during World War II. Courtesy of Dave Eskenazi.

especially San Francisco, their closest rival for fourth place. They beat the Seals 17 games and lost only seven to them. They did almost as well against Portland, winning 17 and losing 10. They had only a four-game bulge on Hollywood and a five-game advantage over Oakland. But the Padres could not beat the three teams that finished ahead of them with any consistency. Seattle gave them the most trouble, winning 17 and losing only seven to San Diego while LA won 16 and lost 10 and Sacramento won 16 and lost 12 to the Padres.

The Padres and Seattle were tied for third place on July 20, but after Seattle won 13 of 14 on a homestand, the Padres were no longer able to get above fourth place. However, the race for fourth place and a spot in the postseason playoffs were still in doubt.

In August, two umpires who finished a series in Los Angeles had to travel to San Diego for their next assignment. They could not get any train space. One of them owned a 1912 Duesenberg, and the two drove that to San Diego, but it took them two days to make the trip.

When the ban on night baseball began on August 20, San Diego tried an 11 A.M. game but it was very poorly attended. They then switched to late afternoon but could not start as late as teams in the Northwest because the sun set later up there.

San Diego was holding its lead over the Seals for fourth place until early September. The Padres had to travel to Seattle and Portland, playing nine against the Rainiers and eight against the Beavers. The Padres ran into a buzz saw in Seattle, losing eight of nine games up there, playing four double-headers because of delayed travel getting there and an "unplayable condition" one day. This coincided with the Seals taking seven of nine games from Hollywood, so the Padres fell 3½ games behind San Francisco and into fifth place.

But the next week was a different story. The Padres moved into Portland and this club was decimated. They were down to 16 players and had outfielders in the infield and pitchers in the outfield. One game drew only 25 fans, but one double-header in Seattle the previous week drew only 700 people. San Diego fattened up on the weak Beavers, taking seven of the eight games, while the Seals were home to Oakland and losing six of eight. That meant that San Diego now moved ahead of the Seals by two games.

The final week was the showdown. San Francisco moved into Lane Field for seven games with the Padres. San Diego needed three wins to clinch fourth place. The papers told of Seal manager Lefty O'Doul being very angry with Portland for not replacing the players that went into the service and putting such a weak team on the field against San Diego when so much was at stake. The Padres won the first two games of this final series to take a four-game lead with just five games left. But then the Seals began winning, taking the next three, to cut the Padre lead to just one game going into the final day's double-header. But unlike what happened at Sacramento, the Padres would not let that happen to them. They clinched the first division when they won the opener of the double-header and, for good measure, won the nightcap also. They finished three games ahead of the Seals and 14 behind Sacramento.

The Padres were eliminated in the first round of the playoffs in both 1940 and 1941 and the same thing happened again. The Angels were in a foul mood after losing the pennant to Sacramento, but nevertheless agreed to allow the Padres to be home for the first three games. The Angels had their choice and unlike 1940 they wanted the weekend games to be at Wrigley Field. In any case, San Diego started these weekday games at 4:30 and almost did not get the first one in because it went 11 innings. LA won the first two and the Padres won game three, which was the last game played at Lane Field in 1942. In Los Angeles, the clubs played a double-header on Sunday and then again on Monday, with the teams splitting them both, so the Angels won the series, four games to three. It would be seven years before the Padres played another playoff game.

5. San Francisco. Manager Lefty O'Doul did not like the look of his club in spring training but it came close to making the first division, missing out on the last day of the season. This was the only war year that the Seals did not finish in the first division. The roster was very stable all year. After outfielder Don White went into the service in April, the Seals acquired Ralph Hodgin to replace him in the outfield. Brooks Holder and Kermit Lewis, who led the league in RBIs, were the other outfield starters. Ferris Fain was at first, Ollie Bejma and Ray Perry shared second, Don Trower was at short and Ted Jennings at third. Charley Hensen and Frank Hawkins, acquired from Portland, were reserves. The two catchers were Joe Sprinz and Ambrose "Brusie" Ogrodowski. Their pitchers were lefties Al Lien and Tommy Seats, and the right handers were Bob Joyce, "Cowboy" Ray Harrell, Sam Gibson, Ed Stutz, Larry Jansen and Al Epperly.

April and early May were not kind to the Seals. They fell into the cellar after losing six of seven to San Diego, five of six to Sacramento and then another five of seven to San Diego again. But they got healthier the second week of May when the lowly Portland Beavers came to Seals Stadium. The Seals won six of seven in that series to pass up Portland and relegate them to the cellar for the rest of the season. During the Portland series the two umpires, Frisco Edwards and Bill Englin, had their wallets stolen from their locker room while the game was being played.

The Seals had a trip to Portland and Seattle in late May and did not cover expenses because attendance was down in those cities. Seattle fans were probably spoiled after winning three straight pennants and were disappointed with their team not looking like a contender in 1942. Of course, Portland was not drawing because of its very poor club. But because the Seals won each of these two series, attendance picked up when the club returned home in June to play Hollywood and Seattle. The Seals also won both of these two home series to move into fourth place. As long as the Seals were a contender for the first division, the fans supported the team rather well.

On Saturday, June 13, the Seals and Seattle took the day off because the City of San Francisco held a special day to honor General Douglas MacArthur at Kezar Stadium with patriotic speeches and a bond drive.

When the military authorities announced the end of night baseball on the West Coast for the duration, the Seals owner, Charles Graham, predicted that the league would not operate in 1943. Even though he was wrong, his statement did not help attendance. The Angels were in town playing the Seals when the last night game was played. A ceremony was held as Seals Stadium was darkened and taps was played. A crowd of 2,500 saw the last night game and only 1,007 came out to see the "supper" game the next evening. That game started at 6 P.M. but had to be called after seven and a half innings because of darkness. The following week, the Seals decided to start their weekday games at 2:15 instead.

The Seals were in fifth place, two and a half games out of first division when they finished the Angel series on August 23. Seattle came in to Seals Stadium and weekday attendance was barely over 1,200 for each game. The Seals had a three games to two lead going into the Sunday double-header but lost it and the series to the Rainiers and were still in fifth place.

But the Seals next went to Hollywood and won seven of the nine games over the Labor Day week. Practically no one saw these games as Hollywood was out of the race, but the Seals pulled three and a half games ahead of San Diego as the Padres were losing at Seattle.

The final home series for San Francisco was very profitable, as 30,000 saw the Oaks and Seals battle with first division on the line for the Seals. But Oakland took six of the eight games while San Diego was feasting on the weak Portland Beavers. So the Seals entered the final week two games behind the Padres, with seven games at Lane Field in San Diego.

Manager Lefty O'Doul of the Seals and manager Johnny Vergez of the Oaks meet at Oaks Park in 1942. They were teammates of the 1933 World Champion New York Giants. Courtesy of Doug McWilliams.

1—The 1942 Season

O'Doul had been angry at Portland early in the season for trying to evade the 20-player limit but now he was upset about the Beavers not keeping a full complement of 20 players when they played San Diego. In any case, the Seals had to win five of the last seven games to finish in the first division; they lost the first two, falling four back with just five to play. They won the next three to get within a game, but lost the Sunday double-header to end up three games behind San Diego.

Seals owner Graham argued that the very existence of the playoffs caused a fight to get into the first division. As a result, he felt they were worthwhile even if they did not make money. The profit came during the season as teams struggled to make the playoffs.

6. Oakland. The Oakland Oaks were again managed by Johnny Vergez, who also played third base for them. The one satisfaction the sixth-place Oaks had in 1942 was winning the season series from their cross-bay rivals, the San Francisco Seals, 17 games to 12. It was especially satisfying that they were able to win six of eight games from the Seals in the second to the last week of the season before large crowds in Seals Stadium; that knocked the Seals out of first division and into fifth place. Vergez had been a teammate of Lefty O'Doul on the 1933 and 1934 New York Giants, and both wore World Series rings from the 1933 Giant team.

The 1942 Oaks began with a pitching staff of Stan Corbett, Jack Salveson, Italo Chelini, Ralph Buxton, Henry "Cotton" Pippen, John Yellovic and Vince DiBiasi. Left-handed pitcher Tony Ananicz, who had been with the club in 1941, joined the team late because he thought he would be drafted, but he was rejected for service. The infielders were Marvin Gudat at first, Hugh Luby at second, Bill Rigney at short, Johnny Vergez at third. The outfield consisted of Mel Duezabou, Emil Mailho, Mike Christoff, Fred Tauby and Wally Westlake. The catchers were Billy Raimondi, who been on the team since 1932 and Joe Glenn, who also filled in at second base. Mel Duezabou was accepted into the navy's officer program and left the club on June 10; Fred Tauby went into the navy at the end of July.

Gudat was not a first baseman but an outfielder, so on May 30, the Oaks were able to purchase Les Scarsella from Seattle to play first. They also picked up outfielder Fern Bell from Hollywood after Tauby went into the navy. In early August, the Oaks picked up pitcher Norbert "Nubs" Kleinke from the Memphis Chicks. He had pitched for Sacramento in 1940 and 1941. Infielder Herman "Ham" Schulte was acquired from Hollywood.

A government edict that forbade minor leagues from chartering buses for road trips did not affect the Coast League because this loop traveled by rail. But this ruling led to the suspension of several lower minor leagues, making the pool of players larger for the high minor leagues. The Texas League did not operate in 1943, which made some of those players available.

Oakland's longest winning streak in 1942 consisted of nine games from July 29 through August 4. Six of those wins were at the expense of lowly Portland. But this streak did not propel the Oaks into the first division.

When the prohibition against night baseball went into effect on August 20, the Oaks were in Hollywood. Oaks owner Victor Devincenzi said they would watch how the Seals did with various starting times and make his own decision. He decided that 6 P.M. would be the best time to start, and the Oaks were able to finish the few remaining weekday games they had left at home.

The second to the last week of the season saw the Oaks move over to Seals Stadium and play the Seals in an eight-game series. This series drew 30,000 fans, which did not count the servicemen that were admitted for 10 cents on Sunday, September 13. As mentioned above, the Oaks won six of those eight games which caused the Seals to finish fifth.

The last week of the season had the Oaks hosting third-place Seattle, a series the Oaks won four games to three. But the story was pitcher Jack Salveson. On Tuesday, he won his 22nd game of the season and

Manager Johnny Vergez in his patriotic 1942 home uniform. Courtesy of Doug McWilliams.

The Oaks' Bill Rigney in a pre-game workout at Seals Stadium. He later managed the New York and San Francisco Giants and the American League Angels. Courtesy of Doug McWilliams.

then on Sunday he pitched both games of the double-header, winning the first 4 to 0 and the second 10 to 5. He went all the way to win 24 games for a sixth-place club. On the final Sunday, it was a day to honor second baseman Hugh Luby, who had set a Pacific Coast League record by playing in his 679th consecutive game on August 27. He added a few more to that in 1942, making it 707 games by season's end, and then played in 157 games in 1943 to reach 864 before going to the New York Giants in 1944. He was showered with many gifts by appreciative fans and fellow players.

7. Hollywood. The Hollywood Stars were the only team in the Pacific Coast League not to make the first division during the four war years. They did come fairly close in 1944, and did make it in both 1941 and in 1946. However, with the success of their cross-town rivals, the Los Angeles Angels, Hollywood had to play second fiddle to them during the war. Another problem this club faced was the fact that they moved to Los Angeles in 1938 after a dozen years in San Francisco as the Mission club. This made it difficult for them to build a fan base because the original Hollywood club moved to San Diego after the 1935 season and still had many fans in the Los Angeles area. It probably took until after the war before this new Hollywood club could overcome these obstacles.

The Stars, even though they finished fourth in 1941, had a losing record so they fired manager Bill Sweeney and replaced him with Oscar Vitt, who managed the last-place Portland Beavers in 1941. Vitt also had managed the original Hollywood club from 1926 through 1934. But the 1942 Stars were not a good club.

Their two catchers were Bill Atwood and Bill Brenzel, infielders were Bill Garbe at first, Ham Schulte at second, Joe Hoover at short and Bob Kahle at third. Del Young was an extra infielder. In the outfield, they had Johnny Dickshot, Bernard "Frenchy" Uhalt, Frank Kalin and Jack Devincenzi. The popular Babe Herman, who had been with the team since 1939, finally signed his contract and joined the club a week after the season started. But Herman, who was a great hitter, played sparingly in the outfield and at first. The pitchers were Wayne Osborne, Fred Gay, John Bittner, "Pappy" Roy Joiner, Manny Perez, Charlie Root, Bill Bevens and Eddie Erautt.

The Stars opened the season with a night game at Gilmore Field against Oakland. A crowd of 6,500 was there along with Babe Ruth and Governor Culbert Olson. The California state guardsmen raised the flag and the national anthem was played.

The Stars split the four games with Oakland in that short opening series but surprised everyone by winning four of seven from their next opponent, the Solons up in Sacramento. They returned home to take four of seven from Seattle, the team that had won three straight pennants but reality was about to set in. They had to go up to Portland and Seattle and lost five of seven to each team, and were not much of a threat to even make the first division after that.

In their first series with the Angels at Gilmore Field, which the Stars won four games to three, an unusual event occurred at the end of the first game. Bill Schuster, the Angel shortstop who loved to do a lot of crazy things, annoyed the Stars, particularly pitcher Roy Joiner. Schuster made the last out of the game on a ground ball, and as he crossed the mound Joiner decked him with a haymaker, leaving Schuster sprawled out on the mound. The lights were turned out before Schuster was able to make his way to the visitors clubhouse.

The 1942 Hollywood Stars, who finished seventh. Courtesy of Dick Beverage.

During the next few weeks, Hollywood began losing one series after another to convince the fans that this team was going nowhere. After Memorial Day, they traded pitcher Wayne Osborne to Portland for Walter "Whitey" Hilcher. Shortly thereafter, they farmed young Eddie Erautt out to Salem. After their second series with the Angels, which they lost at Wrigley Field, the Stars acquired the versatile Roy Younker, who could catch and play first, second and the outfield.

In mid–July, the Stars were 20 games out of the lead. They picked up a new first baseman, Chuck Sylvester, a left-handed hitter. He had a low batting average and hit no homers.

When Hollywood made its second trip to the Northwest, it was announced that all proceeds of the July 15 game would be donated to the Army-Navy bat and ball fund. But that game was rained out, and while a double-header was played on the 16th, it was not mentioned if those proceeds were given for that cause.

The Stars lost the services of pitcher Johnny Bittner during the third week of July because he went into the navy. The Stars were home facing the Angels and again won that series four games to three as they did the first time the Angels played at Gilmore Field. On August 4, Hollywood hosted the Pacific Coast League all-star game, which the South won 1–0. The northern clubs consisted of Seattle, Portland, Sacramento and Oakland.

In mid–August, the Stars sold Ham Schulte to Oakland probably because Del Young was playing second base most of the time. Hollywood was home when the restriction against night ball took effect on August 20. Prior to that date, the team passed out ballots to the fans to suggest the best starting time for day ball. While the starting time of 5 P.M. received the most votes, voting and attending are two different things as the Stars were soon to find out.

During the last week of night ball, the Stars played an exhibition game against a team of former players who were in the military. A crowd of 2,000 saw Hollywood win. Then a series with Oakland followed, and about 2,000 saw the last night game until 1944, which was a double-header. But the next day, only 594 came out to see the 5 P.M. game. The Stars immediately canceled the Friday evening game and decided to play a double-header Saturday afternoon in addition to the regular one on Sunday. The Stars announced that all future weekday games would start at 3 P.M.

That series with Oakland was the last one the Stars won in 1942. They lost one at Sacramento, a lopsided one to the Angels at Wrigley Field and finally a season-ending one to last-place Portland. The Angels captured the city series from Hollywood by winning both series at Wrigley handily, while losing both at Gilmore by a single game.

The few bright spots for Hollywood concerned individual performances. Babe Herman hit .322 but played sparingly. Johnny Dickshot and Frank Kalin both hit over .300 and got a chance with the White Sox in 1943. Shortstop Joe Hoover hit .327 and went to Detroit and earned a World Series ring with them in 1945.

8. Portland. The Portland Beavers were the basket case of the Pacific Coast League from 1939 through 1942, finishing last each of those four years. The 1942 team was managed by Frank Brazill, the fourth of six managers the Beavers were to have from 1939 through 1944. It was especially irritating to Portland fans that this dismal period coincided with the outstanding success of their northern rival, the Seattle Rainiers, who won three straight pennants from 1939 through 1941.

Just before the 1942 season began, the Beavers got the news that two of their better players, outfielders Danny Escobar and Herman Reich, were headed for military service. In addition, third baseman Marvin Owen was injured and could not play until early May.

The 1942 Beaver pitching staff included the submariner Ad Liska, Whitey Hilcher, Joe Orrell, Harry Johnston, Byron Speece, Walter "Tilly" Schaefer, Syd Cohen, Bill Schubel and Lee Stine, who could also play first or the outfield. They started the season with Frank Hawkins at first, but soon acquired Larry Barton from Wilkes-Barre, so Hawkins was released and picked up by the Seals. At second, they had Al "A-1" Wright, Lindsey Brown at short, and with Owen hurt, they used Henry Martinez at third. In the outfield, they had Ted Norbert, who led the league in batting and homers, Rupert Thompson, John Gill and Danny Amaral. The catchers were Dominic Castro and Johnny Leovich, but when Castro left the team, he was replaced by Ted Mayer.

Norbert started out in a slump, getting only eight hits in 57 at bats, but after that he hit at a .443 clip to end the season at .378. Surprisingly, Portland had five hitters that ended up over .300 for the season: Norbert, Gill, Thompson, Owen and Barton. That did not include Amaral, who was hitting .308 when he left in early July to join the navy. But Portland also had its very weak hitters. Catchers Ted Mayer and John Leovich hit only .213 and .190 respectively. Shortstop Lindsey Brown was a slick fielder but hit only .220.

In July, the Beavers won eight games in a row at home against Seattle, Oakland and Hollywood, before doing an about-face, and losing the next 10 in a row. During the Oakland series, which was interrupted by rain, a big hole opened up in center field, causing play to be stopped. When Emil Mailho of Oakland jumped into the hole, only the peak of his cap was visible as he stood in it. The groundskeeper, Rocky Benevento, said the hole opened up where the tiles drain off the field. They got waterlogged and the ground just melted away.

The Beavers traded pitchers with Hollywood, getting Wayne Osborne for Whitey Hilcher. After Martinez left for the service, the Beavers were down to 18 players, 11 position players and seven pitchers, including Lee Stine, who also played the outfield. But things got really bad in August when the double-play combination, Lindsey Brown and Al Wright, went into the navy. They finished the season with just 16 players, and incurred the wrath of Lefty O'Doul when they lost seven of eight to San Diego, a club battling the Seals for fourth place.

When night baseball was stopped, Portland started its games at 3 P.M., but very few could make it at that hour. The series with Sacramento drew very few fans, so for the final week against San Diego, they started the games at 1:30 P.M., hoping to attract shift workers. One game that week drew only 25 fans. But on Sunday, 3,000 came out for the final home double-header, possibly because there were rumors that this would be the last game until the war was over. Some people doubted the league could operate in 1943.

After the 1942 season, the Portland club was sold by the C.T. Schefter family to six Portland businessmen. Only two of the purchases' names were disclosed: A.J. Cook, sales manager of the Lucky Lager Brewing Company, and William Klepper, a former owner of the Beavers and also of the Seattle club. Mr. Klepper had been out of baseball since 1938 when he sold the Seattle team to Emil Sick. The new owners vowed to improve the team and Vaughn Street Park as much as wartime conditions would allow. They said they could not guarantee a first-division team right away, but that is exactly what they delivered.

2 — The 1943 Season

Final Standings

	W	L	PCT	G.B.	MANAGER
1. Los Angeles	110	45	.710	—	Bill Sweeney
2. San Francisco	89	66	.574	21	Lefty O'Doul
3. Seattle	85	70	.548	25	Bill Skiff
4. Portland	79	76	.510	31	Merv Shea
5. (tie) Hollywood	73	82	.471	37	Charlie Root
5. (tie) Oakland	73	82	.471	37	Johnny Vergez
7. San Diego	70	85	.452	40	Ced Durst/George Detore
8. Sacramento	41	114	.265	69	Ken Penner

By 1943, the demands of the military hit very hard on all of baseball. But the Pacific Coast League was able to operate even though it could not play any night ball. The schedule was reduced from 178 games to 155 with teams playing each other only three series instead of four. That meant that some clubs would make two visits to a particular park but have that team visit them only once. The only exception to this situation involved the two Bay Area teams and the two Los Angeles area clubs. In order to increase fan interest, San Francisco gave up a series with Los Angeles to get a fourth with Oakland and Hollywood gave up a series with Oakland to get a fourth with Los Angeles.

With the exception of Portland and Seattle, all Coast League teams trained near home, as did the major league teams. Most clubs played a lot of service teams rather than other Coast League teams. Commissioner Landis ordered the major league clubs to train in the north because he did not want baseball to offend people while there was a big demand for transportation. But Landis was criticized by Floridians because they lost a lot of business normally connected to spring training. They made the case that circuses, lecturers, singers and other performers were allowed to travel, so why were baseball clubs not allowed? However, in eastern cities up north, attendance at spring training games was averaging 25 percent more than what teams drew in Florida in 1942. Fans even paid to see routine workouts.

As in 1942, some players had to leave teams to enter military service. In addition, some players got deferments by working in war plants. Therefore, these players often could only play for their club at home or in a nearby city, unless they used their vacation time to make a road trip.

Since the whole country was on daylight-saving time (called Pacific War Time in the West), Portland and Seattle could start their home games at 7 P.M. in the summer months, but they moved the starting time up to 5:30 P.M. in April and September. Oakland tried 6 P.M. starts but Los Angeles and Hollywood stuck to afternoon games, with the Angels taking Tuesdays and Thursdays off, and playing double-headers at 12:30 P.M. on Wednesdays and Fridays. Angel home attendance was down a little — 223,000 compared to 237,000 in 1942 — but they had a shorter schedule and played fewer days because of the weekday double-headers. The Seals drew 250,000, which was very good considering they had no chance to overtake the Angels, but were second, the first time they had finished in the first division since 1939. The whole league drew 1,155,034 playing all-day ball, and with Sacramento drawing only 31,000 for its dismal season.

Because the St. Louis Cardinals thought the Pacific Coast League might not operate in 1943, they moved all the players that did not move up to the majors or go into the service from the championship 1942 Sacramento team and placed them with their other farm teams. The Solons barely were able to field a team and ended up with the worst won-lost record in Pacific Coast League history, finishing 69 games out of first place. There were rumors that the team might be moved to Tacoma, Spokane or even Long Beach during the season, but the Sacs struggled along, sometimes drawing fans in double figures.

The player limit was increased from 20 to 25 players for 1943 and no distinction was to be made between veterans and rookies. However, only 20 players could be taken on a road trip and the home team had to designate which 20 players would be eligible to play that week. Part of the reason for increasing the player limit was that there were fewer minor leagues operating in 1943, so there would not be as many teams where players could be sent.

This season, the league again employed some very old and very young players. Byron Speece of Seattle was 46, his teammate Sylvester Johnson was 42 and Spencer Harris was also 42. On the other extreme, Bill Sarni was signed in midseason by the Angels before his 16th birthday. At the end of the season he returned to Los Angeles High School. Nippy Jones of Sacramento just turned 18 during the season.

In addition, the league saw the return to action of players who had been out of baseball for a year or two. Lefty O'Doul talked first baseman Gus Suhr out of retirement to play for the Seals. Seattle outfielder Bill Kats did not play in 1942 but did play in 1943. Seattle also acquired shortstop Joe Dobbins from Hollywood, a player who had not played since 1940.

By this time, all the players and umpires, along with the general public, had to turn in their old toothpaste tubes before they could buy a new one because of the shortage of aluminum. One umpire, the popular one-armed Henry Fanning, would not be back in 1943. League president W. C. Tuttle incurred the wrath of some owners by refusing to rehire Fanning because Tuttle felt the cost of bringing him from his home in Dallas would be too much, and that his salary would be more than the league would be willing to pay. Umpires in 1943 were required to stay a minimum of two weeks in one city to cut down on travel.

The 1943 season was one that contained no suspense. The Los Angeles Angels went on an early 20-game winning streak to achieve 26 wins in their first 29 games. No team came close to them. While the Seals had a good team, they finished second, 21 games behind the Angels. The biggest improvement occurred with Seattle moving up from last place in May to third, ending up four games behind the Seals. Portland played good ball the last two weeks of the season to clinch fourth place, six games ahead of Hollywood and Oakland. The playoffs of 1943 drew far more fans than they did in 1942, when the race for first place and for fourth place went down to the last game.

1. Los Angeles. The Angels felt they should have won the pennant in 1942, so they were very anxious to show the league that they were the best team in 1943. Bill Sweeney, who had coached the Angels under manager "Jigger" Statz in 1942, replaced him as manager for this season.

Sweeney had formerly managed Portland to a pennant in 1936 but was fired after the 1939 season; he then managed Hollywood in 1940 and 1941 before losing his job there. But this Angels team was set to play.

There were not too many player changes for the Angels during 1943. Billy Holm did most of the catching, especially after Harry Land had to go into the service in mid–May. Eddie Fernandes was one backup catcher, but the Angels surprised everyone by signing 15-year-old Bill Sarni out of Los Angeles High School to back up Holm. Sarni did rather well for a youngster.

The Angels had seven pitchers who were with the team all year and these seven accounted for 108 of the Angels' 110 wins and 43 of their 45 losses. The other two wins and losses went to Jake Mooty, who was with the team briefly in May and June. The seven regulars were Red Lynn, Ken Raffensberger, Garmen "Pete" Mallory, Paul Gerhman, Oren Baker, Jodie Phipps and Don Osborn. The infield consisted of Wellington "Wimpy" Quinn at first, Roy Hughes at second, Bill Schuster at short and Charlie English at third. Elmer Mallory was the utility man. The outfield had the league's batting champion, Andy Pafko, Johnny Ostrowski, Cecil Garriott and Johnny Moore, who was used mainly as a pinch hitter. Glen "Rip" Russell agreed to leave his chicken farm in late June and joined the Angels and played mainly left field, but could have played first or second if needed.

The season opened with a single game on Sunday, April 18, with a crowd of 12,000, which was the largest opening day crowd the Angels ever had. But the season had never opened on a Sunday before. Before the game, the Angels retired "Jigger" Statz's No. 8, but this may not have healed the wound Statz felt when he lost his job after losing the 1942 pennant. Another opening day ritual was performed before this game with Oakland, when Sheriff Gene Biscaluz threw out the first ball to Mayor Fletcher Bowron. After winning six of eight from Oakland, the Angels went across town to start a series with the Hollywood Stars at Gilmore Field. The Angels lost the opening game on Tuesday, April 27, but did not lose another game until Thursday, May 20, at home against the Hollywood Stars. They won five at Gilmore Field, but the second game on Sunday had to be called after five innings at a 1–1 tie so the Angels could catch a train for Portland. They were able to play only six games at Portland because of rain, but won them all as well as all seven in Seattle. The Seattle team they beat so easily that week was to be greatly improved before the season was over.

The Angels were to lose only two series all season, both at home,

The 1943 Champion Los Angeles Angels at Wrigley Field. This club won the pennant by 21 games only to be swept in the opening round of the playoffs by Seattle. Courtesy of Dick Beverage.

the first to Portland over Memorial Day, five games to four and the other to Seattle, over the Fourth of July, also five games to four. Briefly, for two days in early June, it looked as if the Angels might be jinxed by the league's worst team, Sacramento. After losing the last five games up there to end the 1942 season, the Angels lost the first two they played there in 1943, for seven straight losses at the capital city. But LA won the last five games of that series and won six of seven each of the two times the Solons came to Wrigley Field, to take the season's series from the Sacs, 17–4.

The Angels played only two series, a total of 14 games, with their closest pursuers, the San Francisco Seals. The second week of June, the Angels won at San Francisco, four games to three. Then two weeks later, the Seals made their only trip to Wrigley Field and lost six of seven, to fall 12½ games behind LA. After that series, Lefty O'Doul angered the Chicago Cubs by stating that the Angels were a better team than the parent Cubs.

Most of the season, the Angels played double-headers on Wednesday and Friday afternoons at 12:30 and did not play on Tuesdays or Thursdays. But those days were often not off days for the team. The Angels played a lot of exhibition games with service teams at various military bases around Southern California. A sportswriter for the *San Francisco Chronicle* urged other Coast League teams to do that too.

Travel delays were common in 1943 because the military trains had priority over civilian travel. This caused delays and teams had to play double-headers later in the week. Two interesting cases involved Angel games. In early July, Seattle got to Wrigley Field in time to start a series but their caps and bats did not, so they had to borrow Angel caps and bats for the opening game of the series. Then in mid–August, one umpire could not get to Los Angeles in time to start a series with Hollywood. Bill Englin was the one who was bumped off the train, so Frisco Edwards asked a player from each team to umpire the bases. The Angels volunteered Red Lynn and Hollywood used "Pappy" Roy Joiner. The next day's box score listed the umpires as Edwards, Lynn and Joiner.

That same week, on Saturday, August 21, the Angels and Stars combined to play a team of service all-stars. The military club had Joe DiMaggio, Red Ruffing, Harry Danning and several other major league players. They beat the Angels and Stars 8–2 before 22,000 fans. The Angels felt that Hollywood did not have a single player that could strengthen their club, so LA played the first four and one-half innings and Hollywood played the last four and one-half innings.

The last two weeks of the season saw the Angels go up to play Portland 10 games and Seattle eight games. The Angels clinched the pennant by winning a double-header on Wednesday, September 1, at Portland. But after that, Portland won five of the remaining eight games to tie the series. Then LA went up to Seattle and played eight meaningless games, because both teams had clinched their respective spots in the standings. In any case, the two teams split the eight-game series, so the Angels ended up winning all but four series they played all season. They lost one each to Portland and Seattle and tied one each with the same two clubs.

At one point in the season, after the game of Saturday, August 28, the Angels had a record of 100 wins and 35 losses, a winning percentage of .741. That was actually better than the all-time Pacific Coast League record of .733, played by the 1934 Angels. But from August 29 on, the 1943 Angels played only .500 ball, winning 10 and losing 10, to end up 110–45, which was a .710 winning percentage, the second best in Pacific Coast League history.

2—The 1943 Season 43

Loyd Christopher batting and 15-year-old Bill Sarni of Los Angeles catching during the last week of the 1943 season at Seattle. Courtesy of Dave Eskenazi.

The jubilation of winning the 1943 pennant was quickly snuffed out by the third-place Seattle Rainiers, who swept the opening round of the playoffs from the Angels, four games to none. The first two games were played in Seattle, and the rest were scheduled for Los Angeles, but the Angels lost at home on Saturday and the first game of a scheduled double-header on Sunday. Since the fans were promised a double-header, the two teams played an exhibition game which the Angels won, but fans were not happy.

The first two playoff games in Seattle and the two opening games at Portland, where the Seals were playing, drew more than double the fans that all of the 1942 playoff games were able to attract. It seems a tight pennant race leaves little enthusiasm for postseason play, but a runaway race arouses fan interest for some meaningful playoff games.

2. *San Francisco.* The Seals returned to the first division for the first time since 1939, missing the playoffs three years in a row. Lefty

O'Doul had a team that was no match for Los Angeles but was better than the other six clubs. Pitching was their strongest asset, especially at home in spacious Seals Stadium. The staff included Bob Joyce, "Cowboy" Ray Harrell, Al Lien, 44-year-old Sam Gibson, Tommy Seats, Al Epperly, and relievers Tony Buzolich, Rudy Parsons and 45-year-old Win Ballou. The latter three saw little action, as the first six won 86 of the Seals' 89 wins and accounted for 61 of their 66 losses. The catchers who were with the team all during the war were 41-year-old Joe Sprinz and Ambrose "Brusie" Ogrowdowski. The infield consisted of Gus Suhr at first, Del Young at second, Don Trower at short and Erwin "Babe" Paul or Bill Enos at third, and the outfield had Henry Steinbacher, Bernard "Frenchy" Uhalt, Kermit Lewis, George Metkovich and Logan Hooper. A valuable utility man was Charley Petersen, who could play both infield and outfield. Uhalt and Young were obtained from Hollywood for Brooks Holder. Kermit Lewis left the team in May to join the Merchant Marine. Don Trower left to go into the military in late June. When Trower left, Del Young moved over to shortstop until the Seals obtained Jimmy Adair from Hollywood, who moved in at short.

The Seals decided to start their weekday games at 1:30 in order to allow war workers, working the swing shift, to see a game. The San Francisco transit company was also pleased with this time because they felt that fans would be off the street cars and buses before the war workers left home. Servicemen all season long were admitted for 30 cents. On opening day against Hollywood, Seals and Stars signed baseballs for fans who bought war bonds. On opening day, which was a single game on Sunday, April 18, the Seals' battery totaled 85 years of age, as Sam Gibson teamed up with Joe Sprinz. Gibson had started nine opening games for the Seals dating back to 1931. The opening ceremonies were highlighted by four marines carrying the flag to the pole in center field and it was hoisted up by managers Lefty O'Doul and Charley Root of the Stars. Private Ferris Fain was in the stands; the 1942 first sacker was on leave.

The war caused some problems for food sales at Seals Stadium, especially on weekends. They could find only 40 venders to work, whereas in 1942 they had 70. In addition, there were shortages of hot dogs and soft drinks, the latter because of sugar rationing.

The opening week against Hollywood drew a total of 36,000 fans, their best attendance for an eight-game series since one against Oakland in 1939. The Seals won that series, five games to three, and then moved across the bay to play the Oaks, where day games would start at 2:30

2—The 1943 Season

during April. For the Oaks' home opener, over 430 wounded sailors from the naval hospital were guests of the Oaks. The Seals also won that series, four games to three, and then headed up to Seattle and Portland for the next two weeks. While the Seals did reasonably well in the Northwest, they fell several games behind the Angels, who were in the midst of the 20-game winning streak. On May 20, the Angels were nine games ahead of the Seals

During the third week of May, the Seals had another series with Oakland, but this one was at Seals Stadium. The results were the same with the Seals winning four of seven but the games on Wednesday and Thursday afternoons went 15 and 18 innings respectively. The 1:30 start allowed both games to be finished in the daylight; a later start, as some clubs were using, could have resulted in the games being called and then having to be replayed in full.

One team the Seals beat soundly in 1943 was the San Diego Padres. This was the team that beat the Seals out for fourth place in 1942, so O'Doul was happy to pound the Padres this year. For the season, the Seals won 17 and lost only four to San Diego, and won the opening series from them six games to one at Lane Field in June. This was just before returning home to play the Angels, who were making their only visit to Seals Stadium in 1943. After losing the first two games to the Angels, the Seals won three in a row before losing the Sunday double-header and the series, four games to three.

The Seals then went to Los Angeles and stayed in the same hotel for two weeks, playing first Hollywood and then the Angels. The Stars were no problem, as the Seals won five of seven, but the Angels were a big problem. In their only appearance at Wrigley Field, the Seals managed to win only the second game of the Sunday double-header as the Angels took the series, six games to one, and extended their lead over San Francisco to 12½ games. During that series, Don Trower left for the military and Del Young played short. That series was well attended, with a total of 31,000 seeing the top two clubs. The Seals took home a paycheck of $10,000, their largest in history, so it soothed owner Charlie Graham's wounds.

Even though the Seals now had no chance to catch the Angels, the management and the San Francisco sportswriters did not want a split season, which they felt was a sign of weakness. They felt the fans, who were turning out quite well, wanted to see good baseball regardless of the standings.

In mid–July, the Seals sold outfielder George Metkovich to the

Boston Red Sox for $25,000. He was their leading hitter at .325 with three homers and 38 runs batted in. But Charlie Graham still owed $190,000 on Seals Stadium, which was built in the Depression year of 1931, so the sale made financial sense. He was replaced in the outfield by Logan Hooper, Bill Enos and, later, Harry Rosenberg, obtained from Hollywood. Rosenberg had been out of baseball since the end of the 1941 season.

While attendance figures were very good at Los Angeles and San Francisco they were abysmal in Sacramento. The Sacramento papers stopped reporting the attendance figures after the third week in the season. When the Seals played there in July, fewer than 200 attended several weekday games. For the double-header on Sunday they had 460, but half of them were Seal rooters. The extreme heat in the capital city made it uncomfortable to attend day games, but with such a weak club, they may not have done much better at night.

The Red Sox sent outfielder Dee Miles to San Francisco for George Metkovich, but he broke his leg after playing only eight games and so was out for the season, never to return. Harry Rosenberg proved to be a more reliable replacement. It was in early August that the Seals got shortstop Jimmy Adair from Hollywood, which allowed Del Young to move back to second base.

In late July and early August, the Seals won 11 in a row, including six over their "cousins" the San Diego Padres. The Padres fired their manager, Cedric Durst, after the Seals beat them six of seven and hired George Detore, their former catcher, who left his war job to take the reins.

The Seals had to play another seven-game series in Sacramento in August and attendance was also very bad. Barely 100 showed up for one game. It was about this time that rumors had the Solons moving to another city, but it did not happen.

Al Lien had to go into the army but was granted a leave and pitched a win over Seattle up at Seattle on September 3. The army also allowed him to pitch in a few playoff games, both in Portland and at home.

With the first four positions decided by the first of September, the last two weeks had very little drama. The Seals' final series was in Portland, where the Beavers won five of seven games. It was decided that the playoffs would start in the Northwest, where the Angels and Seals were at Seattle and Portland, respectively, the teams they were supposed to open with. But only the first two games were to be played at Seattle and

2—The 1943 Season

The SEATTLE RAINIERS of 1943
FRONT ROW
PAUL KINNEY ☆ SYL JOHNSON, JR.
SECOND ROW
NICK BUONARIGO ☆ BYRON SPEECE ☆ FORD MULLEN ☆ JOE DEMORAN ☆ CARL FISCHER ☆ SYLVESTER JOHNSON
BILL SKIFF ☆ PETE JONAS ☆ JOE DOBBINS ☆ BILL MATHESON ☆ JOHN BABICH ☆ HAL SUEME
THIRD ROW
BILL KATS ☆ STAN GRAY ☆ JOHN YELOVIC ☆ BILL LAWRENCE ☆ DICK GYSELMAN ☆ LOYD CHRISTOPHER
LEN GABRIELSON ☆ ED CARNETT ☆ HAROLD HOFFMAN ☆ JIM JEWELL ☆ CLARENCE MARSHALL ☆ GLENN ELLIOTT
PACIFIC COAST LEAGUE CHAMPIONS ☆ 1939, 1940, 1941

The 1943 Seattle Rainiers that rose from last place in May to finish third and then defeat the champion Los Angeles Angels in four straight games in the opening round of the post-season playoffs. Courtesy of Dave Eskenazi.

Portland, with the rest in California. It was also decided that all final-round games would be in California, unless it were to be between the Rainiers and Beavers.

Portland continued its winning ways with the Seals in the first two games of the playoffs, winning both at home in Vaughn Street Park, which was friendly to the more powerful Beaver hitters. But when the series moved to more spacious Seals Stadium, the Seals' better pitching paid off as they won four in a row to send Portland packing. Private Al Lien pitched in the opening game in Portland and in game five at Seals Stadium, where he was the winning pitcher. He was not available for the final round.

The final round was against Seattle, a team that shocked the Angels by winning four straight games. Seattle manager Bill Skiff was a little cocky, saying his team could even beat the Yankees. Maybe so, but they could not beat the Seals, who won the series, four games to two, to take home the most prize money, even more than the champion Angels. This was the first of four straight years that the Seals won the postseason playoffs. Seattle was not allowed to bat last in any of the games at Seals Stadium, even though travel restrictions prevented them from having any home games in the final series. The following season, that privilege was afforded Portland at Los Angeles.

3. Seattle. The Rainiers started the 1943 season with a weak team because so many of their regular players from the 1942 team were either in the majors or in the service. They fell into the cellar in May, but some shrewd trades and purchases, most engineered by manager Bill Skiff in his third year at Seattle, improved the team immensely and allowed them to move up to third place. It was in a season such as 1943 that the playoffs made sense, because without them, it would not have mattered much if a team rose from last to third place unless there was the reward of postseason play.

The few players left over from the 1942 team were third baseman Dick Gyselman and outfielders Bill Matheson, Bill Lawrence and Lynn King. Returning pitchers were Hal Turpin, Carl Fischer, Ed Carnett and 43-year-old Sylvester Johnson. Seattle then picked up 46-year-old Byron Speece from Portland. Turpin had to leave the club in June to work on his Oregon farm because he could not get any workers.

The acquisitions that made Seattle a third-place club were made at various times during the season. One of the key players was catcher Hal Sueme, who was acquired from Los Angeles just before the season started. Sueme had a very good year and was almost an iron man behind the plate, catching several double-headers. Bill Kats, whose real name was Katsilometes, was used as a reserve outfielder, even though he had not played baseball since 1941.

First baseman Len Gabrielson was on the team all year and later platooned at first with Jim Jewel, who could play all infield positions. But the player who helped the most was acquired in May from Hollywood, Joe Dobbins. Dobbins had been out of baseball since 1940 but quickly became a fan favorite as a slick fielding shortstop while hitting .316. Unfortunately, Dobbins came down with the measles in late May and was out for at least two weeks.

Seattle also made a good pickup when they signed Ford "Moon" Mullins to play second base. Mullins had been a star at the University of Oregon. In mid–July, Seattle traded outfielder Lynn King to Kansas City for outfielder Loyd Christopher and pitcher Johnny Babich. Christopher had a fairly good season, hitting .277 with four homers.

2—The 1943 Season

One new pitcher who had been with the team all season was Joe Demoran, who won 16 and lost 15. He was a regular starter along with Carl Fischer, another newcomer, Pete Jonas and Ed Carnett, who also played the outfield. After Hal Turpin had to leave for his farm, the Rainiers picked up pitcher Frank Tincup, an American Indian, who helped out a lot, especially in the playoffs. Tincup was also used as a pinch hitter.

After opening in California, the Rainiers returned home the first week of May to host the Seals and Angels. Rain spoiled the planned opener that was to have the governor general of Canada and his wife as special guests. They were not able to stay another day, so the following day the opening ceremonies were less elaborate. Weekday games were started at 3:30 in May but later, when the days were longer, the games began at 7 P.M. The first home stand was not a happy one for Seattle as they ran into the Angels while in midst of their 20-game winning streak. It was the first time Seattle lost all seven games to Los Angeles at home.

Outfielder Bill Matheson (left) clowns with manager Bill Skiff when the latter was honored on his special day late in the 1943 season. Owner Emil Sick is pictured between the two. Courtesy of Dave Eskenazi.

Attendance was not very good as the team fell into seventh and eighth place. But on their next home stand in early June, fans turned out better for the later-starting games. Seattle's radio announcer, Leo Lassen, urged the players to speed up the game to avoid having games called by darkness. Lassen also wrote a newspaper sports column.

The club turned around in July, getting confidence after going into Los Angeles and wining a series there over the Fourth of July week, five games to four. That was only the second and last series Los Angeles was to lose all year. Seattle won the next two series, also on the road, at San Diego and Oakland.

During July, both Loyd Christopher and Pete Jonas had to report for draft physicals, and while absent for a few games, neither was taken during the season. In August, the Rainiers won 23 of 29 games to move

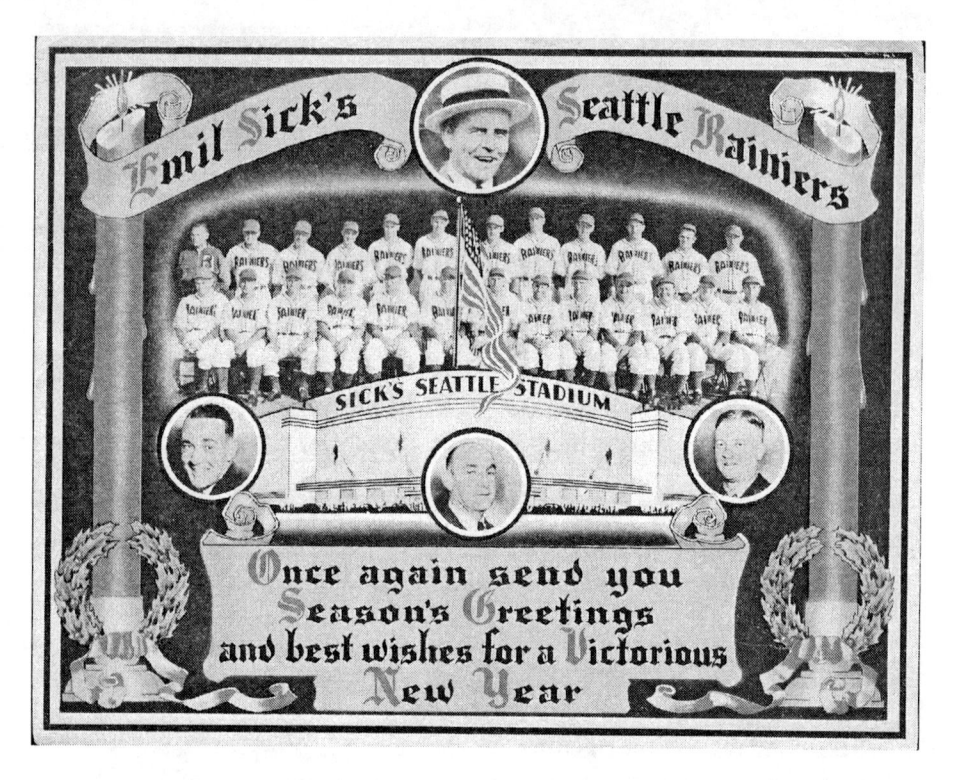

A 1943 Christmas card sent out by owner Emil Sick of the Seattle Rainiers. Courtesy of Dave Eskenazi.

ahead of Portland to clinch third place. But they could not overtake second-place San Francisco.

In late August and September, the Rainiers started their home games at 5 P.M. because it was getting dark earlier. The Seattle club asked permission to play at night because the Vancouver team in Canada was allowed to play at night. However, permission was denied so the fans had to settle for 5 P.M. starts. The last two home series were with the two clubs ahead of them, the Seals and Angels. Even though the Rainiers beat San Francisco seven out of 11 games, they could not get closer than six and one-half games to the Seals. The final series with the Angels was meaningless since all first-division positions were settled. The two teams split the eight-game series.

The postseason playoffs began in Seattle and Portland because the Angels and Seals finished the season at those two cities. But the two Northwest clubs were allowed to have only the first two games at home because the two California clubs finished higher. Manager Bill Skiff was not impressed with the Angel team that ran away with the pennant and claimed his 1941 club was much better. But he also did something no one thought he could do with his 1943 club: beat the Angels four straight games in the playoffs. The third and fourth games were in Wrigley Field, which ruined the season for the champion Angels.

However, Skiff bragged a bit too much. He now thought his current club could even beat the Yankees. The final round of the playoffs was held in Seals Stadium because of the restrictions of wartime travel. The Seals beat the Rainiers four out of six games to win the playoffs and make Seattle settle for runner-up money of $2,500 instead of the $5,000 the Seals earned.

4. Portland. After finishing last for four years in a row, things began to look up for the Beavers in 1943. Their new manager, Merv Shea, who was also the backup catcher, was the fifth of six managers Portland was to employ from 1939 through 1944. One surprising preseason move was Portland's trading of their top slugger, 1942 batting champion Ted Norbert, to Milwaukee of the American Association for four players, only two of whom reported to the Beavers. The two players who became regulars for Portland were Stan "Packy" Rogers, an infielder, and outfielder Ted Gullic, who was to lead the team in homers.

Other new Beavers for 1943 were infielders Leslie "Bubba" Floyd, Mel Nunes, Bill Krueger and Johnny O'Neil. Portland also acquired 42-year-old outfielder Spencer Harris from Seattle after selling them 46-year-old pitcher Byron Speece. The two new catchers Portland acquired before the season, Jack Redmond and Roy Easterwood, both jumped the club in May so the Beavers called up Eddie Adams from Salem. Adams, who had been briefly with Portland in 1938, 1939 and 1940 remained with the club all during the war.

Holdovers from the 1942 club were Larry Barton, Marvin Owen, Johnny Gill and Rupert Thompson. Thompson was late in reporting for spring training because he would not leave his bread truck delivery job until they could find a replacement. Returning pitchers were the submariner Ad Liska, Wayne Osborne, Syd Cohen, Fay Thomas and Joe Orrell. New pitchers included Jack Wilson, Bill Herring, Earl Cook, Earl Escalante and Marino Pieretti.

The new general manager at Portland, Bill Klepper, revived the Portland Baseball Boosters Club in hopes of attracting more fans. After four straight last-place finishes, fan support was down. This group was able to have some fans meet the team at the railroad depot as they returned from their first road trip on May 4th. The team had opened with an eight-game series at Sacramento and then played seven games at San Diego. The Beavers won six of eight in Sacramento but lost five of seven at San Diego to come home 8–7. It took longer to get to Portland from San Diego under wartime conditions, so no game could be played on Tuesday, May 4.

The Booster Club also planned a unique "patriotic" parade for the opening home game against Los Angeles. However, "unplayable conditions" occurred on Wednesday, so the parade had to be postponed until Thursday, May 6. In this parade, there were no gasoline vehicles allowed. Fans came on bicycles or horse-drawn buckboards or walked. Governor Earl Snell and Mayor George Morgan took part in the parade that went from downtown to Vaughn Street Park. Those on bicycles were given free bleacher tickets; about 600 took advantage of this offer, as about 12,400 saw the opener. The Beavers lost that opener and all the rest of the six games that were able to be played that week as the Angels were in midst of their 20-game winning streak. On Sunday, the first game lasted 19 innings, as Wayne Osborne went all the way to lose, 7–6. The second game that day went 10 innings, so the fans who stayed around saw 29 innings of baseball instead of the scheduled 16.

While a big improvement over the last-place 1942 club, this team had trouble at first drawing fans. One reason was the runaway pennant race by the Angels, who swept the Beavers during their first homestand, and the other was the problem of adjusting to day ball during the week. The opening three home series games during the week started at 2:30 but were not well attended. Portland's radio announcer, Rollie Truitt, who had been on the job since 1929, had a hard time encouraging fans to come out to Vaughn Street Park after the Beavers' first homestand resulted in only four wins and 15 losses. The Seals beat them five of six and Seattle beat them four of seven.

The Beavers had a great deal of bad luck in 1943 with injuries. Marvin Owen broke a finger in early May and was out until July 2nd. He returned for four days and sprained an ankle and was out until August 4th. Ted Gullic had to fill in at third so the aged Spencer Harris had to play in the outfield.

After the dismal homestand, the Beavers went on the road and surprised themselves by beating the first-place Angels in a nine-game series over Memorial Day, five games to four. This was one of only two series the Angels were to lose in 1943. Portland followed that with a big six of out of seven series win at Oakland, but then lost four of seven at Seattle. Nevertheless, they had a winning road trip, 14 wins and nine losses. Even though Portland did win at Los Angeles, sportswriter L. H. Gregory of the *Portland Oregonian* urged the league to adopt a split season format and drop the playoffs. Gregory believed the split season format of 1928, 1929, 1930, 1931 and 1935 provided more excitement than the Shaughnessy playoffs. Bill Klepper, the Portland general manager, also advocated the split season format.

When the Beavers returned home after that three-week road trip, they decided to start weekday games at 7 P.M. because it was now in mid-June. The sun set about 8:45 but from 8 to 8:15, the sun shone right into a left-handed batter's eyes. Gregory wanted a 1 P.M. start to allow shift workers to get to work on time but Klepper felt a 7 P.M. start would allow people to have supper at home. But some games had to be called on account of darkness with the 7 P.M. start. Rain was the problem on this homestand with four games being rained out. The Beavers had a four-game winning streak over a seven-day period because of "unplayable conditions."

An embarrassing personnel change occurred on this homestand. The Beavers felt they needed another catcher, so they released rookie pitcher Earl Escalante and purchased a catcher from Milwaukee, whom they thought was Benny Huffman, formerly with the St. Louis Browns. However, they received Hal "Dutch" Hoffman instead, who had played semi-pro ball in Chicago. Manager Shea knew Huffman and was surprised when Hoffman showed up. The Beavers kept him for a month and sold him to Seattle.

On the next road trip, pitcher Wayne Osborne got his draft notice when the team was in Hollywood. It was surprising because Osborne had a finger missing on his right hand, which allowed him to grip his curve ball better. Osborne, who was 9–3 at the time, was allowed to pitch two more games before reporting and lost them both, to end up 9–5.

The Beavers were in third place in late July and safely ahead of Hollywood, Oakland and San Diego. But Seattle went on a hot streak to move to a third-place tie with Portland on August 2. Seattle passed them for good the next day and by August 24 was six games ahead of the Beavers, who held on to fourth place.

Pitcher Syd Cohen had to report to his Dallas draft board in late July. He was rejected for military service, but it took him a month to get back to the club. Mel Nunes also expected to be drafted but he was turned down because he had one leg shorter than the other. Portland also sold pitcher Joe Orrell to the Detroit Tigers and picked up rookie Frank Shone, a pitcher who could also play the outfield.

Just before Labor Day, the Beavers knew they could not overtake third-place Seattle but now they had to worry about hanging on to a first-division spot. Weekday games were now started at 5 P.M. because it was getting dark earlier. The last two home series were against the two top teams, Los Angeles and San Francisco. The Angels series over Labor Day was a 10-game affair, and the following week called for nine games with the Seals. The Angels won the opening double-header on Wednesday, September 1, to clinch the pennant. But after that, the Beavers won five of the remaining eight games to tie the Angels at five games each. Then Portland won seven of the nine from the Seals to finish in fourth place, three games over .500 at 79–76, and six games ahead of fifth-place Oakland and Hollywood, who were tied.

Before the playoffs began, the Beavers lost the services of pitcher Bill Herring, who left to coach at a college in Atlanta. Another pitcher, Jack Wilson, had bone chips in his elbow and could relieve only in one postseason game. This left Portland with only three veteran pitchers, Ad Liska, Syd Cohen and Earl Cook, and two rookies, Frank Shone and Marino Pieretti. Cook, a Canadian, had to live on $50 a week all season because the Canadian government required that the rest of a player's salary be turned over to a Canadian bank, which credited the player with the 10 percent exchange rate premium for U.S. funds.

The Beavers were in the playoffs for the first time since 1937. They opened at home against the Seals, a team they had just beaten seven of nine times. They won the first two games at home in their hitter-friendly Vaughn Street Park, but then they had to play all the rest of the series in spacious Seals Stadium. There the superior Seal pitching took over and the Beavers lost four in a row and were eliminated in the first round. While the Beavers were to appear in the playoffs in 1944, 1945, 1947 and 1951, they never won another postseason series after the opening round of 1937.

5. (tie) Oakland. Manager Johnny Vergez was in his fifth and last year as manager of the Oaks. During his tenure, the Oaks finished in the first division only once, in 1940 when they came in third. There was not much optimism for this 1943 team because it did not compare favorably with teams like the Angels and the Seals.

During spring training, the Oaks and Seals both trained close to their home but did not play each other. They both played only service

2—The 1943 Season

Oaks Park in Emeryville decked out in patriotic bunting, 1943 season. Courtesy of Doug McWilliams.

teams and Oakland lost far more than they won. Three Oakland pitchers had jobs in shipbuilding or other war plants. Jack Lotz at first thought he would have to keep his job and pitch only in home games but he was given permission to leave his war job without being drafted. Ralph Buxton at first also said he was going to keep his shipbuilding job but he did leave it and pitched full time, but was called by the military even though he was allowed to finish the 1943 season. Lefty George Darrow did keep his war job and pitched only when the Oaks were home or in a nearby city.

Manager Johnny Vergez stayed on the active roster all season and started at third base. But in late May, the Oaks picked up Chet Rosenlund from the Seals, who became the regular third baseman. Jake Caufield replaced Bill Rigney at short, Hugh Luby was back at second and Les Scarsella at first. The outfield consisted of Emil Mailho, Fern Bell, Joe Gonzales and Jack Devincenzi. The latter, who was obtained in a trade with Hollywood for Marvin Gudat, was not related to Oaks' owner Victor Devincenzi. Billy Raimondi was back at catcher along with newcomer Will Leonard, who had formerly been with the Seals. Billy Raimondi had been with Oakland since 1932 and was one of four Raimondi brothers to play for the Oaks at one time or another. His brother Walter was an infielder on the 1943 Oaks but was drafted early in the season.

The Oaks pitchers returning were Ralph Buxton, Norbert "Nubs" Kleinke, Italo Chelini, Vince DiBiasi and Henry "Cotton" Pippen. The newcomers were Hub Kittle, Floyd Stromme and Earl Jones, who joined the team in late July.

The Oaks had to open the season with eight games at Los Angeles, and the 1943 champions won six of eight from Oakland. They returned to host their big rival, the Seals, but only 3,000 showed up for their home opener at 2:30 on a Tuesday. Crowds were disappointing until Sunday when over 11,000 jammed into Oaks Park. But the following week, with a very weak Sacramento club in town, the Oaks drew only about 400 fans to weekday afternoon games. During that series, second baseman Hugh Luby was beaned by a pitch and had to come out of the game. Walter Raimondi filled in for him but Luby started each game and came out after one pitch to keep his consecutive playing streak going.

The San Diego Padres followed Sacramento into Oaks Park and the first game of that series on Tuesday, May 11, was broadcast by station KWID on shortwave to servicemen overseas because there was no major league game played that day. The Oaks and Padres did not play on Friday because a special double-header was scheduled on Saturday at 1 P.M. for shipyard workers, who were allowed in at reduced prices. A crowd of 3,500 saw that double-header, which the teams split.

The Oaks kept their 2:30 starts for the San Diego series and, after a week in Sacramento, for another home series against Portland in early June. While down in Hollywood, the Oaks announced that their next

Front of scorecard, May 9, 1943. Sacramento at Oakland. Courtesy of Doug McWilliams.

homestand against Los Angeles would have 6:30 P.M. starts for weekday games. While at Hollywood, one umpire got sick so Henry Pippen and Fay Thomas of Hollywood umpired the bases on Wednesday, June 9.

When the Oaks returned home to face the league-leading Angels, the first twilight game drew only 1,700 fans. A crowd of 2,200 saw the next game but on Thursday, the teams played to a 3–3 tie after 10 innings because it got dark That game drew 3,100 but had to be replayed as part of a Saturday double-header. But the largest crowd was still on Sunday, as 8,500 saw the Oaks split that day but still lose the series, five games to two. Owner Vic Devincenzi felt the Angels were a good draw for the league and therefore opposed Portland's suggestion of having a split season.

The next week, which began on June 22, the Oaks moved the starting times up to 6 P.M. to have a better chance of getting the game in before dark. But Hollywood was not the draw that Los Angeles was, and some weekday crowds were below 1,000. Even one of these games had to be called when the teams were tied 5–5, so another double-header had to be played on Saturday. The Sunday crowd was down to 6,000, either because the Stars were not an attractive draw or the fans felt the Oaks were not going to make the first division. This was especially true after Oakland lost six of nine over the Fourth of July week at San Diego and then lost another six of seven to the Angels at Wrigley Field.

On Tuesday, July 13, a combined team of Seals and Oaks played a team of players that were in the military. A crowd of 6,395 came out to Oaks Park to see the servicemen pound the two Bay Area clubs 14–3. Several major league stars were on the service club.

After this exhibition game, the Oaks' schedule was somewhat repetitive. They had a home series with Seattle, then went north to Portland,

Pitcher Jack Lotz of Oakland at Seals Stadium in 1943. Courtesy of Doug McWilliams.

then to Seattle, then back to Portland for another week. Their traveling for 1943 was over on Monday, August 9, as the Oaks returned home to play Seattle again. The Oaks had the misfortune to run into a hot Seattle ball club, losing all three series to them. The Rainiers won the season series from Oakland, 15–6. But the repetition did not stop with Portland and Seattle. They had 14 straight games with the Seals because they gave up a series with Hollywood to play an extra one with their cross-bay rival. Perhaps the one satisfying result of the 1943 season for Oakland was its 15 wins against the Seals compared to 13 losses.

The final two weeks, the Oaks were home to San Diego and Sacramento, two very poor draws. In the Thursday game against Sacramento, catcher Will Leonard pitched a shutout and on the final Sunday, Billy Raimondi played all nine positions in the first game of that doubleheader, one inning per position. First baseman Les Scarsella pitched and won the second and last game of the season. By winning all 10 games in that last series, the Oaks were able to finish in a fifth-place tie with Hollywood.

5. (tie) Hollywood. The Stars had a new manager for 1943, pitcher Charlie Root, who had been with the club in 1942. Root had a very good season himself, winning 15 and losing five, but the team did not and suffered in comparison to their cross-town rivals, the Angels, who won the pennant handily. In both 1943 and 1944, the Stars lost every series to the Angels, unlike 1942 when Hollywood was able to win both series from the Angels at home, even though they lost the season's series to them because they did very poorly at Wrigley Field. The 1943 Hollywood club came within a single game of the first division in late July, but quickly fell back to the point where they were no longer a threat to fourth-place Portland.

Hollywood made several roster changes as the season went along, giving up three players that helped other Coast League clubs. Shortstop Joe Dobbins was released but hooked on with Seattle and became its top hitter and most popular player. Another shortstop, Jimmy Adair, joined the Seals and was their regular shortstop in the playoffs after Don Trower was drafted. Marvin Gudat, whom the Stars obtained from Oakland, was picked up by San Diego after Hollywood released him. The Stars used two catchers most of the season, Bill Brenzel and Jim Hill, but Roy Younker also caught some games and also played in the outfield. Butch Moran was the regular first baseman, but Babe Herman filled in there occasionally, in addition to playing in the outfield and pinch hitting. Art

2—The 1943 Season

Lilly and Billy Knickerbocker shared second, Tod Davis was at short and Harry Clemens was at third. In the outfield, Hollywood had Johnny Dickshot, who hit in the first 33 games of the season and was named "Athlete of the Month" for April; Brooks Holder, obtained from San Francisco for Frenchy Uhalt; Kenny Richardson, who could also play the infield; Younker and Herman. Late in the season, the Stars picked up Connie Creeden to play right field.

Joining Root on the pitching staff were "Pappy" Roy Joiner, Bill Thomas, Ronnie Smith, Cy Blanton, Eddie Erautt, Pat McLaughlin and Earl Escalante, who was picked up when Portland released him. In July, the Stars got Russ Messerly but he failed to win a game, losing three along with a few no-decisions.

The Stars lost their opening series at San Francisco, five games to three, and then had to come home and open with the red-hot Angels, who began their 20-game winning streak. Hollywood started their weekday games at 2:30, but this was not a popular hour. In later weeks, they moved the time back to 3:30, but avoided the twilight games that were popular with Oakland, Portland and Seattle. At their home opener on April 27, some army planes flew overhead and dropped leaflets urging people to buy war bonds. That was the only game the Stars won from the Angels that week.

The schedule called for teams to have long homestands and long road trips to cut down on travel. After the Angels left Gilmore Field, Hollywood hosted two more series, one with San Diego and the other with Sacramento. The Stars won both of those, five games to two, with Johnny Dickshot maintaining his consecutive game hitting streak. But then the Stars had to play Los Angeles at Wrigley Field. They lost the Wednesday double-header, which extended the Angel winning streak to 20 games, but finally were able to stop it the next day when Pappy Joiner pitched his team to a 4–2 win. Johnny Dickshot's hitting streak stopped when he failed to get a hit on Saturday, May 22. The Angels won this series, five games to two.

After playing four straight weeks in the Los Angeles area, the Stars traveled only 125 miles south to San Diego for a nine-game series over Memorial Day. This time the Padres took the series, six games to three. The Tuesday game was an experimental morning game at 11, but only 757 showed up for this "breakfast special." San Diego did not try any more morning games.

The next two weeks after the San Diego trip found Hollywood back at home playing Seattle and Oakland, with 3:30 P.M. starts on weekdays.

The 1943 Hollywood Stars, who finished in a tie for fifth place. Courtesy of Dick Beverage.

Even though the Stars won both these two series, they still were in fifth and sixth place, because each series was only a four to three win. But Hollywood was still not traveling yet. The following week, the Seals came to Hollywood and knocked off the Stars, five games to two. This shoved Hollywood deeper into sixth place. On Monday morning, June 21, the Hollywood Stars still had not traveled any farther from home than that opening week in San Francisco. After that, it was the Memorial Day week in San Diego. But now the Stars had to pack their bags. The next three weeks they would be playing at Oakland, Sacramento and San Francisco. The games at Oakland were played at 6 P.M. on weekdays, but even one of those had to be called on account of darkness, with the score tied. This meant the whole game would have to be replayed as part of a Saturday double-header. Hollywood lost the series at Oakland, four games to three.

The next series was a nine-game affair at Sacramento over the Fourth of July week. Attendance was very low, making it difficult for Hollywood to cover travel expenses. Not only was the home team buried in last place, but the extreme heat discouraged fans from coming to the park for day games. Sacramento, being an inland city, wanted to play at night, but was refused permission by the military authorities. What was more disappointing was the Stars losing the holiday double-header to the lowly

2—The 1943 Season

Sacs. Nevertheless, Hollywood did manage to win the series, five games to four.

The Stars then made their last trip to much cooler San Francisco, but they did not do well there. The Seals won that series four games to three, pushing the Stars 23½ games out of the league lead, and three and one-half games out of first division.

From July 13 through August 15, the schedule makers wanted the Stars to become well acquainted with the two Northwest clubs. Hollywood had five straight weeks of playing just Portland and Seattle. Although the Stars had played Seattle in early June at home, they had not yet played the Beavers. Their first series with Portland was at Gilmore Field the week of July 13. The Beavers won that series, four games to three, but Hollywood salvaged some respect by winning the Sunday double-header.

Next, the Stars were off on a three-week road trip to Seattle and Portland. Because of the long train ride and military priorities, Hollywood could not get to Seattle in time to play on Tuesday, so the series began on Wednesday and called for a double-header on Saturday as well as on Sunday. This series was just the opposite as the previous one with Portland. The Stars won four of the first five but lost the Sunday double-header. On Monday, July 26, Hollywood was as close to the first division as it was ever to get in 1943, only one game out of fourth place. Next, the Stars made their only visit to Portland and won that series by only a four to three margin, but on Monday, August 2, they were three games out of first division. Portland was starting these weekday games at 7 P.M. and the Thursday night game had to be called with a 5–5 tie, necessitating a double-header on Saturday afternoon. The third week of this road trip called for the Stars to go back up to Seattle again, but this time the Rainiers were not as hospitable. Seattle took five of seven from Hollywood to send them back home five games out of first division.

The team the Stars had to face when they got back to Gilmore Field was Portland again. Because of the travel distance, no game could be played on Tuesday, so the clubs played a double-header on Saturday. Portland won this series, four games to three, pushing Hollywood six games out of the first division. So over a five-week period, the Stars won 16 and lost 19 to the two Northwest clubs.

Actually, when the Stars returned from Seattle on August 10, they were all through traveling for 1943. The next two weeks they played the Angels, first at Wrigley Field, and the next was a split week, with three at Wrigley and four at Gilmore. While this was going on, San Francisco and Oakland were also playing each other 14 straight games because Hollywood gave up a series with Oakland to get a fourth series with Los Angeles. Needless to say, the Angels won both series from the Stars, who were now just playing out the string.

The final two series were with unattractive opponents, nine with Sacramento over Labor Day and eight with San Diego over the California Admission Day holiday. The Stars beat the Sacs seven of nine and the Padres five of eight. Attendance was light because nothing was at stake. The Stars finished in a fifth-place tie with Oakland, 37 games behind champion Los Angeles.

7. San Diego. The Padres were beginning the start of six dismal seasons in the second division in 1943. They would not return to the playoffs until 1949, and only then after winning a one-game playoff with Seattle for fourth place. San Diego was managed by Cedric Durst, whose first year as manager was 1939. However, Durst was fired in August while the Padres were up in San Francisco, and replaced by George Detore. Detore, a catcher, had been with the team since 1937, but began the 1943 season as a part-time player because he had a war job. But he gave up that job when named the team's manager.

In addition to Detore, the other Padre catchers were left-handed batters Bill Salkeld and Del Ballinger. At first base was long-time Padre George McDonald. McDonald began his career when he was 17 back in 1934 when the team was still playing in Wrigley Field as the original Hollywood team, and moved with the club to San Diego for the 1936 season. The rest of the infield was unsettled. Jack Calvey played most of the games at short, but at second was Ed Wheeler, 18-year-old Lou Estes, George Morgan and Al "Frenchy" Cailtreaux. The latter three also played some at short and at third. Walter Lowe, who had been with Oakland in 1938 and 1939, played mostly at third, but also filled in at first and in the outfield. In the outfield, Hal Patchett was in center, but the other two positions were in a state of flux. John "Swede" Jensen was in left but got called into the service in late May. Jack Whipple and the Canadian Morry Abbott flanked Patchett as did Marvin Gudat, who was picked up in June from Hollywood after Jensen went into the service.

The pitching staff included lefties Jim Brillheart (40) and "Chesty" Chet Johnson and right-handers Charley Schanz (formerly with the Seals), Frankie Dasso, Rex Cecil and another Rex, Dillbeck. These six pitchers accounted for all but three of San Diego's 70 wins in 1943. Two of the other three wins were credited to lefty Al Olsen, who had been a mainstay of the staff, but had to report for military service. He did not return until 1946.

The Padres opened the season at home playing Seattle in an eight-game series. The Seattle club, which was to improve greatly in the second half of the year, was rather weak to begin with, so the Padres were able to win six of the eight games played. The following week, the other Northwest club came into San Diego and the Padres were able to win five of seven from them. Thus, San Diego started out well, winning 11 and losing only four from two clubs that would end up in the first division. But the next week, the Padres lost their first of many series, this one to Hollywood at Gilmore Field.

The month of May was not a good one for the Padres. They lost five of seven at Hollywood and then went up to Oakland and lost another five of seven. Returning home, they just barely beat the extremely weak Sacramento Solons, four games to three. By the end of May, they were over 20 games out of first place and with very little prospect of making the first division. But the first week of June was even worse for San Diego. The San Francisco Seals came to Lane Field and Lefty O'Doul was anxious to get even with the Padres, who edged his Seals out of the first division at the end of 1942. San Francisco won six of seven from San Diego, leaving little doubt that this Padre team was not going to contend for the first division in 1943.

The two top clubs, Los Angeles and San Francisco, really pounded the Padres in 1943. San Diego was able to win only five games from the Angels while losing 16, but it was one game worse with the Seals. O'Doul's club beat San Diego 17 times and lost only four. So the Padres were 24 games under .500 with the two top teams, making their performance against the other five clubs somewhat respectable. The Padres won 61 and lost 52 against the rest of the league, with their 14 wins and seven losses against hapless Sacramento their best achievement. They even had a two-game edge on Seattle and a one-game edge on Portland, the other two first-division clubs.

It was in San Francisco in early August that manager Cedric Durst was fired and replaced by George Detore. Detore was a fine hitter and hit .321 in only 73 games while filling in at first, second, third, outfield and even pitching three innings in one game. All this was in addition to playing his main position, catcher. But he had very little success as a manager, finishing seventh in 1943 and last in 1944, his final year with the club. He took over just as the Seals were in an 11-game winning streak that started against Sacramento and ended with six wins over the Padres.

To the Padres' misfortune, the schedule called for San Diego to play a seven-game series in San Francisco from July 20 through July 25 and then again from August 3 through August 8. San Diego won only three games and lost 11 to the second-place Seals in those two series.

Being a navy town, San Diego had special reduced rates for sailors or other military personnel. The sailors were mostly in attendance on Sundays. Some visiting players did not find San Diego a friendly town in which to play because some sailors questioned why they were not in military uniform.

8. Sacramento. After winning the pennant in exciting fashion in 1942, the St. Louis Cardinals stripped the Solons of any talent they had left after the best of the 1942 squad went up to the major leagues or into the military. Even their manager, Pepper Martin, was transferred to Rochester, leaving the thankless job to the 1942 pitching coach, Ken Penner. Owner Phil Bartelme even took out an ad in the *Sporting News* in February seeking ballplayers for his depleted team. There were no regulars back from 1942; only pitchers Henry Polly and John Pintar, who had very small roles in 1942, were back. No position player returned.

Two players from the 1942 team refused to report. Infielder Mel Serafini decided to keep his war job in Los Angeles and second baseman Gene Handley also refused to give up his defense plant job. Left-handed pitcher Larry Kempe left the club to be a switchman on a railroad in Idaho. Outfielder Bill Ramsey had to report to his draft board in Arkansas but flunked his physical and did not report to the team until early June. George Jumonville, driving from Mobile, had car trouble and arrived late. Jumonville played third but left the team in early August to take a war job in Mobile. While with the Sacs, he actually pitched in five games, winning none and losing two.

Pitcher Clem Dreiswerd, who won nine and lost 20 in 1943, gave up a war job in New Orleans, and started to drive to California. He was pulling a trailer and broke an axle, but all the mechanics were booked up. Luckily, he found one who was a baseball fan and got it repaired. He also had to borrow several gas coupons and experienced several blowouts on his journey.

The parent St. Louis Cardinals had lost patience with Sacramento. They complained that even winners did not draw well there and were in no mood to stock this club with top prospects. The Cardinals also announced that they would pull up any prospect that could help them regardless of how that particular minor league team was doing in its pennant race. They regretted not calling up Howie Pollet in 1941 from Houston until the Texas League race was over. They felt that this hesitation may have cost them the tight race with Brooklyn that season.

This attitude of the Cardinals cost Sacramento its best pitcher in 1943. Alpha Brazle had the lowest ERA of any Coast League pitcher in 1943 and had won 11 and lost eight when the Cardinals called him up in mid–July. Brazle had set a club record of 40 scoreless innings in a row, which broke the record of 36 set by Tony Freitas.

The Solons moved players all over the field and often had pitchers playing in the outfield. But mainly they used Jack Angle at first, Vernal "Nippy" Jones, who turned 18 on June 29, at second, Ora "Mickey" Burnett at short and Jumonville at third, although Earl Petersen and Fred Hensley also filled in there. Dick Cole and Jake Suytar also played different infield positions. The outfield, besides Bill Ramsey, consisted of Manny Vias, Joe Molina and Gene Kavanaugh, who had been out of baseball in 1942. Eddie Malone, who was later to play for Los Angeles, Oakland and Hollywood, did almost all of the catching, but Earl Petersen backed him up until he went into the service.

Besides Brazle, the pitchers were Clem Dreiswerd, Bud Byerly, John Pinter, Henry Polly, Jean-Pierre Roy, "Old Folks" Herman Pillette, who was 47 years old, "Smokestack" Steve LeGault, and Jim McFadden, who left the team early to finish high school. Roy and Byerly often had to substitute in the outfield. Polly left the team in June to report to his Nebraska draft board and never returned.

On opening day, Sunday April 18, Governor Earl Warren was on hand to throw out the first ball. There was a flag-raising ceremony to raise the 1942 championship pennant. On hand were two star pitchers of that 1942 team, Tony Freitas and Bill Schmidt. Both were in military uniform. A crowd of 5,906 was on hand, which represented about 18 percent of the 1943 total attendance. On weekdays, when games started at 3:30, only 200 to 300 would show up. The Sacramento papers stopped reporting the attendance because it was so discouraging. When Oakland played a series there in late May, the Oaks took home a check of only $208 for the whole week. The league-leading Angels, a much better draw, got a check of just $650 for a week in early June. The Seals took home only $429 in August. Columnist Dick Edmonds of the *Sacramento Union*, urged the team to play twilight games because of the summer heat. He went on a crusade to keep the team from moving to another city, such as Spokane, Tacoma or Vancouver. But other team owners were very unhappy playing before such sparse attendance in Sacramento.

Edmonds wanted the playoffs scrapped and replaced with a service team playing each club in the league a couple of games in local ballparks from San Diego to Seattle. There were a lot of good ballplayers stationed at various military posts along the West Coast. Edmonds also pointed out the good that a baseball team could do for Sacramento, especially for young teenagers. The team made every weekday a ladies day and Edmonds suggested the same for youngsters.

When Earl Petersen had to report for military duty in late August, it left Eddie Malone the only catcher. Malone did iron man duties and was voted the most popular player by the few fans that chose to vote. Malone hit .262 for the Sacs in 117 games.

Nippy Jones joined the Marines in August but was allowed to play up until the second to the last week of the season, which was at Hollywood. He could not accompany the club to Oakland for its last week. By this time, shortstop Mickey Burnett was pitching a couple of games, which he lost. Fred Hensley, who appeared in 133 games, left the club early and returned to Sacramento and was suspended. He never played again in the Coast League.

The Sad Sacs of 1943 ended up 69 games behind the pennant-winning Angels and 29 games behind the seventh-place San Diego Padres. Their record of 41 wins and 114 losses was the worst in Pacific Coast League history, a .265 winning percentage. Their final attendance of 31,694 was even worse that the 49,932 they drew as a last-place club in 1936, a Depression year. It was the last year they were a farm club of the St. Louis Cardinals. Their ballpark, originally called Moreing Field, would no longer be called Cardinal Field. In 1944, it became Doubleday Park.

3—The 1944 Season

Final Standings

	W	L	PCT	G.B.	MANAGER
1. Los Angeles	99	70	.586	—	Bill Sweeney
2. Portland	87	82	.515	12	Marvin Owen
3. (tie) Oakland	86	83	.509	13	Dolph Camilli
3. (tie) San Francisco	86	83	.509	13	Lefty O'Doul
5. Seattle	84	85	.497	15	Bill Skiff
6. Hollywood	83	86	.491	16	Charlie Root
7. Sacramento	76	93	.450	23	Earl Sheely
8. San Diego	75	94	.444	24	George Detore

With the war progressing better for the Allies, the Pacific Coast League was allowed to play night ball this season for the first time since August 20, 1942. This could have been a big factor in the league setting an all-time attendance record of 2.3 million, which stood for exactly one year. New attendance records were set in 1945, 1946 and again in 1947, the latter year being the all-time high through 1957, the last year San Francisco and Los Angeles were in the league.

Even though Los Angeles again won the pennant and San Francisco repeated as the winner of the playoffs, this season was much more exciting than the previous year. In the month of July, six clubs occupied first place, including San Diego which ended up in the cellar. There were weeks when the first seven clubs were separated by less than five games. While Los Angeles began to pull away from the pack in early August, the race for the first division was very close. Five clubs were vying for three spots until the Sunday before the season ended, and after that, four teams had a chance to make it until the very last day.

With night ball returning, most clubs had to replace some of the lights that had not been used for 20 months. Many popped while games were in progress, causing poor lighting until they were replaced for the next game. But the return of night ball was welcomed by everyone, especially since it meant that the war was going well.

The postseason playoffs had been called the Shaughnessy system up until this season. They were named for Frank Shaughnessy, president of the International League, who got the idea from hockey as a way to sustain fan interest as teams fought to get into the first division. But in 1944, they were renamed the Governors' Cup, since the winning team received a cup with the signatures of the governors of Washington, Oregon and California. The payout to the players was still not very high, but the players' salaries were continued another week or two, giving them the incentive to make the playoffs. The total amount of prize money remained at $12,500 in 1944, but in 1947, it rose to $50,000.

The 1944 season was also the year that some teams dominated others. The most lopsided season series was Hollywood's winning 20 of 22 games from Oakland. But Oakland won 17 and lost 13 to the champion Angels and won 16 of 21 from second-place Portland. Portland papers referred to Oakland as the "Poison Oaks" but the Beavers won 16 and lost eight from San Francisco, including a seven-game sweep in Seals Stadium in August. Portland also took 20 of 29 from Sacramento. The Angels, in addition to having a bad time against Oakland, also lost 14 of 22 to San Francisco, but had winning records against the other teams. They especially punished Portland, Hollywood and Sacramento, beating Portland 14 out of 21, Hollywood 22 out of 30 and Sacramento 17 of 24. The Seals, besides beating LA, also won 18 of 30 from Hollywood but lost 13 of 21 to Sacramento as well as 16 of 24 to Portland.

Even though the war was going better, players still had to leave their clubs in midseason if called into military service. Others, such as pitcher Tommy Seats of the Seals, kept their war plant jobs and played either at home or just on a Sunday away if they could get a flight to and from that particular city. The versatile Charley Petersen was traded from the Seals to Portland so he could keep his war plant job there and play for the Beavers when they were home, or on the road when he took his vacation.

1. Los Angeles. The Angels lost a good many players from that championship 1943 team and as a result were a very mediocre ball club

3 — The 1944 Season

when the season began. Instead of Bill Schuster and Roy Hughes at short and second, the Angels opened the season with 17-year-old Roy Smalley and George O'Gorek at those positions. Charley English was reluctant to leave his war plant job so Guy Miller and Pete Elko both played third. Rip Russell moved in from the outfield to play first because Reggie Otero, the first baseman the Angels acquired over the winter, had trouble getting out of Cuba. The only regular outfielder back from the 1943 club was Cecil Garriott, who played the whole season in center field, but had to go into the service before the final playoff series. Johnny Moore, now 42 years old, was used mainly as a pinch hitter but did play a bit in the outfield early in the season before other players joined the club. Catcher Eddie Fernandes had to play in the outfield for the first two or three weeks, which left the catching to 16-year-old Bill Sarni and the inexperienced Don Grigg. Until help arrived from the Cubs, outfielders Manuel Salvatierra and Tom Skaff filled in.

The ace of the pitching staff was Ray Prim, now 37, and back after a year with the Cubs. He won 22 games for LA in 1944. Pete Mallory was back but had to report for military service in May. Don Osborn returned, as did Jodie Phipps, but the latter was nowhere near as effective as he had been in 1943. Newcomers were Pancho Jorge Comellas, also from Cuba; Red Adams, who had been with the team briefly in 1942; lefty Boyd Tepler; Dick Conger and Claude Horton, who joined the team in late June.

Starting with two of the clubs the Angels handled very well in 1944 masked the weakness of this club until it had to travel to the Bay Area. LA opened at Sacramento and won that series six games to two, and then came home and beat Hollywood five games to two. On hand again for the opening ceremonies at Wrigley Field were Mayor Fletcher Bowron and Sheriff Gene Biscailuz. But also joining them was Ohio governor John Bricker, who later that year ran for vice president on Tom Dewey's ticket.

The Angels headed to the Bay Area in first place with an 11–4 record. But they quickly fell out of the lead and ended up in sixth place after tangling with the Oaks and the Seals. Oakland won six of seven from LA and the Seals won five of seven. The only bright spot for the Angels occurred in the second game of the Sunday double-header at San Francisco when Pancho Jorge Comellas pitched a seven-inning no-hitter. The only base runner he allowed was in the first inning when he hit Dino Restelli. The Angels went into the seventh inning of that game tied 0–0, but got two runs off Win Ballou, who entered because starter Sam Gibson hurt his ankle.

The 1944 Champion Los Angeles Angels at Wrigley Field. This team won the pennant by 12 games but lost the final round of the playoffs to San Francisco, four games to three. Courtesy of Dick Beverage.

When the Angels returned home on May 9, they got the good news that Charley English would join the team. He got three hits in his debut against San Diego on May 10. The Angels also purchased outfielder Ted Norbert from Milwaukee. Norbert, now 36, had a sensational year for last-place Portland in 1942, leading the league in both batting and homers. But with the 1944 Angels, he hit only .289 and just 10 homers. But his arrival meant that Eddie Fernandes no longer had to play in the outfield.

While home in April against Hollywood, the Angels played all games in the afternoon. Their first night game since Friday, August 7, 1942, was on Thursday, May 11, against San Diego and the Angels lost that night as they had to Oakland back in 1942. Even with Norbert and English in the lineup, the Angels lost the series to the Padres, four games to three. The following week, Oakland came to LA and even though the Angels finally won a series, it was not very satisfying since they won the first four and lost the last three games. Reggie Otero was finally able to join the team, but was used mainly as a pinch hitter until he got into shape.

The following week of May 23–28, the Angels went to San Diego and took that series by a single game. But another player who was to help

3—The 1944 Season

the club arrived, Johnny Ostrowski, who went into the outfield. With slick-fielding Otero finally at first, Rip Russell moved over to second, replacing the weak-hitting George O'Gorek. Nevertheless, the Angels came home for Memorial Day week in sixth place and stayed there as the Seals took five of eight from them at Wrigley Field. Russell had some broken fingers, so O'Gorek had to go back to second base.

When LA next went up to Portland and Seattle, their game on Tuesday, June 6, was not played. It would be nice to say it was called off because of the invasion of France by the Allies, but it was because the Angels could not get there in time. But, as will be mentioned later, the Hollywood Stars did call off their game with San Diego that night. While in Portland, the Angels got another key player who was to help them win the pennant. He was Eddie Sauer, another outfielder, but he also played a few games at first. With Sauer and Ostrowski on the club, and Rip Russell's fingers mended, the Angels sent Manuel Salvatierra to Nashville and Goerge O'Gorek to Portsmouth. Even though the Angels lost this series to Portland, four games to three, the club was shaping up. The infield was now Otero at first, Russell at second, Guy Miller replacing Roy Smalley at short and Charley English replacing Pete Elko and Miller at third. The outfield now had a bit of a jam with Norbert in left, Garriott in center and either Ostrowski or Sauer in right. Johnny Moore was now almost exclusively a pinch hitter. Fernandes did most of the catching and Sarni was his backup.

The Angels next went up to Seattle and took four of the six games that the teams could get in with the rain. On June 19, the Angels were still in sixth place, but the next week was a weird one that saw the team improve. It was a split week with the Angels supposed to play three games in Portland and then Portland play the last four in Los Angeles. The person back in Massachusetts who drew up the schedule should have consulted a map. But the Beaver management did the best it could. The Beavers persuaded the Angels to play the opening game on Monday instead of Tuesday, and the third game was moved up to the afternoon on Wednesday. Then the Beavers and Angels boarded a train for Los Angeles and got there in time to play Friday night. This was the beginning of the Angels' move up the ladder, as they took five of seven from the Beavers, with an especially come-from-behind win in the first game of the Sunday double-header. The Beavers got two runs in the 10th, but the Angels came back with three, and then won the second game in a rout. By Monday, June 26, the Angels were tied for fourth place, only three and one-half games off the lead.

The following week was a disappointment for the Angels, as they had a three games to one series lead over Seattle, and the Rainiers won the final three games to take the series at Wrigley Field. During this week, Ted Norbert was used mostly as a pinch hitter while Sauer, Garriott and Ostrowski played in the outfield. When this series was over on July 3, the Angels were in fifth place but only three games off the pace.

The month of July began with San Diego and Oakland vying for the lead, with San Francisco and Portland close behind. Even Seattle led for a day or so. But before this month was over, the Angels were in first place to stay and San Diego fell into the cellar, from which it never emerged.

The Fourth of July series began for the Angels with a double-header at Hollywood. That was a very well-attended series, with some fans behind the ropes in the outfield. The Angels won six of the eight games from the Stars, to end up tied for second place, just a game off the lead. The Stars were one of the teams the Angels did very well against, and another was moving into Wrigley Field the following week.

That team was the Sacramento Solons. As the series opened on Tuesday, July 11, only one and one-half games separated the first five teams. During this series, the Angels' new pitcher, Claude Horton, made some appearances. He had considered retiring from baseball but changed his mind. After losing the first three games of the series, the Angels won the last five of this eight-game series to end up in second place, only a half game behind first-place Oakland. Very large crowds were attending the Sunday double-headers at Wrigley Field. A total of 16,541 saw the Angels take two from the Sacs on July 16.

The week of July 18–23 was an important one for the 1944 race. The Angels pounded San Diego six out of seven games, putting the Angels into the lead and the Padres into the cellar. On Friday night, July 21, LA took the lead for the first time since April 27 and never relinquished it. And on Sunday, July 23, the Padres lost a double-header at Wrigley Field before 15,000 and plunged into the cellar, from which they never emerged. Yet, in early July, the Padres were in first place. At the end of this series, the Angels led the second-place Seals by two games.

The week of July 25–30 saw the Angels up at Seals Stadium for a seven-game series. Pitcher Dick Conger was lost for the season to LA because he had to go into the service. During this series, a significant lineup change was to take place for the Angels. Right fielder Johnny Ostrowski moved to third base, Eddie Sauer moved over from left to right field, Ted Norbert moved from the bench to left and third baseman Charlie English moved from third to the bench. Manager Bill Sweeney

3—The 1944 Season

was upset with English because he had been slumping and his fielding had fallen off. This was attributed to his keeping his war plant job to avoid military service. But English also angered Sweeney when he drove his car to the series in San Francisco without permission.

The Angels led the Seals by two games, but the Seals never caught the Angels even though they won this series, four games to three. The Seals won the first, third, fifth and seventh games, while the Angels won the second, fourth and sixth, so each time the Seals got to within a game, the Angels won the next day to go back up by two, except for the last game. So the series ended with LA leading the Seals by just one game on July 31.

When the Angels returned home, they acquired another player from the Cubs, infielder Tony York. It was mentioned that Charley English had a bad back. Catcher Eddie Fernandes had a bad finger, so the catching had to be shared between Bill Sarni and Don Grigg, who had been released from the army air corps before the season. This series at home was against Portland, starting with a double-header on Wednesday afternoon. But the Beavers were delayed getting there by a train wreck in Mojave, and had to take a bus 65 miles to the ballpark. The first game started 45 minutes late and the Beavers were shut out 3–0 by Ray Prim. The Angels pounded Portland six of seven times in this series to push the Beavers into a tie for fifth place, nine games behind LA, who led the Seals by three games on Monday, August 7. Eddie Fernandes returned to the lineup on Sunday. Tony York filled in at short late in one of the games.

The next week finished the Seals as a threat to the Angels. LA went up to Sacramento and won six of eight games from the Solons while the Seals lost all seven games at home to Portland. By the end of this week, Hollywood was second to LA, six games back. Charley English was on the bench this whole series in Sacramento.

The week of August 15–20 saw a personnel change for the Angels. They were at home against the Oaks, a team that gave them a lot of trouble in 1944. In the Wednesday double-header, which was split, Charley English pinch-hit for the Angels. On Friday night, he played second base for Oakland. He was sold outright, a move that could have hurt the Angels in the playoffs. In any case, the Angels managed to beat Oakland in this series, four games to three to stay six ahead of Portland, who was now in second place.

The following week of August 22–27 saw the Angels host their crosstown "cousins," the Hollywood Stars. The Angels lost the opening game and then won the last six to push the Stars into the second division and increase their lead over Portland to 10½ games. From this point on, the pennant race was over, but the race for the first division was in full swing. On Saturday, August 26, a combined team of LA and Hollywood played a team of service all-stars as they did in 1943. This year the Angels suggested combining the two squads, but the Hollywood general manger, Oscar Reischow, flatly refused because of the Angels' attitude in 1943. In that season, when they were leading the league by a huge margin, they stated that Hollywood did not have a single player that could strengthen their club, so in 1944, Reischow refused to combine the teams, and LA played the first four and one-half innings and Hollywood played the last four and one-half innings. But the servicemen prevailed even more lopsidedly this year than they did in 1943. The final score was 16–6, as many of those players had major league experience.

The Angels had a nine-game series at Oakland over Labor Day week, which they lost, five games to four, but no team made up any significant ground on the league leaders. LA then went to Gilmore Field for its last series with Hollywood and knocked Hollywood out of contention for the first division by taking five of the eight games played. The Angels again won the city trophy for taking the season's series with the Stars. A crowd of 10,500 came out Sunday, September 10, to see the Angels cop the final two games from Hollywood. With a week to go in the season, the Angels had cut their magic number to one.

The final series was at Wrigley against Seattle, the team that had humiliated the Angels in the 1943 playoffs. It was an eight-game series because of California Admission Day. Seattle won the first game of the series on Tuesday night, September 12, but when Portland lost at Oakland, the Angels were the 1944 Pacific Coast League champions. Manager Bill Sweeney said that he would not rest his squad for the playoffs but go full bore against Seattle the rest of the week. Sweeney apparently was not pleased with Seattle manager Bill Skiff's attitude in the 1943 playoffs. The Angels proceeded to win six of the last seven games to take the series, six games to two, and push Seattle into fifth place. This was the first time since 1937 that Seattle did not finish in the first division and also the first time since that year that they finished under .500. The Angels won 99 games in 1944, the first time a first-place pennant winner did not win 100 games since the 1936 Portland Beavers won only 96. In 1937, Sacramento finished first and won 102 games but third-place San Diego won the pennant in the playoffs with only 97 regular season wins.

Because of wartime travel restrictions, all playoff games were held in California. The league got railroad priorities only for the regular season, and not for the postseason. Second-place Portland opened at Los Angeles while San Francisco and Oakland played each other because they tied for third place. The Beavers surprised the Angels by taking the first two games, but the Angels won on Friday night to break a seven-game losing streak in the playoffs, going back to the final game of 1942. Saturday was an off day, and on Sunday, the Portland club was given the privilege of being the home team by batting last. This was of no help as the Angels pounded them 14–3 in the first game and 11–1 in the second to take the lead in the series. On Monday night, the Angels eliminated Portland by winning game six, 3–2. This was the last game that Cecil Garriott, the team's most valuable player, could appear in because he had to report for military duty.

The loss of Garriott could have been the crucial factor in the Angels loss in the final round to the Seals. LA had the option of opening at home but chose to play the first three games at Seals Stadium to have the weekend double-header at home. In San Francisco, the Angels were colder than the night weather as they lost all three games up there, scoring only a single run in those three games. But the return to Wrigley Field brightened LA's outlook. The Angels won the Sunday double-header before over 12,000 fans, and followed that by another win on Monday night to tie the series. All three Angel wins were by one run. Then on Tuesday night, October 3, a crowd of 13,385 came out hoping to see the Angels pull off a great comeback. Instead, the crowd saw the weirdest play of the season in the top of the fifth inning. With LA leading 2–1, the Seals got men on first and second with no one out. Ben Guintini laid down a bunt, and pitcher Pancho Comellas assumed he had a play at third. He threw the ball to third but third baseman Stan Gray started in for the ball and then started back to cover the base. But he got his feet tangled up and fell over backwards with his feet and arms waving in the air as the ball whizzed past him into the left field corner. Left fielder Ted Norbert was slow getting to it, and by the time he did, both runners and the batter, Guintini circled the bases for a home run on a bunt. The Bay Area writers chided Bill Sweeney for getting rid of Charley English, whom they felt was a better third baseman. If Garriott had been available, Ostrowski would have been at third, instead of in center field. So the Seals won their second of four straight playoffs. The 1944 Angels were the only pennant winner to lose the playoffs in the final round. Eight times the pennant winner won the playoffs and seven times they were eliminated in the first round, but in 1944 the Angels lost in the final round to share the same amount of prize money as the Seals, $5,000 each.

2. Portland. The 1944 Portland Beavers made another jump towards the top as they improved over their 1943 fourth-place finish. This season, their sixth manager in six years was third baseman Marvin Owen, who had played for the Detroit Tigers in the 1934 and 1935 World Series.

The new manager was faced with a major pitching problem when his star hurler, Ad Liska, held out for a two-year contract, something minor league teams never granted. There were stories that he would be suspended and that the team would have to make do without his "underhanded" services. (He was a submariner!) But during the second week of the season the team relented and signed Liska for two years. He pitched his first game for Portland on Friday night, April 28, which was the third week of the season, but the Beavers' first series at home.

Other pitchers on the 1944 Portland club were Marino Pieretti, who was to win 26 games; Syd Cohen; Joe Sullivan, who had won 25 games for the original Hollywood club back in 1934; Roy Helser, who was to win 20 games in his third try to make the club; Clarence Fedemeyer and Don Pulford. Others who were with the team briefly were Al Ott, George Windsor, Wandel Mossor and Jack Wilson. Sullivan, who had been with the Boston Bees and Detroit Tigers, came to the Beavers from Buffalo in a trade for Rupert Thompson and Packy Rogers. Rogers, however, went into the navy.

The Beavers got catcher Gilly Campbell from Memphis. Campbell had previously been with Seattle and Los Angeles but now was past his prime at age 36. He was considered to be a smart receiver who never suffered a broken finger because he learned to catch one-handed. The other catcher was Eddie Adams, who would become the starter as the season went along.

Larry Barton, Johnny O'Neill and Marvin Owen were back at first, short and third, but second base was unsettled. The Beavers started with 21-year-old John Ciccimarro, but he failed to hit and could not turn the double play. Mel Nunes replaced him and occasionally Charley Petersen would play there. Petersen was acquired from the Seals because he had a war plant job in Portland that kept him out of the service. Petersen, who could play just about everywhere, including catcher, was mainly used at home, or when the team was in Seattle. He made only one road trip to California, and that was during his two-week vacation period.

3—The 1944 Season

The Portland Beavers of 1944, who came in second. Notice the patriotic patch on the left sleeve. Courtesy of Dave Eskenazi.

An infielder from the 1943 club, Les Floyd, decided to stay with his defense job rather than play.

In the outfield, John Gill, 43-year-old Spencer Harris and former pitcher Frank Shone were back from 1943, but were joined by Norm DeWeese, who was obtained in the trade with Buffalo that brought Joe Sullivan to the team.

The new president of the Pacific Coast League was Clarence "Pants" Rowland, who had been the general manager of the Los Angeles Angels. He won some plaudits from the owners by rehiring the popular one-armed umpire Henry Fanning, and holding a preseason meeting with all the umpires, something that W. C. Tuttle, the former president, never did.

As usual, the Beavers spent the first two weeks of the season in California, this year against San Francisco and Sacramento. During this season, the Beavers handled both these clubs very well, winning 16 of 24 from the Seals and 20 of 29 from the Solons. But the opening week at San

Francisco was a rocky one for Portland. Their pitching had not jelled and the wind was very strong. It especially bothered Joe Sullivan, who had a shutout for five innings, but when the wind came up in the sixth, he was toast. It was a 10-game series, which Portland lost, six games to four, but after that, the Seals were able to win only two games from Portland all year, while losing 12.

In Sacramento, the clubs could get only six games in because of rain, but Portland won four of the six, to finish the road trip at eight and eight. The team then headed home and when they got off the train at the Portland depot, a large number of the Beaver Boosters Club were there to greet them with a big sign congratulating them for being able to play .500 on the road.

The home opener was held at 4 P.M. on Wednesday, April 26, at a time that schoolchildren could attend. Over 12,000 made their way into Vaughn Street Park to see the San Diego Padres beat the Beavers 5–3 in 15 innings. Both pitchers, Joe Sullivan and Chet Johnson, went all the way. The home opener had to be played on Wednesday because San Diego could not get to Portland by Tuesday afternoon. Portland's first night game since August 1942 was held on Thursday April 27, and Ad Liska won his first of 18 games for the 1944 Beavers. The Saturday night game was rained out, so the Beavers persuaded San Diego to stay over for Monday to make up the game and get all seven games played. Since the Padres were only going to Seattle, they agreed. The first game of the Sunday double-header turned out to be one Beaver fans would cherish. The Padres got five runs in the top of the 12th to break a 5–5 tie, but Portland came back with six to win it, 8–7. Frank Shone got two doubles in that final inning, the last one the game-winner. The Beavers won the San Diego series, four games to three to go one game over .500.

The next two weeks were very good ones for the Beavers. The Sacramento Solons came to Vaughn Street Park and won only one game while losing six. This put the Beavers very near to the league lead. The following week, the third straight week Portland was home, the Hollywood Stars came to town and, as in the case with Sacramento, were able to win only once while losing six. That gave Portland a 16–5 homestand and put them in first place by two and one-half games over the Seals. This was the first time Portland had led the league since early 1937. The only drawback to the visit by Hollywood was the uncertainty if they could get there in time to play Tuesday. It made it difficult to sell tickets. As it turned out, the Stars could not make it for Tuesday, so a double-header was played on Thursday night.

3—The 1944 Season

On May 15, the Beavers embarked on a three-week road trip that would keep them away from home until June 7. The first stop was in San Diego, a city that the Beavers did not like visiting. It was a long rail trip with changes in Martinez and in Los Angeles and, with so many sailors and war workers there, it meant standing in long lines to get food. In addition, the Beavers had to leave three players at home: Gilly Campbell, who hurt his arm and could not throw; Mel Nunes, who dislocated his thumb; and Charley Petersen, who could not leave his war plant job.

One bright spot for Portland was the pitching of Roy Helser, who was also a very good pinch hitter. He was to get 28 hits, including three doubles in 1944. The Beavers won the series at San Diego, four games to three, just as they had done when they met in Portland. But Hollywood was a different matter. The Stars won this series, five games to two. Gilly Campbell was able to join the team in Hollywood and give Eddie Adams a rest behind the plate. With Mel Nunes out, Robert Hedington played rather well at second base. He played all four infield positions for the Beavers in 1944. Portland released John Cicimarro while in Hollywood, in addition to two other players who had hardly played at all. But even being six and eight on this road trip, the Beavers still were leading the league as they entrained for the long rail trip from Los Angeles to Seattle.

Submariner Ad Liska, whose 1944 holdout gained him a two-year contract, something very unusual for a minor leaguer. Courtesy of Dave Eskenazi.

In Seattle, the two clubs encountered rain. It took until Friday night before the two northern foes could play, and Portland won both games from the Rainiers at Sick's Stadium. Seattle won Saturday and the teams split on Sunday, giving the Beavers the series, three games to two. Charley Petersen was able to play second base in this series. When the team got back to Portland after a trip of nine wins and 10 losses, they were tied for the league lead, but had left on the trip two and one-half games ahead. Outfielder Ted Gullic had missed several games with a bad hip.

On Tuesday, June 6, the invasion of France occurred. There was no game in Portland, but it was because the Angels could not get there in time. One night game was called because of a curfew while tied at 7–7, so a double-header was scheduled for Monday night, June 12, a normal travel day, but since the Angels were only going to Seattle, there was no problem. The Beavers won three games and had one tie with Los Angeles as of Saturday, June 10. This gave them a two-game lead over the second-place Seals and a nine-game lead over the fifth-place Angels. But since the Angels finished 12 games ahead of Portland at the season's end, they gained 21 games on the Beavers from June 10. The Angels won the Sunday double-header and split the Monday double-header, giving the Beavers the series, four games to three. This was the only series Portland would win over Los Angeles in 1944.

By the end of the Angels series, the Beavers had had just four home series but they had already drawn 103,259 fans, which was more than they drew during all of 1942 when they finished last, and within 26,000 of their 1943 total, when all games had to be played in the daytime.

The following week, June 13–18, the "Poison" Oaks came to Vaughn Street Park and won all six games that could be played. Portland was able to win only five games while losing 16 to Oakland in 1944. On Thursday night, Oakland won 17–2 with Les Scarsella pitching for the Oaks. He was a first baseman who led the league in 1944 but he batted cleanup that night and went four for six. Since Portland had lost the last game of the Angel series, it now had a seven-game losing streak that reached eight when the Angels won on Monday night, June 19. But on Tuesday, Portland finally won over the Angels to break the streak. The club had now fallen to fourth place.

The second Angels–Beavers series was a scheduling mistake. It was a split week with the first three games in Portland and the last four in Los Angeles. To get these games in, the Thursday game was moved to Monday night, and the Wednesday night game was moved up to the afternoon so the two clubs could get on the train for LA in time for the Friday night contest. This was accomplished, but Portland lost five of the seven games to the Angels. Charley Petersen made this his one trip

3—The 1944 Season

to California and played third base because Marvin Owen was hurt. Larry Barton was also hurt, so Spencer Harris and Ted Gullic played first, with Norm DeWeese moving in to play second base.

Portland next went to Oakland and was able to win three games in a row from its nemesis, the Oaks, to take a 3–0 lead in the series. However, Oakland won the last four games to take the series, four games to three. So Portland won three of its five victories from Oakland in 1944 on three straight nights in late June. Marvin Owen was able to play third in the Oakland series, so Charley Petersen played second. When Owen's back acted up again, Ted Gullic moved to third base. After the July 4 double-headers, the eighth-place Sacramento Solons were only five and one-half games out of the league lead, which at this point was held by the Seals.

The Beavers returned home after winning only four and losing seven on the road to LA and Oakland. For the next three weeks, from July 4 through July 23, Portland would be home to Seattle, San Francisco and Hollywood. During these three weeks, Charley Petersen played first, second, third and center field. Barton at first was in a slump and Owen still was having trouble with his back. Sportswriter L. H. Gregory considered Owen the spark plug of the team because the Beavers played much better when he was in the lineup.

Since Lucky Lager Beer was a large owner of the Portland club, the company wanted to call the team the "Lucky Beavers" and change the name of Vaughn Street Park to Lucky Beaver Stadium. Most observers would not call the team lucky with all the injuries the players were having. Pitcher Ad Liska had to miss some starts with a bad leg which prevented him from getting as low a delivery on his submarine pitch, but he tried to compensate for this by keeping his arm closer to his leg.

The Seattle Rainiers barely made it from Los Angeles in time to play in the July 4 night double-header at Portland, but they managed to split the twin bill with the Beavers. The two clubs were tied in the series at three games each until Seattle won the Sunday double-header on July 9 to take the series five games to three.

The Seals followed the Rainiers into Portland and the Beavers were able to win five of the seven games from San Francisco. During this series, Portland released pitchers Jack Wilson and Al Ott and signed outfielder Frank Demaree. Demaree had won the triple crown with the Angels in 1934 and had a successful major league career with the Cubs and Giants, but recently had moved to the Braves, Cardinals and Browns before the Beavers acquired him. However, it took another week before he appeared in the Portland lineup.

After the Seals series, a combined team of Hollywood and San Francisco players defeated a team of Portland and Seattle players at Sick's Stadium on Monday, July 17, for charity. This meant that many players had to give up their off day, but since this was during the war, sacrifices were expected of ballplayers.

The Hollywood Stars began their series at Portland on Tuesday the 18th but the game was stopped by rain, so a double-header was scheduled for Friday night. This was the last week that catcher Gilly Campbell was with the Beavers. He was released because Eddie Adams was playing very well and Campbell was not hitting. The Oaks picked up Campbell for the rest of this season. Hollywood won four of the seven games from Portland this week, giving the Beavers an 11–11 homestand. At this point, Portland was one game under .500 but in fourth place. Momentous world events were taking place this week while Hollywood and Portland were innocently playing baseball. In Tokyo, Premier Tojo was kicked out as leader of his country because the war was going badly for Japan. The next day, an unsuccessful attempt was made on Hitler's life by a group of German generals, which led to a massive purge of those suspected in the conspiracy.

The Beavers now embarked on a three-week road trip to Seattle, Los Angeles and San Francisco. It was to be a trip of highs and lows. The Seattle series was an eight-game series to make up for a rain out during early June. This time, the Beavers turned the tables on Seattle, winning five of the eight games played, just as Seattle had done in Portland three weeks earlier. Seldom-used catcher Earl Norager had to fill in for the injured Eddie Adams by catching most of the games in Seattle, including two double-headers. With Gilly Campbell gone, there was no one else to catch because Charley Petersen could play only the opening game before getting back to his war job in Portland. Norager got quite a workout that week. The Wednesday night double-header called for the first game to go seven innings, but it went 12, and the second game still had to go nine innings. Then on Sunday, the second game was supposed to be the seven-inning affair, but it went 10.

The Portland club now embarked on a trip to California to play the Angels and the Seals. The Angels had been scheduling Wednesday afternoon double-headers all season, rather than play on Tuesday. Even this proved to be difficult for Portland to make on the trip from Seattle. There was a train wreck ahead of their train in Mojave and the team had to be bused 65 miles to Wrigley Field. They arrived 45 minutes late but the Angels made them pay by taking both games that day. In fact, the Angels

3—The 1944 Season

won every game except the one on Saturday afternoon, winning the series six games to one. Eddie Adams was now getting back into the lineup.

Before the series with San Francisco, another charity all-star game had to be played, this time in San Francisco. A combined team of Angels and Seals beat a composite Portland and Sacramento team on Monday night, August 7. But this was the only bad experience the Beavers were going to have this week at Seals Stadium.

The Beavers were four games under .500 before play began on the night of August 8. For the first time during Lefty O'Doul's tenure as manager of the Seals, a visiting team came into Seals Stadium and won all seven games. During that seven-game sweep, Ad Liska got two shutouts, Roy Helser one and Syd Cohen one. The Beavers finished the week three games over .500 in third place. Manager Marvin Owen had a policy that whenever his club won seven games in a row, he would have the entire team over to his home for steak dinners. He probably had to ask each player to bring his ration book and red points so he could buy the steaks.

The Beavers returned home for their last homestand which included series with Seattle, Sacramento and San Diego. At this time, Portland had four good starting pitchers: Ad Liska, Roy Helser, Syd Cohen and Marino Pieretti. The Seattle series was supposed to start on Tuesday, August 15, but the Rainiers, who were coming from Hollywood, could not get there in time. They were to change trains in Martinez but the train from Oakland to Portland was overloaded, so the team had to spend the night in that small town (where Joe DiMaggio was born) and take the morning train north; it did not arrive in Portland until late Tuesday night. There were 4,600 fans in the park on Wednesday night to see if the Beavers could extend their seven-game winning streak, but Seattle won the game 3–2. With Johnny O'Neil sick, Mel Nunes had to play short and Charley Petersen played second base and led off. The clubs split the Thursday night double-header, then traded wins the next two days. Portland won the Sunday double-header to take the series, four games to three. A crowd of 9,683 saw that double-header in which Pieretti won his 20th game with a 4–0 shutout. Portland was now in third place, four games over .500. They ended up tied for the season's series with Seattle at 15 wins each.

The Sacramento Solons were the second of three clubs to come to Portland for the Beavers' last homestand. This was not a good series for Portland. Not only did they lose four of seven to the Sacs, but catcher Eddie Adams went on a one-day sit-down strike. He demanded a sweetener to his contract and did not get it so he watched the opening game with Sacramento from the stands, as his team lost 5–3. Earl Norager caught that game and the next evening too, even though Adams called off his strike. Adams was back behind the plate on Thursday night. On Friday night, only a few hundred fans showed up to see the Sacs win 4–2 because there was a prizefight at Multnomah Stadium that drew 5,240 fans. But a steady drizzle held both crowds down. Even though Sacramento took the series, Portland was now in second place, three games over .500 but 10½ games behind the Angels.

The last home series for Portland in 1944 called for San Diego to play nine games there because of Labor Day. The Beavers got the word that all playoff games would be held in California unless the final series were between Portland and Seattle. A former Beaver, Rupert Thompson, was now playing for San Diego, having joined the team in early August.

This final home series started out splendidly for the Beavers as they won five straight games to go eight games over .500 and take a game-and-a-half lead over the third-place Seals. But just when large crowds turned out, the Beavers flopped. Before 8,237 fans on Sunday they lost the double-header to the Padres; then, before a Labor Day crowd of 7,429, they lost another double-header to the cellar dwellers. One bright spot was a two-run double by 17-year-old catcher Don Cook, who filled in for Earl Norager. In any case, Portland ended its home play in 1944 in third place with a 78–74 record. Portland's home attendance was 270,907 in 1944, compared to 133,000 in 1943.

The last two-week road trip took the Beavers to Sacramento and Oakland. The Tuesday night game at Sacramento had to be postponed because the Solons could not get there in time from Seattle. A double-header was then scheduled for Thursday night. On that evening, which saw the Beavers win both games, Ad Liska won his 150th game as a member of the Portland club, which he first joined in 1936. This was a nine-game series because of the rain outs back in April, when the Beavers made their only other appearance in Sacramento. Double-headers were played on Thursday, Friday, Saturday and Sunday and the Beavers swept three of them and split the other to take the series, seven games to two. Portland was now in second place with an 85–76 record, eight games behind LA with just eight to play, and three ahead of Seattle and San Francisco and five ahead of Oakland.

But the final series was against the "Poison Oaks" at Oaks Park. When the Beavers lost the opening game at Oakland, they were eliminated from the pennant race. They lost the second game of the series also, but then managed to win the next two, but then lost all the remaining games of this eight-game series. Gilly Campbell was now catching some games for Oakland. But Charley Petersen could not make the road trip and could not be used in the playoffs, since they were all in California. Even though the Beavers lost this final series to Oakland, six games to two, they clinched a playoff spot on Saturday, while losing that game to Oakland, 3–2 in 13 innings. When Portland swept that seven-game series at San Francisco in mid–August, they went over .500 and never fell below it. The Beavers ended up 12 games behind the Angels in second place, and Oakland, thanks to its domination of Portland, was able to tie San Francisco for third place, one game behind Portland.

Normally the playoffs called for the first- and third-place teams to play in the opening round, but since San Francisco and Oakland tied for third, the latter two were to play each other, leaving Portland to play the champion Angels.

The first game of the playoffs did not begin until Wednesday, September 20, so the Beavers had time to rest and work out before facing the pennant-winning Angels on their home field. Even though Portland won only seven of the 21 games they played with the Angels during the regular season, and just two in Los Angeles, they surprised the fans by winning the first two games of the series. Ad Liska won the first, 4–2 and Marino Pieretti won the second, 3–2. But Roy Helser was not as successful as he lost 5–4 on Friday night.

The Angels, even though trailing two games to one, gave Portland the advantage of batting last for the rest of the series. It was also reported that the Beavers talked the Angels into paying their hotel bill in Los Angeles for compensation of not having any games in Portland. After taking Saturday off to allow college football to have center stage, the teams played a double-header on Sunday. As the "visiting" team, the Angels pounded Portland 14–3 and 11–1 before 13,166 fans, to take a 3–2 lead in the series. On Monday night, over 5,000 turned out to see the Angels wrap it up with a 3–2 win. Liska, Pieretti, Helser and Cohen took the four Portland defeats. The first-round loss, as in 1943, netted the Beavers $1,250 to divide up, but they all received an extra week's salary for that first round of the playoffs.

3. (tie) San Francisco. Manager Lefty O'Doul had quite a few players returning from his 1943 team that finished a poor second to Los Angeles. The pitching staff in particular was experienced with Bob Joyce,

Seals Stadium with a large daytime crowd, 1944. Courtesy of Doug McWilliams.

Tommy Seats, Ray Harrell, Sam Gibson and Bill Werle back. Gibson was 43 and a seldom-used hurler, Win Ballou, was 46. Three other pitchers had minor roles for the 1944 Seals; Okey Flowers, Rudy Parsons and Joe Knowles Piercey, who had just turned 20.

    The right side of the infield was back with Gus Suhr at first and Del Young at second. But at short the Seals had Joe Futernick and Johnny Cavalli, who had just been discharged from the Coast Guard, At third was John Trutta for most of the season. Jim Adair, who played short in 1943, was drafted very early in the season after playing in just 23 games. Bernie Uhalt, Will Enos, Logan Hooper and Henry Steinbacher returned in the outfield and were joined by Dino Restelli and Ben Guintini, who could also play third. Restelli was leading the club in batting when he got drafted in May. The same two catchers returned; Joe Sprinz, who was now 42 years old, and Ambrose "Brusie" Ogrodowski.

    Lefty Tommy Seats, who was to win 25 games for the 1944 Seals, had a job in a shipbuilding plant and pitched mostly at home. However, he would try to get transportation on a weekend to pitch an away game

3—The 1944 Season

if he could get back to his job on Monday. In August, he pitched a shutout in both games of a Sunday double-header in Sacramento.

Before the season started, the Seals counted four players who were over the draft age, eight who were 4-F, and nine in 1-C, who had been discharged for medical reasons. But there were also nine who were 1-A and subject to call up.

Servicemen again were allowed into Seals Stadium for 30 cents in 1944, while other prices ranged from $1.50 to $1. On opening day, against Portland, 16 marines—eight men and eight women—marched down from left field to home plate to pick up the two teams and then marched out to the center field flag pole. Unfortunately, the marines could not raise the flag because the halyard broke.

San Francisco games were broadcast on station KLX while the Oakland Oaks broadcast on station KROW. Road games away from the Bay Area were recreated for the home audience.

The opening series against Portland went rather well for the Seals. It was a 10-game series, beginning on a Saturday, followed by a Sunday double-header, and then seven games as in a regular series. The Seals won six and lost four to Portland but could win only two more games from the Beavers in 1944. Portland and Sacramento were the teams that gave the Seals the most trouble this season. The first night game since August 1942 was supposed to be played during this opening series on Tuesday night, but it rained, so the reintroduction of night ball was postponed one night. The rained out game was made up with a Saturday double-header.

After the opening series, the Seals went across the Bay to play archrival Oakland at Oaks Park. Another night game was rained out but also made up with a Saturday double-header. The Seals had a very good series, taking five of the seven games.

The Seals next went to Hollywood and again rain encroached on night baseball. Two games were rained out so only one could be made up with a double-header on Saturday. Tommy Seats was able to make it down there to pitch one of the games on Saturday but he lost. However, the Seals won four of the six games played with the Stars.

The Seals returned home for a series beginning May 2 with the Angels. The defending champions were really suffering at this time, having just lost six of seven at Oakland. So O'Doul was anxious take on this slumping squad. He was not disappointed as the Seals won five of seven from LA, and were to win every series from them in 1944. But a Sunday double-header crowd of 15,400 was treated to something they might not have wanted to see. After Tommy Seats won the opener, Pancho Jorge Comellas of the Angels pitched a seven-inning no-hitter in the nightcap. The only Seals base runner was Dino Restelli, who was hit by a pitch in the first inning. Sad Sam Gibson was also pitching a shut out through six innings, but he hurt his ankle and was relieved by Win Ballou in the seventh, and Ballou gave up the only two runs scored in that game. The two Seals pitchers in that game totaled 89 years of age.

The Seals thought they were going to lose second baseman Del Young to the military, and even planned a special "going-away" day for him, but he was rejected for service and remained with the team all season. But they did lose Dino Restelli and another outfielder, Wally Carroll, to the military.

The week of May 9–14 was not a good one for the Seals. They had to go north to play Seattle and then return home to take on Hollywood. It was very rare for a California club to go to the Northwest and play only one of those teams. Later in the season, they did play at both Portland and Seattle on a trip up north. But this trip to Seattle was marked by two rainouts, and only one could be made up. The Seals won only one game and lost five to the Rainiers and fell out of first place, two and one-half games behind Portland. Returning home, the Seals won four of seven from Hollywood but lost four of seven the following week to Seattle.

The Seals then went to Los Angeles for an eight-game series over Memorial Day week at Wrigley Field. After losing the holiday doubleheader to the Angels, the Seals won five of the remaining six games to take the series, five games to three. Tommy Seats could not get either a train or plane reservation from San Francisco, so he did not pitch in this series. But at the end of this series on June 4, the Seals and Portland were tied for first place.

Tommy Seats did win his 10th game on Tuesday night, June 6, D-Day, at home against Sacramento. These teams, unlike Hollywood, did not take that night off. But the Seals were able to win only one more game that week against the Solons, as they lost the series five games to two. One night the Seals blew a 6–1 lead in the ninth inning as the Solons got nine runs off Bob Joyce and Win Ballou. Tommy Seats lost on Saturday and 10,774 disappointed fans saw the Sacs take two from the Seals on Sunday, June 11.

The following week was a much better one for Lefty O'Doul's crew. The San Diego Padres came to Seals Stadium and got pounded six times out of seven. So on Monday, June 19, the Seals were back alone in first place, with a three-game lead over second-place Seattle. Unfortunately, the schedule called for the return of the pesky Sacramento Solons to Seals Stadium, and the Seals lost another five of seven to the then last-place Solons. However, this was a split week, with only three games at San Francisco and the last four at Sacramento.

On the Monday night prior to the second Solon series, June 19, the Seals had to play an army team, and lost 5–1. On the good side, $28,000 worth of war bonds were sold that night, which was the price of admission. The Friday night contest in Sacramento was also a war bond night, with box seats going to purchasers of large bonds and bleachers to those who bought the $25 bond. Tommy Seats was able to get to Sacramento for one of the Sunday games, but he lost a tough one, 1–0 on Ogrodowski's throwing error.

The following week of June 27–July 2, the Seals went to San Diego and had more trouble with them than they did in San Francisco. The Padres won the series four games to two, but what irritated Lefty O'Doul was San Diego's stalling in the second game of Sunday's double-header. At the end of the regulation seven innings, the score was tied 3–3, but the Seals got several runs in the top of the eighth; with the Padres' stalling, the game was called on account of darkness before the inning could be completed, and so the score reverted to a 3–3 tie. In those days, lights were not allowed to be turned on to complete a day game. Tommy Seats was able to get to San Diego to pitch one of the night games, but he lost it 5–4 in 10 innings.

The Seals returned home to play their big rival, the Oaks, at Seals Stadium for an eight-game series that included a Fourth of July double-header. At the start of that week, only three games separated the first seven clubs. A holiday crowd of 19,888 saw the Oaks win that doubleheader but the Seals righted themselves and won four of the next six to tie the series at four games each. A Sunday crowd of 19,128 saw the two rivals split that double-header of July 9. Outfielder Wally Carroll, who was already in the navy, was allowed to play on July 4. He was hitting .446 when he left the team.

The next two weeks, extending from July 11–23, the Seals invaded the Northwest and this time played both Portland and Seattle. They probably would rather have spent both weeks in Seattle because Portland won five of the seven games from them. Tommy Seats got off the train on Sunday morning, July 16, and went straight to Vaughn Street Park but lost 5–2.

Before the Seattle series, the Seals and Hollywood had to combine to play an exhibition game against Seattle and Portland in Seattle for the Army-Navy bat and ball fund. The Seattle series was an eight-game affair to make up for a previous rainout. The Seals won six of the eight games against the Rainiers, with Tommy Seats winning on Thursday night, a rare midweek road appearance for him.

The Seals now returned home to take on the Los Angeles Angels, who had just moved into first place. The Angels held a two-game lead over the second-place Seals and they never relinquished this lead. The Seals won the first, third, fifth and seventh games of this series, each time cutting the Angel lead to a single game, but the Angels won the second, fourth and sixth games to go back up by two games, So after the last game, the Angels left town with a one-game lead. Tommy Seats won two of the Seals' four victories that week and over 35,000 saw the series. The Sunday crowd was held down to 13,374 because of the oppressive heat.

But it was even hotter where the Seals went next. They had to play a seven-game series in Sacramento, which is very hot in August. The Seals were trailing in this series three games to two after Saturday's game, but on Sunday, Tommy Seats got away from the shipyard long enough to pitch two shutouts to give the Seals the series, four games to three. The Seals won the first game 6–0 and the second 3–0 with Brusie Ogrodowski catching both games on a hot day. The crowd of 8,636 at Sacramento gave Seats a big hand at the day's end because not only did he pitch well, he got three hits in four times at bat in the opener and went one for three in the nightcap. Seats hit .271 in 1944.

But things were going to turn sour very quickly for the Seals. Before they could start the next series at home against Portland, they were forced to play another exhibition game for the benefit of servicemen's sports equipment. On Monday, August 7, a combined Seals–Angels team beat Portland and Sacramento 5–4 before 4,510 fans. But the uplifting performance against Sacramento was going to be followed by a monstrous downturn against Portland. The Beavers won all seven games from the Seals, the first time that ever happened to Lefty O'Doul's club. This series jumped Portland over the .500 mark from which it never retreated. It also ended any thought the Seals might have entertained of catching the Angels.

The Seals were now going to play two series each against Hollywood and Oakland, a total of 32 games from August 15 to September 10. Outfielder Neil Sheridan, who was 22 years old, joined the team for the Hollywood series after having a good year at Chattanooga. He hit .293 with

3—The 1944 Season

four homers the last month of the season. He was acquired to replace Logan Hooper, whom the Seals thought was going into the service. But Hooper was allowed to finish the season with the Seals. Technically, Sheridan joined the team too late to appear in the postseason playoffs, but he was allowed to play in the opening round against Oakland because the Oaks wanted to use Charley English. But Sheridan was not allowed to play in the final round against the Angels. The Seals lost the series at home to the Stars, four games to three. Tommy Seats lost on Sunday, 3–2, when the Stars got three runs in the top of the ninth.

The Seals then moved over to Oakland for seven games. The visitors won the odd game of the series, so the Seals gained one game that week on Oakland. Over 12,000 jammed their way into Oaks Park for the Sunday double-header, which the two clubs split. Seats was able to pitch twice in this series because it was just like being home. He split the two decisions.

The Seals then went down to Hollywood for a 10-game series, which included a Labor Day double-header. The Seals won seven and lost three to the Stars with Seats winning twice, on Friday night and again on Monday afternoon. This series, along with the next one against LA, ended Hollywood's chances to make the first division.

The Seals then returned home for their final home series against Oakland, which was a series to remember. On Tuesday night, September 5, the two teams were ready to play but no umpire showed up. Because there was a good crowd in the stands, the clubs decided to use a couple of veteran catchers as umpires, with the Oaks selecting Gilly Campbell and the Seals picking Joe Sprinz. After the third inning, an amateur umpire came down from the stands to call balls and strikes, so the two catchers moved to the bases. Oakland won the game, 8–7. This was an eight-game series because a double-header was held on Saturday, September 9, which is California Admission Day. The Oaks won the series, five games to three, but the Sunday double-header, which was split before 15,058 fans, caused quite a stir among the fans, many of whom were for Oakland. There were several fights in the stands during the second game, which the Seals won 14–1. Perhaps the Oakland fans were goaded by the ceremony between games in which the Seals players were awarded their rings for winning the 1943 playoffs. Or the fans on both sides may have consumed a bit too many adult beverages. Nevertheless, this was San Francisco's final regular season home game, in which they set a new record for attendance which would be broken in the near future.

The Seals, even though losing the final home series to Oakland, were very close to clinching a spot in the Governors' Cup. The last series was in San Diego, which called for eight games because of the suspended game on July 2. After winning the first three games at Lane Field, the Seals did clinch the first division. But they lost three of the last four games to end up tied with Oakland for third place, one game behind second-place Portland, and 13 games behind the Angels.

Because the Seals and Oaks tied for third place, they were scheduled to meet in the opening round of the playoffs. If bad blood had existed from the last series in San Francisco, it was to boil over during the Governors' Cup series. The Seals won 16 and lost 14 to Oakland during the regular season, but it starts over in the postseason. The first three games were scheduled for Oakland, and if one team did not sweep those three games, it was decided that the fourth game would be played Saturday night at Seals Stadium. If a sweep occurred, they would wait until Sunday to play the fourth game in San Francisco because they wanted to get the big Sunday crowd.

Neither team swept the first three games but there was no Saturday night game at Seals Stadium; instead there was one at Oaks Park. This came about because of a protested game in which Lefty O'Doul's protest was upheld. In the opening game, held on Wednesday night, September 20, the Oaks pulled out an exciting win over San Francisco 6–5, in 13 innings. Or so the fans thought! The Seals broke the tie with two runs in the top of the 13th, only to have the Oaks come back with three to win the game, apparently. But in the top of the second inning, Bob Joyce hit a grounder which hit Seals first baseman Gus Suhr's mitt, which was lying in foul ground. The ball bounced off the mitt into fair ground and the Oaks' first baseman picked it up and stepped on first and Joyce was called out. Lefty O'Doul argued correctly that when the ball hit the mitt it was a foul ball, but umpire Powell allowed it to be fair. The next day, Clarence "Pants" Rowland upheld O'Doul's protest, and the game was rescheduled for Saturday night in Oakland, which meant there would be no game that night in San Francisco.

The Oakland players were infuriated and so were their fans. The Oaks threatened to go on strike unless the receipts of that game were given either to charity or to the players. Nothing came of this protest, but the anger did not die down. The next night, the official "game one" was played at Oakland before 9,000 belligerent fans. There was a lot of verbal abuse heaped on O'Doul and the Seals players. However, the Oaks won the game 5–1, to take the series lead. On Friday night, the 22nd, the

Seals evened the series with a 1–0 win. But Seals outfielder Ben Guinitini was hit with a bottle, which did not cause injury but much anger. A controversial call at third base in which the umpire was out of position allowed the Seals runner to get into scoring position. Since this was the only run the of the game, it ignited the Oakland fans. Only two umpires were used in the first round of the playoffs, which made it difficult for them to get into the right position.

From then on it was all Seals. They won the make-up game on Saturday night in Oakland 9–3, and then knocked Oakland out of the playoffs by taking the Sunday double-header at Seals Stadium 9–7 and 2–0 before 15,200 fans. O'Doul said he was never so glad to win a series because of the viciousness of the Oakland fans and their abusive behavior after the protest was upheld.

The final round was against the champion Angels, whom the Seals had beaten 14 out of 22 times during the season. The Angels could have opened at home, but they wanted the Sunday double-header at home, so they agreed to play the first three games at Seals Stadium. Neil Sheridan could not play in this series because he joined the team after August 1, but because Charley English also joined Oakland after that date, the Seals and Oaks agreed to let both play. But the Angels would not be as generous. The Seals made quick work of the Angels in San Francisco, winning three weekday night games in which the Angels could score only one run in Seals Stadium. But when the two teams went to Los Angeles, the Angels played better, winning the Sunday double-header and the Monday night game to tie the series with three one-run victories. But on Tuesday night, October 3, before 13,385 fans, the Seals won their second of four straight playoffs by overcoming a 2–1 Angel lead with a bizarre play in the fifth inning. With men on first and second and no one out, Ben Guintini laid down a bunt and LA pitcher Pancho Comellas threw to third but third baseman Stan Gray fell down, and the ball went down the left field line, allowing Guintini to circle the bases for what amounted to a home run on a bunt. The Seals won the game 4–2, and took the series, four games.

3. (tie) Oakland. The Oaks had a new manager in 1944; Dolph Camilli, the former slugging first baseman of the Brooklyn Dodgers. He was a playing manager so Les Scarsella had to play in the outfield. It was important to keep both bats in the lineup, especially Scarsella's, because he was to lead the league in batting in 1944.

The Oaks lost pitchers Ralph Buxton, Italo Chelini and Vince Di-

Oakland Oaks team photograph for 1944, the only war year they finished in the first division. Courtesy of Doug McWilliams.

Biasi to the military but had Floyd Stromme, Norbert Kleinke, Henry "Cotton" Pippen and Jack Lotz back from the 1943 club. After the season began, Oakland picked up pitcher Manny Salvo from the Boston Braves, who became an 18-game winner. Salvo had previously pitched for Sacramento and San Diego in the 1930s. In July, Salvo pitched a no-hitter against Sacramento. Two other pitchers acquired in midseason were Damon Hayes and Kenny "Coral" Gables. Hayes was signed after he pitched batting practice for the Oaks and the Rainiers when Oakland was playing Seattle in late June. Dolph Camilli outmaneuvered Seattle to sign Hayes. In August, Oakland got pitcher Joe Sullivan and catcher Gilly Campbell when they were released by Portland. The Oaks also started the season with a very old and a very young pitcher. The elderly one was Archie Campbell, age 41, who had pitched for the original Hollywood club in the early 1930s and moved with them to San Diego. The youngster was Ray Martinez, who was 18. Another youthful pitcher was John Marshall, who was just 21. The latter two pitched very little in 1944.

 Bill Raimondi was the old standby at catcher, but his brother, Al, a pitcher, got called into the service after appearing in 21 games, winning two and losing four. The backup catcher was Sam Fenech, who had been out of baseball since 1941. While Fenech did not play a great deal, he did catch Manny Salvo's no-hitter.

With manager Camilli playing most of the time at first, the rest of the infield consisted of Al "A-1" Wright at second, Jake Caufield at short and Chet Rosenlund at third. Jim Herrera and Lin Storti also played a lot at second until the Oaks acquired Charley English from the Angels in August. The 1943 second baseman Hugh Luby was now with the New York Giants and Johnny Vergez, who played third, had retired. As mentioned, Scarsella moved to the outfield, and was joined out there by Emil Mailho, John Kreevich, Jack Devincenzi and Frankie Hawkins. Kreevich's brother, Mike, was to play in the 1944 World Series with the St. Louis Browns.

The War Department announced that the last hour of selected major league games was to be broadcast to our troops overseas. The Pacific Coast League had some of their games carried on this overseas network also. The last hour of some Coast League games was broadcast to troops in South America, the Caribbean and Alaska. In addition, some major league games were re-created for troops in the Pacific theater.

Before the 1944 season could get underway for Oakland, a snag occurred in getting the team from its training camp in San Bernardino to San Diego. No buses could be chartered for civilians. There was no rail service that the team could take from its training camp. The problem was solved by the U.S. Navy. They wanted their sailors to be able to see the opening week of baseball, so the navy sent two large buses to pick up the Oaks and take them to San Diego.

The opening week was not a good one for Oakland as the Padres won seven of the 10 games played. The season began on Saturday, April 8, followed by a double-header the next day, and after taking Monday off, the regular seven-game series format was followed.

The Oaks had trouble getting out of San Diego too. After the Sunday double-header on April 16, they had to crowd onto a 7:30 P.M. train to Los Angeles with no time to eat before boarding, and no meal service on board. They got to their LA hotel after 10:30 P.M., and had to get up at 6:30 A.M. to catch the Valley Daylight train to Oakland. That train was also overcrowded, with servicemen standing in the aisles and some sitting in the rest rooms.

On Tuesday, April 18, the Oaks opened their home season with their archrivals, the Seals. Both the players and the fans were pleased to find that Oaks Park, built back in 1913, had been spruced up over the winter.

The clubhouses and the umpires room were cleaned up and painted, as was the entire ballpark. Neon signs were installed over the concession stands, the rest rooms were cleaned up and the team flattened out some of the walking surfaces that formerly had been steep ramps. The owner, Victor "Cookie" Devencenzi, felt that if the fans were not treated well, they would go to movies, the beach or to other sports. The 1944 crowds at Oaks Park were very good, especially on Sundays and holidays.

Even though the Oaks lost their home opening series to the Seals, five games to two, they drew very well. With a rain out on Wednesday, the teams played a double-header on Saturday, as well as the usual one on Sunday. A crowd of 10,800 saw the final two games of that series.

The next visitor to Oaks Park was the eventual pennant winner, Los Angeles. But in April, this was not a very good club and the Oaks beat them decisively, six games to one. For the Sunday double-header on April 30, over 3,000 fans had to be turned away. A night game was also rained out in this series, necessitating a double-header on Saturday, as in the previous week. The Oaks won 17 and lost 13 to the Angels in 1944, so after this first series, the two clubs battled on fairly even terms.

After this great success with the Angels, the Oaks had to travel down to Gilmore Field to play the team that was to be their nemesis, the Hollywood Stars. The Stars won all seven games from the Oaks, several by lopsided scores. The schedule then called for Oakland to return home to play Sacramento before going back to Los Angeles to play the Angels. The series against Sacramento was going very well with the Oaks taking four of the first five games, but with a big crowd expected on Sunday,

Front of Oakland scorecard, 1944. Courtesy of Doug McWilliams.

the double-header was rained out, costing the Oaks their largest gate of the week.

Before embarking on the train back to Los Angeles, the Oaks announced the acquisition of pitcher Manny Salvo from the Braves. However, Salvo did not pitch that week in Los Angeles. The Oaks started out as badly as they did when over at Gilmore Field, playing Hollywood. The Angels won the first four games of the series, but then the Oaks got up off the floor and won the final three games, including the Sunday double-header. Les Scarsella started the opener on Sunday but was relieved by Archie Campbell, who got the win. But Scarsella stayed in the game and went to left field.

The Oaks then went to Sacramento and on Tuesday night, Scarsella relieved Floyd Stromme and got the win. On Saturday, Scarsella pitched the whole game, won it 9–1, and batted fourth. On Friday night, the one-armed umpire, Henry Fanning, collapsed on the field after an argument with manager Dolph Camilli. But he was able to continue the following day. The Oaks took four of seven from Sacramento, and on Sunday, Manny Salvo won his first start for the Oaks.

But now it was time to face Hollywood again, this time at Oaks Park and in an eight-game series over Memorial Day. The Stars were just as difficult in Oakland as they were in Hollywood, taking seven of the eight games. Manny Salvo suffered his first loss on Saturday. A crowd of 8,200 saw the Stars take the Sunday double-header on June 4, to give Hollywood 14 wins in 15 games.

After that dismal Hollywood series, the Oaks were glad to get out of town. They were to embark on a successful but peculiar trip to the Northwest. They had a week at Seattle, a week at Portland and then returned to Seattle for just three games, with the final four against the Rainiers at home. Because of a rain out, only six games were played in Seattle that first week with the Oaks taking four of the six. One night game loss was especially hard for the Oaks to take because they blew an eight-run lead, to lose 9–8 in 12 innings. The following week in Portland was even better. The Oaks took all six games played, with one rain out. Scarsella pitched one of those wins while batting fourth.

Oakland then had to return to Seattle where they won two of the three games scheduled up there. It was in this series that pitcher Damon Hayes was picked up by the Oaks. Because the split week called for the teams to finish the series in Oakland, there was no game on Friday. In fact, the Saturday game had to be moved to an 8:30 P.M. start to allow the teams to get there. The Oaks won the three games played in Oakland to win the Seattle series, five games to one. A crowd of 10,500 turned out to cheer their team in the Sunday double-header win.

It was now the last few days of June and only three and one-half games separated the first seven clubs in the league. The Oakland fans were anxiously looking forward to the next series, which called for the Portland Beavers to play at Oaks Park. This time, the Oaks were a bit surprised, as Portland, having lost all six games to the Oaks up north, won the first three games of this series. But the Oaks righted themselves and won the last four games to win the series. A crowd of 11,000 saw the Oaks take two on Sunday, July 2, from the Beavers. New pitcher Ken "Coral" Gables made his debut that Sunday but was not involved in the decision.

The following series was the one that drew the most fans all season long. It was an eight-game series over the Fourth of July at San Francisco; over 55,800 fans took in those games. The Oaks won the Fourth of July double-header and split the Sunday double-header, the latter drawing 19,128 fans, which was the largest crowd in San Francisco history. But when the series was over, each team had won four games. Scarsella pitched twice, winning one and getting a no decision. But he batted fourth in every game.

The next week, July 11–16, saw the Oaks move into first place when they took six of the seven games from San Diego at home. Ken Gables won his first game in that series with a 2–0 shutout. Another big crowd of 11,653 turned out for the Sunday double-header and the Oaks did not disappoint the home crowd, taking both games.

But the following week, July 18–23, saw the Oaks tumble from the top spot, never to return. The troublesome Sacramento Solons came to Emeryville and won six of the nine games in this series. The two extra games were to make up for the Sunday double-header rained out on May 14. This was also the week that the Angels took over the lead and began pulling away from the pack. It was also the week that the Oaks lost two players: pitcher Henry "Cotton" Pippen had to go into the service and outfielder Frankie Hawkins hurt his leg and was out for the year. To replace these players, the Oaks picked up catcher Gilly Campbell and pitcher Joe Sullivan, who had been released by Portland. One bright spot this week was that one of Oakland's three wins was a no-hitter by Manny Salvo on Wednesday, July 19. Another noteworthy game was played on Saturday when the two teams started two 18-year-old pitchers, Ray Martinez for Oakland and Lou Penrose of Sacramento. This was the second game of a double-header in which Penrose won his only decision of the year, while Ken Gables lost after relieving Martinez.

3—The 1944 Season

If ever a team did not want to make a road trip, it was the 1944 Oaks on Monday, July 24. After losing six of nine to the Solons, the Oaks had to go to Hollywood for another pounding. That is exactly what they got. The first two games were lost by scores of 12–2 and 9–2, but the third was a bit more respectable, 4–2. That made it 17 wins in 18 games for Hollywood over the Oaks, but on Friday night, Oakland finally won 8–5, with four unearned runs in the ninth inning. But then it was back to their old ways for the Oaks, as they lost on Saturday and the doubleheader on Sunday before 11,000 Gilmore Field fans. The Stars won 20 of 22 games from Oakland in 1944.

By this time, it was apparent that Oakland was no longer a pennant contender. But it was one of five teams trying for the other three first-division spots. The Oaks returned home on August 1 for an eight-game series with Seattle, the extra game due to the travel day during that split week in June. There was a double-header played on Wednesday night and Seattle won both those games as well as both games on Sunday. But Oakland won the four single games, so the series ended up a 4–4 split. Friday night was Les Scarsella Night as the fans honored the player who was not only to win the batting title, but also the most valuable player award. He returned the fans' gratitude by driving in the winning run that night. But a disappointed crowd of 9,000 came out Sunday to see Seattle take both games from Oakland and tie the series.

Before Oakland was to go to San Diego, for the first time since the opening week of the season, some of its players had to stop off at Gilmore Field in Hollywood to play in an all-star game in which Oakland and Seattle opposed San Diego and Hollywood. This was done throughout the baseball world to raise money for servicemen's athletic equipment. One of the most unusual exhibition games was played at the Polo Grounds in New York in late June when the Dodgers, Giants and Yankees played a three-way game in which the Dodgers got 5, the Giants 1 and the Yankees 0. Each team batted six times, three against each opponent, and also was in the field six times, three times against each club.

Down in San Diego, the Oaks did not fare as well as they did at home against the Padres. San Diego, now falling into the cellar, nevertheless beat Oakland four of seven games. During that week the two clubs pulled a trade: the Oaks gave up pitcher Norbert Kleinke for outfielder Mel Steiner. Steiner was to be insurance for the loss of Frankie Hawkins.

The Oaks then made the short trip to Los Angeles where they again lost a series four games to three, and picked up two new players. One of the players was Charley English in a straight cash deal. He pinch-hit for LA on Wednesday and played second base for Oakland on Friday, Saturday and Sunday. The other new player was 17-year-old Vic Picetti, a high school all-star who played in New York in the East-West all-star game for high school players. He had always liked Dolph Camilli so he signed with Oakland after turning down several offers from major league clubs. Even though Picetti was a first baseman, Camilli let him play there and either benched himself or played in the outfield. Picetti got four hits in 20 at bats in Los Angeles. Unfortunately, this lad died before his 19th birthday.

After the Angels series, the Oaks were all through traveling for the season. They had a series with the Seals, one the Oaks lost four games to three, but one that was very well attended. A crowd of 11,000 saw the Sunday double-header. They then had a nine-game series with the Angels over Labor Day, a series Oakland won five games to four. Then the Oaks went across the bay to take on the Seals again, a series Oakland won five games to three. Nevertheless, San Francisco won the season's series between the two Bay Area clubs, 16–14. Large crowds attended this series at Seals Stadium even though neither club was in the pennant race, but both were struggling to get into first division. But Oakland lost pitcher Ken Gables, who was called up to the Pittsburgh Pirates.

The opening game in the Seals series was the one that no umpires showed up for, so Gilly Campbell and Joe Sprinz did the umpiring. After the third inning, they moved to the bases when an amateur umpire came down from the stands to call balls and strikes. The Sunday double-header before over 15,000 was marred by fights among fans in the stands. No players were involved. This attitude was only to get worse when the two teams met in the opening round of the playoffs.

The final week of the season saw the Oaks entertain their "cousins," the Portland Beavers. Portland had already clinched the first division, the Seals were almost in and Hollywood was now out of it. So the final week was one of scoreboard watching between the Oakland and Seattle players. At the start of this final week, Oakland's record was 80–81 and Seattle's was 82–79. The Rainiers had a two-game lead but fortunately for Oakland, Seattle was down in LA losing six of eight to the champion Angels while the Oaks took six of eight from the Beavers. On the final day of the season, Oakland ended up tied with the Seals at 86–83, while Seattle fell to fifth place, with a record of 84–85.

Because Oakland and San Francisco were tied for third, they met in the first round of the playoffs. It was a bitter series indeed. The first game on Wednesday night saw the Oaks rally from a two-run deficit in the 10th inning to win the game 6–5. But Lefty O'Doul protested the game on a play in the second inning. A ground ball hit by a Seal hit a mitt in foul territory and bounded back into fair ground, and the umpire allowed the Oaks to retire the batter. This protest was upheld and that game had to be replayed in its entirety on Saturday night in Oakland. Originally the Saturday night game was to be played in San Francisco. The Oaks won on Thursday but the Seals evened the series with a 1–0 win on Friday, when a controversial call allowed a Seal runner to be safe at third. When this man scored the only run of the game, it further angered the Oakland fans, who claimed the umpire was out of position. From that point on, it was all Seals, and so the Oaks were eliminated from the only wartime playoff series in which they participated.

5. Seattle. The 1944 season was the only wartime year that the Seattle Rainiers did not finish in the first division. In fact, it was the first time since 1937 that Seattle missed the playoffs. But they were in the hunt for the first division until the final day of the season.

Seattle had some old pitchers returning from the 1943 season. Sylvester Johnson, the last man to pitch to Babe Ruth back in 1935, was 43, Byron Speece was 47 and Hal Turpin was 41. Carl Fischer was 38 but the rest were younger. These included Joe Demoran, Frank Tincup, John Yelovic and Glenn Elliott. After the season began, the Rainiers were able to acquire John Babich after he left his war job in Oakland. One newcomer, Al Libke, showed such promise with the bat that he often played outfield or first base.

Hal Sueme was back at catcher along with seldom-used Hal Hoffman and Nick Buonarigo, who was later sold to Hollywood. Hoffman was released when Seattle was able to get Hal Spindel in midseason. Spindel, who had been with Seattle from 1934 to 1938, had the highest batting average in the league but did not have enough plate appearances to win the title.

Other position players returning from 1943 were third baseman Dick Gyselman, shortstop Joe Dobbins, infielder Stan Gray and outfielders Loyd Christopher, Bill Kats and Bill Matheson. Newcomers were infielder Bill Lyman, formerly of Oakland; Connie Creeden, formerly of Hollywood; Paul Carpenter, formerly of the Angels; and Roy Johnson. Johnson, who was 41, played third and outfield and had been with the Seals from 1926 to 1928. Carpenter had been out of baseball in 1941 and 1942.

Hal Turpin, who had to leave the team in mid–1943 to work his

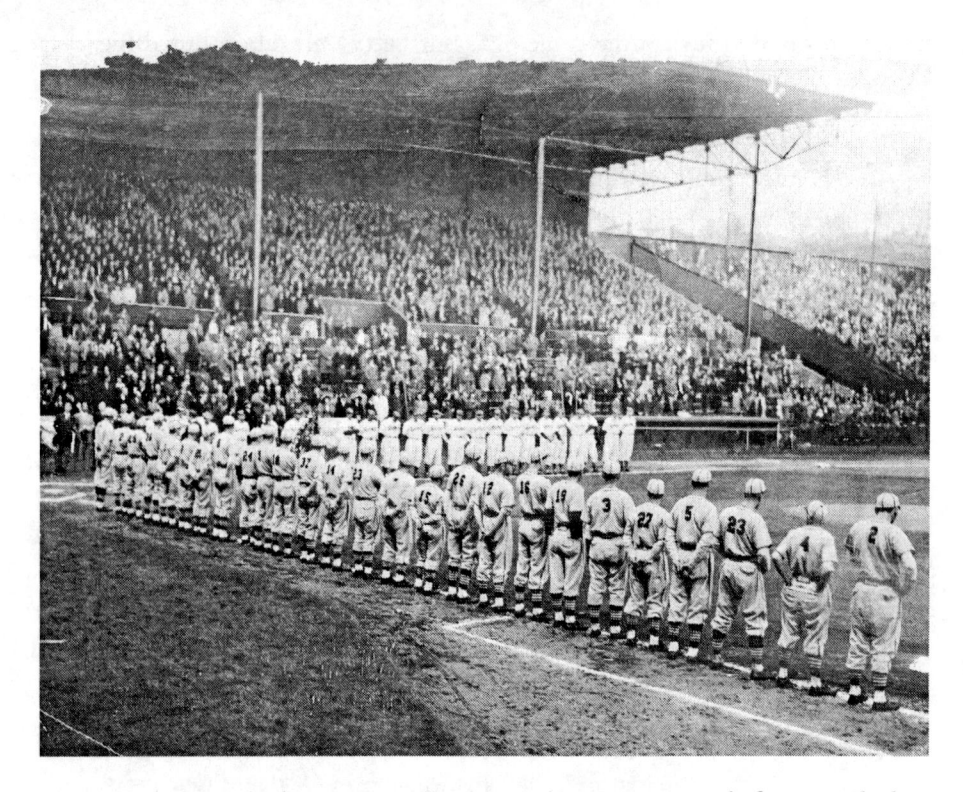

Seattle opens its home season in 1944 against Sacramento before a packed Sick's Stadium. This was to be the only wartime year that Seattle failed to finish in the first division. Courtesy of Dave Eskenazi.

Oregon farm, got his first starting assignment in 1944 at Hollywood. He pitched well, but lost to the Stars 2–1. However, he beat them later in the series, 4–3. The season began with a game on Saturday, then a Sunday double-header before the regular seven games that were played from Tuesday through Sunday. Seattle did not start out well, losing the first three games, but then won four of the last seven games, thereby losing the series at Gilmore Field, six games to four. The Seattle players were annoyed with the reading of news bulletins over the loudspeaker by the Gilmore Field announcer, because they felt fans came to the park to forget the war news for a while.

The Rainiers then went to San Diego where they won the series four games to three by winning the Sunday double-header. Hal Turpin could not pitch in this series because he had to visit his sick mother in Oregon. During this series, manager Bill Skiff used five different first basemen,

3—The 1944 Season

but he never quite found the ideal man this season. Even catcher Hal Sueme began playing there later in the season when Seattle acquired Hal Spindel.

The Seattle Boosters Club planned on meeting the team at the rail station when they got home from San Diego. It took until Tuesday night for the team to get there, so the home opener with Sacramento was postponed until Wednesday night. A patriotic theme was a major part of the opening ceremony. A crowd of 12,464 saw the Rainiers behind Joe Demoran beat the Solons, 8–0. The Seattle Boosters won a 45-pound salmon from the Portland Boosters because their home opener outdrew Portland's by 788 fans. The following night, April 27, Loyd Christopher got Seattle's first home run of the season, but Sacramento won the game 4–2. Sick's Stadium was not an easy park to homer in, especially at night, but the 1944 baseball was not as lively as the prewar baseball. During this week, the Rainiers picked up Bob Gorbould, a Canadian, who played second and short.

During this series, Hal Turpin rejoined the team only to leave very soon when he got word his mother had died. Because of the missed game on Tuesday, the teams played a double-header on Friday night, which was split. Unlike Portland, Seattle still scheduled the second game of night double-headers for seven innings, rather than play seven in the opener. On Saturday, catcher Hal Sueme split his finger and was to be out for over 10 days. That meant that Nick Buonarigo and Hal Hoffman had to catch, but neither were good hitters. That is when Bill Skiff began trying to get Hal Spindell from Toledo, where the St. Louis Browns had sent him.

Seattle was able to win the odd game of the Sacramento series and then the San Diego Padres came to town for an eight-game series. Nick Buonarigo caught all eight games as well as the last three of the Sacramento series, but was hitting under .200. Hal Turpin returned in time to pitch a shutout over San Diego in the first game of the Sunday doubleheader. Seattle won the San Diego series, five games to three but got word that outfielder Bill Matheson and pitcher John Yellovic had to report for their draft physicals. Up until this point, third baseman Dick Gyselman was the only player to appear in all the games and he showed up on opening day with no spring training.

The San Francisco Seals were the third and last team to come to Seattle on this opening homestand. Both the Tuesday and the Thursday games were rained out so only one could be made up with a Friday night double-header. After observing what Portland had done, the Rainiers decided to schedule the seven-inning game first for night double-headers. The idea behind it was that fans showing up at the normal time of 8 P.M. could see the end of the first game and then watch a regular nine-inning second game. That seven-inning opener of the Friday night double-header was the only game the Seals could win on this trip, so the Rainiers took the series, five games to one. Hal Sueme was able to return to the lineup during this week. On Saturday, Byron Speece, the 47-year-old submarine pitcher, shut out the Seals on seven hits. So Seattle was able to win 14 of the 21 games played on this first homestand. Even though the team was playing well, Bill Skiff was not happy with his leadoff hitters. He tried several players there but finally settled on Bob Gorbould by mid-season.

The Rainiers next embarked on a two-week road trip to Sacramento and San Francisco. To Seattle's embarrassment, the Solons won their first series since 1942 when they won the last game. All four of Sacramento's wins were by a single run with scores of 1–0, 2–1 and two of 4–3. Seattle's pitchers were doing their job but the hitters were not. But the team picked up the following week in San Francisco. Seattle won four of the seven games in the only series that they were to play in Seals Stadium in 1944. So the trip, which concluded on May 28, ended up with seven wins and losses. Outfielder Bill Kats was sent to Kansas City but was recalled later in the season.

Seattle returned home to host Portland, Oakland, Los Angeles and then Oakland again for half a week. This homestand covered the period from Memorial Day through June 22. The May 30 double-header was played at night, with the first game now being the seven-inning game. Portland was in first place, a game and a half ahead of Seattle but when the Rainiers won that holiday double-header they took over the league lead. The Wednesday game was rained out so a double-header was scheduled for Thursday night, but that too was rained out. By this time, the

Manager Bill Skiff, who managed Seattle from 1941 to 1946, shown here during spring training. Courtesy of Dave Eskenazi.

Aerial view of Sick's Stadium in Seattle, as players work out before a game. Courtesy of Dave Eskenazi.

Pacific Coast League rosters had to be trimmed down to 20 veterans and five rookies and both managers, Bill Skiff of Seattle and Marvin Owen of Portland, protested that the limit was too severe.

Finally the rain let up to allow the two clubs to play a Friday night double-header. The visiting Beavers won both games to go back into the league lead by a game and a half. The Rainiers' win on Saturday cut Portland's lead to a half game. The teams split the Sunday double-header to give Seattle the series win, four games to three, but the Beavers held a half-game league lead. The second game Sunday, scheduled for seven innings went 15, with Seattle winning 5–4.

But extra innings were just beginning for the Rainiers. After a day off on Monday, the Oakland Oaks came to Sick's Stadium and beat Seattle, 5–2 in 13 innings. On Wednesday night, Seattle won 4–3, but it took 12 innings. Then on Thursday, Seattle won 9–8 in 10 innings after Oakland blew an 8–0 lead. So in the last four games, Seattle played 50 innings instead of the 34 scheduled (the second game Sunday was to be a seven-inning game). The rest of the Oakland series consisted of regulation games, with the Oaks taking four of the seven.

The Los Angeles Angels next appeared at Sick's Stadium. Up until this point, the Angels had been playing poorly but help was on the way from the Chicago Cubs, which was to make the Angels the 1944 pennant winner. The Angels won the first three games of the series in Seattle, but the Friday night game was rained out. Seattle won Saturday and the teams split the Sunday double-header, so Seattle lost this series, four games to two. They also lost a catcher, but were about to gain a much better one. Nick Buonarigo quit the team to go into business in Los Angeles but after much perseverance, Bill Skiff was finally able to get catcher Hal Spindell from Toledo.

The next week, June 20–25, was a split week with the Oaks back in Seattle for three games and then the teams moved to Oakland to finish the series. Monday was an off day and the Rainiers did not request that Oakland play that night instead of on Thursday, as was done in Portland between the Beavers and Los Angeles. So the Oaks and Seattle played the usual Tuesday, Wednesday and Thursday nights and then entrained for Oakland. The teams not only did not get there in time to play Friday night, but the Saturday afternoon game had to be moved to night to get that one played. This was a bad series for Seattle; they lost two of three at home to the Oaks and all three in Oakland, thereby losing five of the six games.

Outfielder Connie Creeden was left behind in Seattle in order for the team to sell him to Little Rock. Bill Skiff was not happy with his playing. In addition, Joe Dobbins was slumping after having had a fine year in 1943.

The Rainiers then went to Los Angeles to play the Angels. At first, it looked like another bad week for Seattle. The Rainiers lost three of the first four games, which made Seattle's record nine losses in the last 11 games. Hal Spindell made his debut in the Friday night game, which Seattle lost 4–2. But then things turned around for the Skiffmen, and Seattle won the last three games of the series to win it, four games to three. Two ex–Angels, Hal Sueme and Paul Carpenter, had very good games against their former club. The Rainiers were now only two games out of the league lead, but in fourth place.

Seattle then went to Portland for the first time in 1944 for an eight-game series over the Fourth of July week. The holiday double-header

3 — The 1944 Season

was played at night to allow the Rainiers to get there from Los Angeles. After winning three of the first four games of that series at Vaughn Street Park, Seattle moved to within a half game of the league lead. But the clubs split the final four games, giving Seattle the series, five games to three, but they were a game out of first place. During this week, Seattle released infielder Stan Gray and signed outfielder Jimmy Ripple, who had been in two World Series with the New York Giants and one with the Cincinnati Reds. Stan Gray was picked up by the Angels.

Seattle now moved back to Sick's Stadium for a 23-game homestand with Hollywood, San Francisco and Portland which extended from July 12–31. The Stars brought with them a former player on Seattle's great pennant-winning team of 1940, Frankie Kelleher. Kelleher really hurt his former club in this series by homering three times, including a grand slam. The Stars won four of the first five games but Seattle did win the Sunday double-header, to lose the series by only one game. The new acquisition, Jim Ripple, was used only as a pinch hitter in this series because he had a bad leg.

Before the next series with San Francisco could start, the clubs were required to play an all-star game for the servicemen's bat and ball fund. On Monday night, a combined team of Hollywood and San Francisco beat Portland and Seattle, but it was for a worthy cause, even though the players could have used the rest. The Seals then proceeded to take six of the eight games from the Rainiers, removing them from serious pennant contention. During this series, Jim Ripple was used in left field but he was almost a one-legged man. At the end of the series, he was released by Seattle and the Seals gave him a chance, but they also kept him only a short while.

The Portland Beavers next came to Sick's Stadium and took great pleasure in winning five of the eight games from their northern rival. At the end of this series, Seattle was in seventh place, six and a half games behind the pennant-bound Angels. On this homestand, Seattle won only eight games while losing 15. Royal Brougham of the *Seattle Post Intelligencer* wrote in his column that one former member of the Seattle team left owing money to several Rainier players but he did not say who it was. The recent castoffs were Stan Gray, Connie Creeden and Jim Ripple.

Seattle left on what looked like a funeral train for a three-week road trip to Oakland, Hollywood and Portland. The Oakland series was an eight-game affair because the teams could not get there from Seattle during that split week in June. The teams played a double-header on Wednesday night and Seattle won both games as well as both games on Sunday.

But Oakland won all four single games, so the two clubs tied the series, four games each.

Seattle went to Hollywood and won the first two games of the series to extend their winning streak to four games. But then the club went into a slump. The Rainiers lost the last five games of the series to the Stars. While in Hollywood, Loyd Christopher had a groin injury and went to a specialist. He was replaced in the outfield by rookie Bill Derflinger. Derflinger got only one hit in seven at-bats but he did make the news in Los Angeles. He and rookie pitcher Gene Holt were outside their hotel in downtown Los Angeles after a game and were attacked by a gang of zoot suiters, who had been causing trouble in the LA area. The gang pulled knives and Derflinger used his left leg to ward off the blows, but was cut, while Gene Holt was cut in the head. After this incident, both players were released by the Rainiers.

Seattle was now going to Portland but the club missed its train connection in Martinez, California, and had to spend a night there before taking the day train to Portland. They got there too late for a Tuesday night game so a double-header was scheduled for Thursday night. During this series, Hal Sueme played a few games at first base. Outfielder Bill Kats was recalled from Kansas City to replace Derflinger. Seattle had a 3–2 lead in this series at Vaughn Street Park going into the Sunday double-header but lost both games and the series by a 4–3 margin. On this road trip, Seattle won only nine and lost 13 to fall to sixth place, 12½ games behind the Angels. But they were only four games out of fourth place.

Bill Skiff still harbored thoughts of Seattle finishing in the first division. The team returned home for its last homestand on August 22, for seven games with San Diego and nine with Sacramento over Labor Day. These two weeks gave the fans hope. Before this homestand began, the team got word that Paul Carpenter and Bill Lyman both passed their army physicals, but they were given 21 days to report, which would allow them to finish the regular season.

With the return of Bill Kats, Skiff inserted him into the lead-off spot with Bob Gorbould batting second. Hal Spindell was hitting at a pace that would have him finish at .355, but with too few at-bats to claim the title. He caught both games of double-headers on consecutive days, with Hal Sueme playing first. Loyd Christopher was also back in the lineup after his groin injury. Seattle got back into the race for the first division with six wins in seven games over the cellar-dwelling Padres. After this series, they were only a game out of fourth place.

The Solons followed the Padres into Sick's Stadium for the last series to be played there in 1944. Dick Gyselman was hurt so Bill Matheson played a few games at third with Al Libke going to the outfield. Seattle won six of the nine games from the Sacs to finish their homestand with 12 wins and four losses. Over 330,000 saw the Rainiers play this season. The team left town on its last road trip in third place, a game ahead of fourth-place Hollywood and two games behind second-place Portland.

At this point in the season, Seattle had hit only 20 home runs compared to 56 for the Angels, and their team batting average of .253 was the lowest they had experienced in years. They had to make the longest trip possible, a 1,200-mile journey to San Diego. They could not start that series until Wednesday night, with a double-header which the teams split. Another game was postponed by fog, so the teams had to play double-headers on Saturday and Sunday. The Rainiers won five of the seven games from San Diego, to tie the Seals for third place, two games behind Portland. In three weeks of playing just San Diego and Sacramento, the team revived, taking 17 of the 23 games played, and moving to three games over .500, at 82–79.

The final series called for eight games with the Angels in Wrigley Field, a place where Seattle had won four of seven earlier when they won the final three games of that series. Things started out very well when they won the opening game, 3–1, to go four games over .500 with their fourth win in a row at Wrigley Field. But even though the Angels clinched the pennant that night they said they were going all out to win every game and not save themselves for the playoffs. The Angels went on to win six of the final seven games of the series to knock Seattle into fifth place with an 84–85 record, two games behind the Seals and Oaks, who tied for third place. This was the first time since Emil Sick owned the club that it did not make the playoffs. Bill Skiff blamed the injury to Loyd Christopher as the main cause. But the Angels were anxious to avenge the humiliation they suffered in 1943 when the Rainiers beat them in the first round of the playoffs, after Los Angeles won the pennant by 21 games. This was Bill Sweeney's revenge for the bragging that Bill Skiff did in 1943.

6. Hollywood. The Hollywood Stars were managed for the second year in a row by pitcher Charlie Root, who continued on the active roster despite being 45 years of age. This would be the final year for Root to manage the club. The 1944 season was the one wartime year that the Stars had a good chance to make the first division. They were as high as second place on August 21 but began a tailspin that dropped them to sixth place. Even so, they ended up only three games behind San Francisco and Oakland, which tied for third place.

Besides Root, the pitchers returning for Hollywood were Earl Escalante, Ronnie Smith and Cy Blanton, who joined the team in July. Blanton, like many other wartime players, continued with his defense plant job and pitched only when the Stars were home or at Los Angeles. Newcomers to the pitching staff were Joe Mishasek, John Intelkofer, Jim Sharp, Alex Weldon, Earl Embree, 17-year-old Clint Hufford and Don Hanski, who was sold to San Diego in August. Knut Kimball, a former Angel pitcher from the 1930s, joined the club in June as a part-timer who also pitched only when the Stars were home because of his war plant job.

Butch Moran was back at first, Kenny Richardson at second, Tod Davis at short and Harry Clements at third. Brooks Holder was back in center field, along with Roy Younker, who could play several positions, and 41-year-old Babe Herman, who mainly pinch-hit. Jim Hill retuned as catcher. New infielders were Ray Olsen, who left in early September to take a war plant job, and 16-year-old Gordon Goldsberry, who was a first baseman. New outfielders were Otto Meyers, who was later sold to Sacramento; Del Jones; Joe Gonzales, who was sold to Mobile in July; and Les Powers, who had been with the Seals and Solons in the mid–1930s. A new catcher, Ernie Potocar, backed up Hill early in the season, but was released when Root decided to use Roy Younker as a catcher.

In May, the Stars received an outfielder who was to become the most popular player ever to wear a Hollywood uniform, Frankie Kelleher. Kelleher had been on that great Seattle team of 1940 but he was to have his best years while with Hollywood. In 1944, he missed the batting title by a fraction of a point to Les Scarsella of Oakland.

The wartime theme was present even in preseason games. Before one game at Gilmore Field between the Stars and the Angels, 30 marines from Camp Pendleton put on a demonstration of hand-to-hand fighting with clubs, machetes, bayonets and knives. The fans seemed to appreciate it and gave the marines a big hand.

The Stars opened the season at home against Seattle on a cold Saturday afternoon, April 8. Sheriff Gene Biscaluz made his usual appearance along with actor Joe E. Brown and Jack Norworth, who wrote the famous song *Take Me Out to the Ball Game*. A crowd of 5,000 braved the cold to see the Stars get off on the right foot with a 2–1 win. The next day, Hollywood won a double-header to go 3–0. After an off day Monday, the teams played a regular seven-game series, with Seattle winning four of the last seven, but Hollywood still won the series, six games to

The 1944 Hollywood Stars, who finished sixth but just three games out of the first division. Courtesy of Dick Beverage.

four. One real bright spot for Hollywood occurred on Thursday night when 17-year-old Clint Hufford pitched a 10-inning shutout, as the Stars won, 1–0.

The next week was not as nice for the Stars. They had to play their cross-town rivals, the Angels, at Wrigley Field. The opening ceremony, which was the Angels' home opener, again featured Sheriff Gene Biscaluz, along with Mayor Fletcher Bowron and the governor of Ohio, John Bricker. The Angels, who won every series from Hollywood in 1943 and 1944, won this one five games to two. Hollywood, still hurting for outfielders, used Steve Sitek in right field for a few games. But Sitek, a former Giants farmhand, worked the graveyard shift in a rubber factory, and was available only when the Stars were at or near home. But his job may have hurt his playing, because Hollywood released him after five games.

The San Francisco Seals came to Gilmore Field for the third week of the season and beat the Stars four games out of six. Two weeknight games were rained out and only one of them could be made up. Hollywood won the first game of the Sunday double-header despite a rather unusual circumstance. Third base coach for the Stars, Marty Krug, left the coaching box in the eighth inning and walked across the infield as three Hollywood runners were scoring. Krug thought it was the last of the ninth and the game was over. Because of this, Ray Olsen had to bat again and singled in two runs, so the Stars won anyway.

The next visitor to Gilmore Field was most welcome, the Oakland Oaks. The Stars owned this club in 1944, winning an astounding 20 of 22 games from them. Seattle was the only other team that Hollywood had a winning record against this season. This series, the first week of May, was a seven-game sweep for Hollywood. A crowd of 11,000 came out for the Sunday double-header and was not disappointed.

It was now the second week of May and the Stars had not been further from home than the one week they spent at Wrigley Field. But now it was time to pack their bags for a strange trip to Portland and San Francisco. It was almost a given that any California team that went up to the Northwest would play both Portland and Seattle, but the schedule was drawn up by someone in Massachusetts who should have consulted a map. Because of wartime travel, the Stars could not get to Portland in time to play on Tuesday, so the teams began the series on Wednesday and played a double-header on Thursday night. Hollywood started out by winning its eighth game in a row on Wednesday night but then lost the final six games to the Beavers, including two double-headers. The Stars were without two of their outfielders for the Portland series because Del Jones hurt his knee and Brooks Holder had to report to his San Francisco draft board for a physical. Pitcher Earl Escalante played right field in one game and catcher Ernie Potocar played out there in another.

In San Francisco, the Stars lost the first two games to extend their losing streak to eight games, after winning eight in a row. But the addition of Frankie Kelleher in the outfield helped spur the team out of its slump as Hollywood won the next two games; still, the Seals managed to win the series, four games to three. At this point in the season, May 22, the Stars were in sixth place, seven games behind league-leading Portland.

Portland was the team the Stars were to play next, at Gilmore Field. This time the Beavers were not as tough as they had been up north. Hollywood won five of seven from them with Kelleher making a big hit with the hometown fans by his game-winning hit in the ninth inning on opening night. The Sunday double-header was started at 12:45 P.M. rather than at 1:30 to allow the Beavers to catch a train home. After this successful series, the Stars were now fourth, only four games behind first-place Portland.

The next week was a pleasure trip for Hollywood, as the stars went to Oakland for an eight-game series over Labor Day. On Thursday night,

3—The 1944 Season

June 1, the Oaks won their first game of the season from Hollywood 2–1, but it took 11 innings. But the Stars won the other seven games of this series, including the Memorial Day double-header to start the series and the Sunday double-header to end it. After this successful trip, the Stars were tied for third place, only a half game out of the lead.

After a successful one-week road trip came an unsuccessful two week homestand. The San Diego Padres came to Gilmore Field and won five of the seven games from the Stars. The first game of the series, scheduled for Tuesday June 6, was postponed to honor our forces that invaded France earlier that day. The game was made up with a double-header on Thursday night, which the Padres swept. In this series, 16-year-old Gordon Goldsberry was used as a pinch hitter.

The following week, June 13–18, the cellar-dwelling Sacramento Solons came to Gilmore Field and surprised Hollywood by overcoming a 3–1 series deficit by winning Saturday and the double-header on Sunday to take the series, four games to three. During that week, Hollywood acquired third baseman Buck Faucett, who was to manage the team next year. They also got pitcher Knut Kimball, but he was limited to part-time duty at home. To make room for them, the Stars released catcher Ernie Potocar.

Things were not going to improve for Hollywood any time soon. The San Diego Padres were back in town for a split week, with three games at Gilmore Field and the last four down in San Diego. The Stars began using Les Powers at first base in this series, a veteran who had played with the Seals and Sacramento in the early 1930s. Powers hit .280 with three homers in 1944. This split week caused no travel problem for the Padres and Stars as it did for the Angels and Portland. But San Diego won two of three in Hollywood and three of four down in Lane Field to take the series, five games to two. Even so, Hollywood was tied for fourth place, only three and one-half games behind the league-leading Seals.

The Stars now had to go up to Sacramento to face the Solons, who beat them when they came to Gilmore Field. The result of this series was the same, as the Solons beat the Stars, four games to three, but not as dramatically as they did in Hollywood when they won the last three games of that series. But with all the teams playing close to .500 ball, the Stars were now only three games off the pace, but in fifth place.

It was now the Fourth of July and Hollywood returned to Gilmore Field to face its big rival, the Los Angeles Angels. A crowd of 13,000 jammed in to see the holiday double-header as the teams split that day. But the Angels were now starting to roll, and they proceeded to win five of the remaining six games to take the series, six games to two. This series put Hollywood in seventh place, five games off the lead. Over the past five weeks, the Stars had lost five series in a row, two each to San Diego and Sacramento and one to LA. But things were about to improve.

The Stars were now embarking on a *normal* two-week road trip to the Northwest, playing Seattle and Portland. As was expected with wartime conditions, the Stars could not get to Seattle in time for the Tuesday game, so the teams played a double-header on Wednesday night, which was swept by Hollywood. Frankie Kelleher was giving his old Seattle club a very bad time by hitting three homers, one a grand slam. The Stars won four of the first five games but then lost the Sunday doubleheader, but still won the series. They were still in seventh place, but now five and one-half games behind first-place Oakland, the team they dominated.

The next stop was at Portland, where Hollywood had been badly beaten when it appeared there in May. But this time the Stars won the series, four games to three, to end their trip to the Northwest by winning eight and losing six. On July 24, they were in sixth place, six and one-half behind the Angels, who had taken the lead for good.

Hollywood was now playing its best ball in 1944. After the successful northern trip, the stars returned home to take on their "cousins," the Oakland Oaks. During this series, the Stars sold outfielder Joe Gonzales to Mobile. On Friday night, Hollywood lost only its second game of the season to Oakland, 8–5, with four unearned runs in the ninth inning. But the other six games of that series were won by Hollywood, to make it 20 wins in 22 games for the Stars over the Oaks. At the end of this series, on July 31, Hollywood was in third place, only three and one-half behind the Angels.

The first week of August saw the Stars go to San Diego and this time Hollywood was able to beat the Padres, four games to three. This series was won in dramatic fashion as the Stars were down three games to one, and then won the last three games to cop the series. Knut Kimball was able to get away from his war plant job to pitch on Sunday and he won his game.

Hollywood was still on a roll as it returned home to face the Seattle Rainiers. It had been four months since Seattle had opened the season at Gilmore Field but it was still having trouble with the Stars. Seattle won the first two games of the series, but Hollywood won the last five. In this series, first baseman Butch Moran was suspended for one game in a salary dispute and was replaced by Les Powers at first. But things were

3—The 1944 Season 115

resolved the next night as he returned to the lineup. During this series, Roy Younker was doing most of the catching. A crowd of 10,000 turned out for the Sunday double-header as Knut Kimball and Ronnie Smith got credit for the wins. The Stars were now in second place, six games behind LA on August 14.

The only sour note of this series happened off the field. Seattle reserve outfielder Bill Derflinger and relief pitcher Gene Holt were slashed with knives by a gang of zoot suiters in front of the Rosslyn Hotel, in downtown Los Angeles. Both received injuries and were released by the Seattle club shortly after the incident.

The Stars now embarked on a week's trip to San Francisco to play the Seals, a team that had beaten them in each of the two previous series. But this time Hollywood was able to take the series, four games to three, for its sixth series win in a row, after having lost five series in a row before this hot streak began. The Stars were still in second place, six games behind the Angels.

The last team to beat Hollywood in a series was the Los Angeles Angels over the Fourth of July week at Gilmore Field. Now the Stars returned from San Francisco to the Southland to play the Angels again, this time at Wrigley Field. Normally the Angels started their home series with an afternoon double-header on Wednesday, but this time they began with a night game on Tuesday, followed by that afternoon double-header. The reason for this change was an exhibition game that was to be played on Saturday, August 26, between a group of service all-stars and a combined Angels–Stars team. This had been done in 1943 also, and this year the Angels suggested combining the two clubs for the full nine-inning game, but the Stars rejected it because the Angels refused to do in 1943 when they felt they had such a great team than no Hollywood player could strengthen it. So as in the previous year, the Angels played the first four and one-half innings and Hollywood the last four and one-half as the service team smashed the two local clubs, 16–6. Many former major league players were on the service team.

Hollywood started out this series with the Angels by winning the opener on Tuesday night, 7–3, with Knut Kimball beating his former team. But from that point on, it was all Los Angeles as the Angels won the series, six games to one. So the Angels put an end to Hollywood's streak on winning six series in a row. Now, on Monday, August 28, the Stars were in third place, 11 games behind the Angels.

That series was the one that put the Stars on the skids, from which they never escaped. The Seals came to Gilmore Field for a 10-game series that extended over Labor Day. The tenth game was a make up from the first time the Seals came to Hollywood. So there were three double-headers in this series, and the teams split all three. But the Seals won all the single games to take the series, seven games to three. Before Hollywood won the second game of the Sunday double-header, it had lost 12 of the last 13 games, counting the last six lost to the Angels. But even after this dismal series ended, the Stars were tied for fourth place, 12½ games off the lead.

But the next series was with the Angels again, this time at Gilmore Field. Before this series began, the Stars lost the services of second baseman Ray Olsen, who quit to take a war plant job. They also added a catcher to their club, Nick Buonarigo, who had been with Seattle earlier in the season. This was an eight-game series because of Admission Day in California. The Stars lost five of the eight games to the Angels, and fell to sixth place, 14½ games behind Los Angeles, which had clinched a tie for the pennant with its double-header win on Sunday before 10,500 fans. The Angels, with some help from the Seals, ended all hope Hollywood had of finishing in the first division.

There was only one week left in the season and that called for the Stars to go to Sacramento. But with Oakland playing Portland, a team it beat soundly, and the Seals playing last-place San Diego, there was no chance for the Stars to make the playoffs. The Stars did manage to win four of seven from the Solons but that was small comfort. Frankie Kelleher lost the batting title to Les Scarsella by hitting .328542 compared to Scarsella's .328857. But Scarsella had 109 more at-bats than Kelleher and 36 more hits, because Kelleher joined the team in mid–May.

7. Sacramento. The 1944 season almost did not happen for fans in Sacramento because the St. Louis Cardinals came very close to selling the club to interests in Tacoma, Washington. With less than two months before the season was to start, it looked as if the deal with Tacoma would go through, but the Sacramento Chamber of Commerce and the sports editor of the *Sacramento Union*, Dick Edmonds, put on a drive to get local people to buy the team and keep it in Sacramento. The story is well told by John Spalding in his book on the Sacramento Solons. Edmonds, who was only 30 at the time, got a 28-year-old entrepreneur, Yubi Separovich, to invest $5,000 to help buy the team. Those two made a successful effort to get enough people to put up the money to pay the Cardinals' asking price, which finally amounted to $50,000 for the ballpark and $40,000 for the franchise and players.

The final agreement of the league owners came at a meeting in Los Angeles on February 23. But even this came only after a dramatic appeal by Edmonds and Separovich. Those two took the train to Los Angeles but a snowstorm halted the train in the mountains south of Bakersfield and both men had to catch a bus to the city, arriving at the league meeting three hours late. By that time, the owners had already voted to allow the club to be moved to Tacoma, but Edmonds and Separovich showed the $60,000 in checks to league president Clarence Rowland and the owners were persuaded to vote again, and this vote allowed Sacramento to keep its team.

After this success, the Sacramento Baseball Association was incorporated for $125,000, with each share of stock sold for $50. When the new manager, Earl Sheely, was hired, he agreed to take $2,000 of his $10,000 salary in association stock.

Sheely had played in the Coast League with Salt Lake City in the late teens and then spent most of the 1920s as the first baseman for the Chicago White Sox. He returned to the Coast League in 1928 and had a great year with to Solons, hitting .381. In 1930, he hit a league-leading .403 with the San Francisco Seals, and later finished up his career with Portland and Seattle in 1934 at the age of 41.

Because the St. Louis Cardinals no longer owned the ball club, the ballpark was renamed Doubleday Park before the 1944 season. It had originally been called Moreing Field after its owner, but was changed to Cardinal Field in 1936 when he sold the team to the Cardinals. When Edmonds died tragically from pneumonia in 1945, the ball club was renamed Edmonds Field in his honor, because he did so much to save the team for Sacramento.

Manager Sheely had a big job ahead of him, taking over a team that finished 69 games out of first place in 1943. His only returning pitcher turned out to be his ace, Clem Dreiswerd, who was to win 20 games in 1944 after losing 20 in 1943. Dreiswerd won those 20 games by August 19, just before he was sold to the Boston Red Sox. Herman "Old Folks" Pillette also returned, but at age 49 he was more of a pitching coach than a pitcher, but he was on the active roster. The only returning infielder was Charles "Jake" Suytar, but Jack Angle joined the team in June. The two returning outfielders were Bill Ramsey and Manny Vias, but the latter was released at the end of May. The club resembled a revolving door in April and May as many players were released as some were hired from amateur ranks while others were acquired in trades or from war plant jobs. Several players had to report to their draft boards for physicals during the playing season, causing Sheely much uneasiness. One infielder, Jim Jewel, acquired from Seattle in April, was able to play only eight games before having to go into the military.

Some of the newcomers that stayed with the club for most of the season were pitchers "Smokestack" Steve LeGault, "Grumpy" Guy Fletcher, Gene Babbitt, Larry Kempe, Earl Porter, Dick Powers, catcher Lilo Marcucci, infielders Paul Bowa, Ralph Watson and Forrest Rogers, and outfielder Ted Greenhalgh.

Sheely did receive some good news when the club's 1942 second baseman, Gene Handley, decided to quit his war plant job and report to the team after he was rejected for military service. His first game was May 10. Another member of that championship 1942 team, Mel Serafini, also reported to Sacramento on May 25. Unlike Handley, Serafini was not a regular in 1942, but he did get into 96 games in 1944 at third base.

At the end of April, the Solons purchased two players from Memphis, outfielder Al McElreath and infielder Bill Krueger. Krueger, who had been with Portland in 1943, played until June 12, when he went into the navy. McElreath stayed with the club for two years.

While Marcucci was with the team all season, he divided his time between catching and the outfield. The starting catcher was Joe Rossi up until mid–June, when he left to join the navy. He was replaced by Jim Steiner, a catcher who had played at Jersey City in 1943, but did not want to return there. The Solons made a deal for him and his first game was on June 9. Steiner, who had caught for the Angels in the mid–1930s, hit .312 for Sacramento and was voted the team's most valuable player, the third year in a row that a catcher won that honor.

The Solons opened the season at home on Saturday, April 8, against the 1943 champion Angels. A crowd of 6,384 saw this game, which was larger than the other three opening games drew, but some blamed the cold weather for lower turnouts elsewhere. The next day, the Sunday double-header drew 6,981, which was good by Sacramento standards, but not so for Los Angeles, San Francisco or Seattle. Two night games were rained out on the following Tuesday and Wednesday nights, and were not made up during this series. The first night game Sacramento was able to play since August 1942 was on Thursday, April 13. Unfortunately, the Angels won their fourth in a row that evening and extended the Solons' losing streak to six games when LA beat them on Friday night and Saturday afternoon. The Friday night game drew only 858 fans. But on Sunday, April 16, the Solons got into the win column by taking the Sunday double-header from the Angels by identical scores of 2–1. But

3—The 1944 Season

only 2,484 saw this double-header. Shortstop Ralph Watson had to report for his draft physical in Los Angeles, so outfielder Manny Vias played short on Friday night, making two errors. So Paul Bowa moved over to short and newcomer Jim Jewel played third, but soon left for military service.

Unfortunately, in 1944 there was no live broadcast of Sacramento games as there had been in the past on station KFBK with Tony Koester doing the broadcasts. The station devoted just 15 minutes to summing up baseball from 10:15 to 10:30 P.M. A good announcer can bring out more people to the park by building fan loyalty.

The next series was not much better for the Solons. The Portland Beavers came to Doubleday Park the next week and won four of the six games that the teams could play. There were two weeknight rain outs but one was made up with a Friday night double-header. The Saturday afternoon game drew only 816 but 2,872 saw the teams split the Sunday double-header. Ralph Watson returned to the lineup and was able to stay with the team all season.

The Solons now had to embark on a three-week road trip to Seattle, Portland and Oakland. The Rainiers could not get to Seattle in time for their Tuesday night home opener, so the teams made it up with a Friday night double-header. Close to 13,000 were on hand for the Seattle home opener, which must have made the Solons envious. Jim Jewel had to leave for the service and did not get to play against his former club. The Solons lost the series at Seattle, four games to three, but were blown out by Portland the following week at Vaughn Street Park. The only game the Solons won was on Saturday when the Sacs scored five runs in the 10th inning to win 9–4. The Beavers won the series six games to one and the Sacs were in the cellar.

When the Solons went to Oakland the week of May 9, they were happy to have Gene Handley join the team and play second base. Outfielder Al McElreath also made his first appearance in this series. The Solons also announced that pitcher Jack Pintar, who lost 27 games for them in 1943, could pitch for the Sacs when they were in Oakland or San Francisco because he was employed at a nearby military base. But Pintar appeared in only five games for the Solons in 1944. As in the previous week in Portland, the Solons were able to win only one game in Oakland and it too went 10 innings. Guy Fletcher won this game on Friday night. Luckily for the Solons, the Sunday double-header was rained out, so Sacramento lost this series only four games to one.

As the Solons returned home on Monday, May 15, they read in the

Sacramento papers that all housewives were urged to save their waste fats by keeping them at the back of the stove in a can, and then putting the can in the refrigerator. They were then to take them to their butcher and he would give them two red points and four cents per pound for these fats, that were used to make munitions and some medicines.

The Seattle Rainiers were the visiting team at Doubleday Park when the Solons returned from that three-week road trip. The Wednesday night game was rained out and so the teams made it up with a doubleheader on Friday night. This time a fairly good crowd saw that double bill, 3,263. But of great joy to the Sacramento fans was the fact that the Solons won this series from Seattle, four games to three, which was the first series they had won since beating the Angels the last week of 1942.

However, the good performance did not carry over to the following week when Oakland came to Doubleday Park. During this week, outfielder Manny Vias was released because Sacramento picked up another outfielder from Hollywood, Otto Meyers. The Sacs also got word that the versatile Jack Angle, who had been on the dismal 1943 squad was anxious to return to the Solons. He had been playing in the Houston Shipyard League while working down there. But the Solons disappointed their fans on the last weekend in May as the Oaks won the last three games of the series to win it five games to two. A sad crowd of 4,545 turned out for the Sunday double-header which the Oaks won by lopsided scores, 6–0 and 15–2. But the total home attendance for the Solons up to this point was 43,378, which exceeded all of 1943's attendance by over 37 percent.

The Memorial Day series followed with the Solons in San Diego. The two clubs split the eight games, but during this week the Solons were happy to hear catcher Jim Steiner was going to join their team the next week in San Francisco. Steiner played for Jersey City in 1943 but refused to return because he lived in Los Angeles. Another addition to the Sacramento team, besides Jack Angle, was pitcher Bud Beasley, a lefty who had been teaching school in Reno and was now out for the summer. Beasley, whose full name was Andrew Alberdine McGill McKnight Arvel Lewis Beasley, delighted the fans around the league with the humorous gyrations that he went through before delivering a pitch.

The following week in San Francisco, things began to pick up for the downtrodden Sacs. Sacramento won the series, five games to two, which was the first of five straight series it was to win throughout the entire month of June and the first half of July. Jim Steiner caught his first game for the Solons this week in Seals Stadium and Joe Rossi caught his last, as he joined the army. Shortstop Bill Krueger also left after playing the whole week to join the navy.

The following week, the Solons traveled to Hollywood and won this series, four games to three, by winning Saturday and the double-header on Sunday. On Wednesday night, Jack Angle made his first appearance in 1944 at shortstop to replace Krueger. Angle, who drove out from Houston, remained in the Los Angeles area for the Solons to come south from San Francisco. On Thursday night, Jake Suytar won a $25 bond as his drive hit a sign on the Gilmore Field fence, which also gave the Solons $1,000 for new uniforms, courtesy of the owner of the Los Angeles Mustangs football team. A week later, Jake Suytar had his picture taken in the new visiting uniform that his hit at Gilmore Field had won for the club.

The following week was a split week with the Solons back at San Francisco for three games and then the teams moved to Sacramento for the last four. The Solons won the first two games at Seals Stadium for their fifth win in a row before the Seals won on Thursday night. The Friday night game at Doubleday Park was a special bond drive game in which admission to the game was with a bond purchase. The more expensive bonds got the best seats. This bond drive raised $2,761,400 for the war effort; over 9,500 fans were at the game but over 15,000 tickets were distributed with the bond sale. The Solons, behind Clem Dreiswerd, won the game 2–1. Pitcher Bud Beasley made his first appearance in relief during the Sunday double-header, which the team split. Sacramento won five of the seven games from the Seals.

The Hollywood Stars next came to Doubleday Park during the last week of June. The opening game on Tuesday night was won by Hollywood 7–5 in 14 innings, but the Solons would have won in regulation if Al McElreath had not pulled a "Fred Merkle" boner in the ninth inning. McElreath was on first when Jake Suytar hit a ball off the left field wall which apparently scored the game-winning run. But Frankie Kelleher in left field noticed that McElreath did not touch second base and threw the ball to center fielder Brooks Holder, who ran in and stepped on second, forcing McElreath for the third out of the inning. Nevertheless, Sacramento won the series, four games to three.

The San Diego Padres came to Sacramento over the Fourth of July week for an eight-game series. The Solons began the series very well by taking the July 4 double-header. In the seven-inning second game, Padre pitcher Frankie Dasso had a no-hitter going into the last of the seventh, and the Sacs got three hits and two runs to win it. This was the week that only three games separated the first seven teams, and Sacramento was last, only seven games back. When Beasley won his first game on July 5, the Solons were still last, but only five games out of first place. Sacramento won five of the first six games of this series, only to lose the Sunday double-header before over 7,000 fans. During this week, the team got word that pitchers Guy Fletcher and Gene Babbitt and shortstop Ralph Watson were rejected for military service. Clem Dreiswerd was accepted but was given no notice of when he would be called.

After winning five series in a row, the Solons traveled to Los Angeles to play the red-hot Angels. This was an eight-game series because they were making up one of the rain outs that occurred during the opening week of the season up in Sacramento. The Solons got off on the right foot by winning on Tuesday and taking both games of the Wednesday double-header. On Thursday morning, July 13, the Solons were still in last place, but only four games behind first-place Oakland. But the Angels were the one of the toughest teams for Sacramento to play in 1944, winning 17 of 24 games from them. Los Angeles went on to take the remaining five games of this series, causing the Solons to lose their first series after five winning weeks, five games to three. During this week, Sacramento picked up a 30-year-old third baseman named Billy Cox, who had been playing in an industrial league. This was not the Billy Cox who later played for the Pittsburgh Pirates and the Brooklyn Dodgers.

Even though the Solons lost the series at Los Angeles, they still had something left. They went up to Oakland for a nine-game series, the two extra games caused by the rain out of the Sunday double-header on May 14. The Solons took six of the nine games played at Oakland, as the Oaks fell out of first place. During this series, Sacramento signed a semi-pro pitcher off the Oakland sandlots, 23-year-old Jack Rossi, who was not related to catcher Joe Rossi who had left for the service. Jack Rossi made very few appearances in relief for the Solons.

An unfortunate situation arose in Sacramento in mid–July when the city was put under a 10 P.M. curfew and the city was designated as "off limits" to all military personnel, except those who lived there. This was because of several fights that had occurred between enlisted men and juvenile delinquents, called zoot suiters, who were causing disturbances up and down the entire West Coast. There were some killings that prompted the action taken. Sportswriter Dick Edmonds wrote that saving the Solons for Sacramento had done wonders for the youth of the city because it gave them some wholesome entertainment, especially now that it was locally owned, and not just a weak link in the Cardinal chain.

3—The 1944 Season

The Solons went to San Diego the last week of July and won this series, five games to two. This was a battle for seventh place, and the Solons actually moved up to sixth place, temporarily ahead of Seattle. Sacramento won the Sunday double-header as Billy Cox drove in the winning run in each game. Cox also played some outfield.

The first week of August saw the Solons return home to take on the Seals. Attendance was picking up as the race got closer. Thursday night, August 3, was stockholders night at which all the people who invested in the club were honored. The Solons won that night, to get to within a half game of the first division in a very tight race. These night games were drawing about 4,500 fans, and 8,638 turned out for the Sunday double-header. With the Solons leading the series, three games to two, Seal pitcher Tommy Seats came up from his war plant job in San Francisco and pitched shutouts in both games as the Seals copped the series. Seats pitched a total of 16 scoreless innings and was given a big hand by the Sacramento fans at the end of the second game. A total of 31,427 saw this series, which was just about the number the 1943 team drew all season.

The Sacramento club had been working on a sale of pitcher Clem Dreisewerd to the Boston Red Sox. Dreisewerd was hoping to get $5,000 of the purchase price, and when told he would be getting only $1,500, he threatened to jump the club. Herman "Old Folks" Pillette talked him out of it, explaining that the purchase price dropped when he lost at Los Angeles before Red Sox scouts. Dreisewerd's last game with Sacramento was on Sunday, August 20, against San Diego.

But on August 8, the league-leading Angels came to Doubleday Park and ended all hope Sacramento had for finishing in the first division. The Angels won the eight-game series, six games to two. On Thursday night, August 10, the club planned an "all out for Sacramento" night. A special program was planned before the game with some entertainers and some races were held between Angels and Solons players. A crowd of 8,362 turned out, but the Angels beat Clem Dreisewerd again, 4–3. After this series, the Solons were five and one-half games out of the first division.

The San Diego Padres, now in last place, came to Sacramento next and won the Sunday double-header to take the series from the Solons, four games to three. Nevertheless, the Sacs held on to seventh place by just half a game.

For the rest of August and over Labor Day, the Solons had to travel to the Northwest to take on Portland and Seattle. Portland gave the Sacs a lot of trouble in 1944, winning 20 of the 29 games played, but surprisingly, the Solons won this series at Vaughn Street Park, four games to three. But things went sour in Seattle. The Rainiers won six of the nine games from Sacramento, finishing up with a double-header sweep on Labor Day over the Solons.

That series win at Portland was the last one the Solons were to win in 1944. The team now returned home for the final two weeks of the season to play Portland and Hollywood. The Beavers and Solons were scheduled for nine games because of the rain outs in April when Portland was at Doubleday Park. This was a dismal series for the Sacs. Portland, fighting to stay in the first division, played very well, taking seven of the nine games, including sweeping double-headers on Saturday and on Sunday. Gene Handley did not show up for Saturday's double-header because he had car trouble and no one could find him. At this point, Sacramento was just a game and a half ahead of eighth-place San Diego.

The final series was with Hollywood, and even though the Sacs lost it, four games to three, they did manage to finish a game ahead of San Diego and avoid the cellar. The Solons were lucky that the Seals were fighting for the first division and went all out to beat San Diego that last week. The 1944 Solons were 23 games behind the league-leading Angels, which was an improvement over the 69 games they trailed by in 1943. Attendance in 1944 was 200,915, which was more than six times what the team drew in 1943.

Catcher Jim Steiner, who hit .312, was named the team's most valuable player, following in the footsteps of Eddie Malone in 1943 and Ray Mueller in 1942 as catchers who won that award. Clem Dreiswerd, now with the Red Sox, won 20 games and lost nine, and was the only regular pitcher with a winning record.

8. *San Diego*. George Detore was back as manager of the Padres in 1944, his last year in that position and his last year in the Pacific Coast League. Detore still caught a few games in 1944 but left most of the catching to Bill Salkeld and Del Ballinger. The pitchers returning from the 1943 team were Rex Cecil, 41-year-old Jim Brillheart, Frankie Dasso, Chet Johnson and Rex Dilbeck. But Dilbeck had to go into the service after pitching only a few games. Newcomers were Joe Wood, son of the famous "Smokey" Joe Wood of the 1912 Red Sox; Joe Valenzuela; Carl Dumler; Earl Jones and Keith Bauer. The latter two pitched very sparingly. In midseason, San Diego acquired pitchers Don Hanski from Hollywood and Norbert "Nubs" Kleinke from Oakland.

3—The 1944 Season

Most of the infield was back. George McDonald returned at first, Jack Calvey at short, Ed Wheeler, who played three infield positions, Walter Lowe at third, Al Cailteaux at second, short and third and George Morgan, who also played several infield positions. The one new infielder was Vern Reynolds, who played mostly at second. The outfield still had Hal Patchett in center, Marvin Gudat in right and Mel Steiner in left. Steiner was traded in midseason to Oakland for Nubs Kleinke. Morry Abbott, the Canadian, was back as an outfielder and occasionally did some catching. Jack Whipple also returned from the 1943 team. Lou Vezlich, who had been in the Sacramento outfield in the late 1930s, was picked up in midseason. Another late season pick up was Rupert "Tommy" Thompson, who starred with the Padres team that won the playoffs in 1937 and had played three years with Portland.

Pitcher Rex Cecil, who won 19 games for the 1944 San Diego Padres, and whose sale to the Red Sox caused the Padres to plummet in the standings. He is shown here in 1947 when he was briefly with Seattle. Courtesy of Dave Eskenazi.

The Padres almost always opened the season at home because Portland and Seattle almost always opened on the road to avoid the rains in the Northwest in April. The Oakland Oaks, who had a great deal of difficulty getting to San Diego, were the opening day opponent. The U.S. Navy had to send special buses to San Bernardino to pick the Oaks up because regular bus companies could not charter a special one for civilians. The first series was a 10-game affair because it opened on a Saturday, April 8, followed by a Sunday double-header, and then the regular seven-game series. The Padres did well in this series, winning seven of the 10 games. But the following week, Seattle came to Lane Field and won the series, four games to three.

San Diego then went on a three-week road trip to Portland, Seattle and Los Angeles. As was usual during wartime conditions, the Padres could not get to Portland in time to play on Tuesday, April 25, so the series began on Wednesday, and a double-header was played on Friday night. The Wednesday opener went 15 innings and Chet Johnson went all the way to win it, 5–3. San Diego lost the Sunday double-header, which cost them the series, four games to three. What was especially annoying to the Padres was the first game on Sunday in which San Diego scored five runs in the top of the 12th inning, only to allow Portland to come back with six.

The next series in Seattle was an eight-game series with a double-header on Friday night. No explanation was given for the extra game. But it did not help San Diego as it lost this series, five games to three.

The last week of this three-week trip went a little better as the Padres went into Wrigley Field and beat the Angels four of seven games. This was the second week of May and before the Angels received the help they were later to get from the Cubs. In any case, the Padres were now one game over .500 on May 15.

The Padres stayed rather close to the .500 mark for the next few weeks as they returned home to play Portland, Los Angeles and Sacramento. They went 11–11 on this homestand, losing the odd game to the Beavers, taking the odd game from the Angels and splitting the Memorial Day series with the Solons at four wins apiece.

When the Padres reported to Gilmore Field on June 6 to play the Stars, Hollywood management called off Tuesday night's game in honor of the big invasion of Europe. This was the only Pacific Coast League game that was postponed for that momentous occasion. The Padres played very well in this series, taking five of seven from Hollywood, to come very close to first place at 36 wins and 32 losses. But the next week was a disaster! The Padres made their only appearance of the year at San Francisco and the Seals demolished them, six games out of seven, to put the Padres under the .500 mark.

But the next two weeks were good ones for San Diego in the tightly bunched race. They returned to Hollywood for a split week, with three games in Gilmore Field and the last four at Lane Field. The Padres won five of the seven to get back over .500 and then entertained the Seals. In San Diego, the Padres played a lot better than they did in Seal Stadium, winning four of the six games to claim the league lead. One game was suspended as a tie game and would be made up the last week of the season when the Seals returned to Lane Field. So on July 4, San Diego stood on top of the league, but several clubs were tightly bunched. Only five games separated the top seven clubs.

But before the month of July would be over, San Diego would be on the bottom of the league to stay. The Fourth of July series at Sacramento was a four-four draw, but the following week at Wrigley Field was the beginning of the end for San Diego. The Angels were now in full gear with several new players from the Cubs and they knocked off San Diego six out of seven games, which put the Padres under the .500 mark to stay. The following week at Oakland was just as bad. The Oaks jumped to the top spot by also winning six of seven from the reeling Padres.

The Padres had two very good pitchers in 1944, Rex Cecil and Frankie Dasso. Dasso stayed with the team all year and won 20 games, which was remarkable for a team in the cellar. But the Padres sold Cecil to the Boston Red Sox, putting a big dent in their pitching staff. The acquisition of Norbert "Nubs" Kleinke from Oakland in exchange for outfielder Mel Steiner did not fill the pitching gap. So the Red Sox purchased two top pitchers from the teams with the two worst records in the Pacific Coast League in 1944. Clem Dreiswerd from seventh-place Sacramento and Rex Cecil from eighth-place San Diego. Neither pitcher had a winning record with Boston in either 1944 or 1945.

During the first two weeks of August, the Padres were home to Hollywood and to Oakland. Even though they finished that homestand with seven wins and seven losses, they were still in last place. They then went on a three-week road trip to Sacramento, Seattle and Portland. They managed to win four of the six in Sacramento to get very close to the Solons in the standings, but the following week in Seattle was a dismal one for the Padres. The Rainiers won six of seven to push the Padres deeper into the cellar, from which there was no escape. They lost five in a row the next week at Portland, making it 11 losses in the last 12 games. But San Diego won the Sunday double-header and the Labor Day double-header to put a scare into the Beavers, who were fighting to stay in the first division.

The last two weeks of the season were played at Lane Field. Seattle continued its dominance of the Padres, winning five of seven. The final week matched the Padres with the Seals. This was an eight-game series because of the suspended game at the end of June. The Seals were also fighting to make the first division and won four of the eight games to tie Oakland for third place. San Diego ended up only one game behind Sacramento, winning 75 and losing 94.

4—The 1945 Season

Final Standings

	W	L	PCT	G.B.	MANAGER
1. Portland	112	68	.622	—	Marvin Owen
2. Seattle	105	78	.574	8.5	Bill Skiff
3. Sacramento	95	85	.528	17	Earl Sheely
4. San Francisco	96	87	.525	17.5	Lefty O'Doul
5. Oakland	90	93	.492	23.5	D. Camilli/B. Raimondi
6. San Diego	82	101	.448	31.5	Pepper Martin
7. Los Angeles	76	107	.415	37.5	Bill Sweeney
8. Hollywood	73	110	.399	40.5	Buck Faucett

The 1945 season was the second of four straight years in which the Pacific Coast League set new attendance records. A total of 2,919,470 fans paid their way in to see the last wartime season. Every club except Los Angeles, the team with the largest park, had an increase over 1944. The Angels had a decrease largely because their team slumped to seventh place, after having won two consecutive pennants and just missing one in 1942. The 1945 season consisted of 183 games, compared to 169 in 1944.

The 1945 season coincided with the death of President Roosevelt, the surrender of Germany and the surrender of Japan. Games were called off on Thursday April 12, the day the president died, and on Saturday, April 14, the day of his funeral. There were no postponements when Germany surrendered on May 8 nor when Japan surrendered on August 15, but some teams, such as Oakland, allowed their military veterans to take the latter night off and celebrate. In San Francisco, only 500 fans came to Seals Stadium on August 15 to see their team play San Diego, as they were out celebrating. Fans in some Coast League cities had trouble getting food the day Japan surrendered because grocery stores and restaurants closed to celebrate the occasion.

Even though the war was winding down, travel was even more of a problem than in previous years. In midseason, the government declared that sleeping cars could not be used by civilians for trips of 450 miles or less because there was such a huge demand for them. This did not affect travel from either Portland or Seattle to California, but it did affect travel within the state of California. Teams going from the Bay Area or Sacramento to the Southland would stay in their hotel or home Sunday night and then take the Daylight to Los Angeles on Monday. The same held true for teams leaving the Southland and traveling to the Bay Area.

One advantage in scheduling in 1945 over 1944 was that the schedule was no longer drawn up by someone in Massachusetts but by Damon Miller, the traveling secretary of the San Francisco Seals. Travel in this last war year was greatly reduced by having teams usually stay home for three weeks at a time. Very few split weeks were scheduled and none that would require teams to go from Portland to Los Angeles without a day off, as in 1944.

The War Manpower Commission declared in March 1945 that ballplayers could give up their war plant jobs and play ball full time, but they would still be subject to the draft. This was a help to several clubs, especially to Portland, which was to win the pennant this year.

Housing was very scare in 1945, with many players having to rent rooms in private homes. When a new player would join a club in midseason, the radio announcer would tell the fans that the player was looking for a place to stay in the hope someone would like to rent a room to him. Hotel space was really at a premium in San Francisco from April through June because of the conference that set up the United Nations. There was even some talk of putting visiting players up in the clubhouses at Seal Stadium, but most were able to find space in Oakland or other hotels on the east side of the bay.

One good thing for the players was the increase in their meal money to $3 a day. It had been cut to $2 in the early 1930s and not been restored. Even so, some complained that this was inadequate in San Francisco and Los Angeles.

During the first three years of the war, major and minor league baseball teams often played exhibition games to raise money so that the military could buy baseball and other sports equipment for their service

4—The 1945 Season

teams. But in 1945, it seemed the situation was reversed. There was a shortage of bats and the major league teams had first call on the reduced supply. So some service teams began donating bats to Pacific Coast League players. Charley English, now of Portland, was able to get some bats for his team from some navy friends after the Beavers played an exhibition game with a navy team.

The 1945 Pacific Coast League season was the longest in all of professional baseball, beginning on Saturday, March 31, and ending the regular season on September 23. But the playoffs did not end until Friday night, October 12, and would have gone to Sunday October 14 if a seventh game had been necessary.

1. Portland. The Beavers reached the pinnacle in 1945, winning this franchise's first pennant since 1936. But unlike the 1936 club, this one won by a comfortable margin and did not have to "win it twice," as Bill Sweeney's 1936 team did. The 1936 season was the first time the Shaughnessy system of postseason playoffs was used to decide the pennant winner. So even though Portland finished first by a game and a half, it did not win the pennant until defeating Seattle and Oakland in the playoffs. But beginning in 1938, the first-place team was declared the pennant winner and the playoffs were just for prize money.

In 1942, Portland finished in eighth place for the fourth year in a row, but after that, things began to improve for this franchise. It moved up to fourth place in 1943, and then to second in 1944 and finally to the top in 1945. Marvin Owen, who still played third base, was in his second year as manager this season and had reason to feel optimistic during spring training in San Jose. The declaration by the War Manpower Commission that allowed players to quit their war plant jobs and play full time was a big help to Portland. Four of its players were affected: pitcher Roy Helser, first baseman Larry Barton, utility man Charley Petersen and newcomer Charley English all had war-related jobs during the winter.

Another reason for Owen's optimism was the acquisition of some new players for the 1945 season. These included right-handed pitchers Jack Tising from Buffalo and Jake Mooty, a former Angel, from Detroit, and three promising rookies, left-handed pitcher Wandel Mosser, backup catcher Hank Sousa and infielder-outfielder Frank Lucchesi. Another rookie, infielder Curt Schmidt, was traded in midseason to Sacramento for the very versatile Roy Younker. The other newcomer, English, who could play second or third, was obtained in a trade with Oakland for outfielder Norm DeWeese.

The Beavers encountered a great deal of rain in San Jose during spring training so were limited to a very few exhibition games, all of them with nearby service teams. Thus, the Beavers got no preseason look at any of their league opponents. Manager Owen once took his team to work out in the San Jose State College gym but most players did not have sneakers, so they got blisters on their feet by wearing just socks.

The housing shortage affected Portland's star pitcher, Ad Liska. When he arrived in Portland with his family from Eau Claire, Wisconsin, they were taken in by Rocky Benevento, the popular groundskeeper at Vaughn Street Park. Players without families usually had to rent rooms in private homes. Liska was the only member of the Portland team that was with them when they won the pennant in 1936.

Manager Marvin Owen, at right, shows his favorite grip on a baseball to Portland pitchers (from left) Ad Liska, Don Pulford and Roy Helser, all of whom won 20 games for the 1945 Beavers. This was Portland's first pennant since 1936 and to date, their last. Courtesy of Dave Eskenazi.

Before the 1945 season began, the Beavers and their fans received the sad news that Henry Martinez, infielder on the 1942 club, was killed in action in the battle of Leyte Gulf in the Philippines. Martinez had played briefly with Oakland in 1938 and with Seattle in 1939.

Two players had much better seasons for Portland in 1945 than they did in 1944; shortstop Johnny O'Neil and outfielder Frank Demaree. Each accomplished this after a change in weight: one up and one down. Demaree, following his nurse-wife's diet, lost 30 pounds and was able to get more bat speed and became a gazelle in the outfield. He raised his average from .276 to .304. O'Neil, who hit only .236 in 1944, bulked up with 12 pounds of pure muscle and raised his average to .309 in 1945. Two other players improved their performance after playing winter ball once a week in Los Angeles. Pitcher Don Pulford won only three and lost 10 in 1944, but won 20 and lost 11 in 1945. Larry Barton raised his average from .252 to .318, claiming that playing just once a week kept him sharp without wearing him down.

Vaughn Street Park, at 44 the oldest in the league, underwent some improvements before the 1945 season, but they were not enough to please the fire marshal. The lobby under the grandstand was redone, some old staircases were replaced with ramps, and the clubhouses were upgraded. But the fire marshal still said the place was a firetrap. He wanted to close the center field bleachers because there were too few exits and the aisles were too narrow; he also felt that the concession booths located under the grandstand could lead to quick combustion from splintered boards nearby. Groundskeeper Rocky Benevento usually spent most of his time going around with buckets of water putting out small fires from cigarettes. Even with these shortcomings, most players, visitors and Beavers alike enjoyed playing there because the fans were close to the action and were knowledgeable, giving ovations for any player who made a great play. There were several articles predicting that Portland would get a new ballpark after the war, but it did not happen. The Beavers played in Vaughn Street Park, renamed Lucky Beaver Stadium, until 1955 and then in 1956 moved to Multnomah Stadium, which had been primarily used for football.

The Beavers, as usual, opened the series on the road, this year in Oakland, on Saturday, March 31. This short series lasted through Tuesday and then the Beavers moved on to Sacramento. Portland won four of the five games from Oakland, but on Sunday, April 1, which was Easter, the clubs had to play in the worst conditions encountered all season. There were 50 mph winds, making fly balls treacherous. Even when the Beavers moved to Sacramento for night games beginning on Wednesday, April 4, the weather was very cold. Portland won the first four games at Sacramento, but lost the Sunday double-header, still taking the series four games to two. Don Pulford, Jake Mooty and Jack Tising pitched very well in the cold, but Roy Helser and Ad Liska did not fare as well. A Pacific Coast League rule required that any pitcher throwing a spitball would be ejected immediately, and Jack Tising was the first to be tossed in Sacramento.

After a day off on Monday, April 9, the Beavers opened a series at

Seals Stadium which was shortened to just five games because of the death and funeral of President Roosevelt. Even though Portland won this shortened series, three games to two, it fell a game behind Seattle after the Tuesday game, then moved into a first-place tie, and fell again a game behind the Rainiers after splitting the Sunday double-header. But this was a very successful road trip, with 11 wins against five losses. While in San Francisco, Lefty O'Doul tried to get Charley Petersen back from the Beavers. Petersen had played for the Seals in 1943, but Portland rejected the sale at this time. It was lucky for them that they did because the Beavers were soon to suffer several injuries and Petersen could play just about anywhere, including catcher when asked.

Manager Marvin Owen weighed only about 165 pounds when he played with Detroit and the White Sox in the late 1930s. He was given a heavy bat by Larry Rosenthal, a White Sox teammate, but could not swing it well because it was too heavy for him. But by 1945, Owen had bulked up to 187 pounds and now found out that he could really hit with this bat. He started out the first few weeks hitting over .400 and would not let anyone near his special bat.

When the Beavers left for home after the San Francisco series, they were greeted at the Portland depot by General Manager Bill Klepper and the Beavers Booster Club on Monday evening. But their home opener could not be played until Wednesday afternoon at 4 P.M. because the

Lefty Roy Helser warms up at Vaughn Street Park in 1945. This was his second of three straight years of winning 20 games for the Beavers. Courtesy of Dave Eskenazi.

visiting Hollywood Stars could not get there by Tuesday. This 4 P.M. home opener drew 12,651 fans, which topped Seattle's home opener against the Oaks by 196, so Seattle had to send a big salmon to the Portland club. Unfortunately, the Stars, who were to finish last in 1945, beat Portland 2–1 to spoil the occasion. Portland won on Thursday and the double-header on Friday night to gain a tie with Seattle. The two Northwest clubs remained tied through Saturday's games, but on Sunday, Portland split its double-header but Seattle lost both games, giving the Beavers a one-game lead and the series win, five games to two. No one knew it at the time, but after the games on Sunday, April 22, the Portland Beavers were in first place to stay the rest of the 1945 season. Seattle got as close as a half a game later, but never could even tie them for the top spot. So the Beavers were out of first place only a few days in April, and never by more than one game.

The Beavers' next foe was Oakland, and the two clubs split the six games that were played. The Saturday night game was rained out and could not be made up that week. During this week the Beavers sold outfielder John Gill to Seattle. Gill had been with Portland for five years, but with Demaree, Frank Shone and Ted Gullic playing well, he was not needed. But the injury bug hit Portland this week against Oakland. Owen hurt his leg, causing Charley English to move to third and Mel Nunes to second. Then English got a charley horse so Charley Petersen went in at third. Larry Barton pulled a ligament so Ted Gullic moved to first and 44-year-old Spencer Harris went to right field. When the team traveled south to Hollywood on Monday, April 30, Barton stopped off at Boyes Hot Springs to see about the ligament in his left knee.

The series at Gilmore Field had to start on Wednesday because both teams were coming from the Northwest. Portland played this whole series without Demaree and Barton but still won it, six games to one. The team now led the league by five games. Charley Petersen played in the outfield each day while rookies Frank Lucchesi and Curt Schmidt filled in on occasion.

On Tuesday, May 8, Germany surrendered but no holiday was declared for baseball. The Beavers moved on to San Diego for their next series and found hotel space so scarce that three players were forced to share each room. That proved harmful to pitcher Jack Tising, who got up in the middle of the night and stubbed his toe, breaking the middle one on his left foot. But this did not prevent him from winning Saturday's game and going the distance. After losing the first two games, the Beavers won the final five, to extend their league lead to six games. In the first 39 games played, Portland pitchers went all the way in 30 of them, winning 21. During the San Diego series, Larry Barton returned, giving the Beavers their fine starting infield of Owen, O'Neil, English and Barton, the best in the league.

After an 11 and three road trip, Portland returned home to start a series with the Angels on Wednesday, May 16. Both teams arrived on the same train, missing a connection in Martinez, which prevented them from playing on Tuesday. At this time, many writers, including L. H. Gregory of the *Portland Oregonian,* were predicting the Angels would win their third pennant in a row. The thought was that the Chicago Cubs would unload a lot of talent on Los Angeles as they had done in 1944; but in 1945, the Cubs won the pennant, so they hoarded players and took the best the Angels had. The Angels finished a dismal seventh, just ahead of Hollywood.

This was not a good series for Portland. The first two nights it rained, so the series did not start until Friday night, with the Beavers taking a double-header. But LA won on Saturday, and took the Sunday double-header, and the make-up game on Monday as well, to take the series, four games to two. The Monday game was especially disappointing because the Beavers blew an 8–1 lead, losing 9–8 on Johnny Moore's pinch homer in the ninth.

The poor homestand continued as the Seals came to Vaughn Street Park. Rain and a key injury hurt the Beavers. The Wednesday night game was rained out, causing the clubs to play two on Thursday night. Then the second game of Sunday's double-header could not be played because of a downpour. The Beavers won only the Tuesday night game and the rain-shortened game on Saturday, so lost the series, four games to two. On Tuesday night, catcher Eddie Adams took a foul tip on his finger and was sidelined until early June. The young catcher Hank Souza caught the Thursday night double-header, which Portland lost, and turned in two bad performances. He was charged with two passed balls and the Seals were stealing bases on him. Charley Petersen went to catch but his days with Portland were numbered. Lefty O'Doul finally convinced the Beavers to sell him back to the Seals, the club he played for in 1943. Petersen, while versatile, did not get along with manager Owen.

The Beavers were now in trouble. They just finished a homestand in which they won only four of 12 games and now had to travel to Seattle to open an eight-game series with the club that now trailed them by only a half game. Portland's six and one-half game lead on May 19 had dropped to a half game on May 28.

4—The 1945 Season

The Beavers opened the crucial series at Sick's Stadium with a 4–3 win in 12 innings, in which pitcher Don Pulford not only went the distance, but also got five hits in six at-bats. This increased Portland's lead to a game and a half and it stayed there the next day as the teams split the Memorial Day double-header. Hank Souza was forced to catch all these games because Eddie Adams's finger was still bothering him and Charley Petersen was now with the Seals. The lead for Portland increased to three and a half games as Syd Cohen and Roy Helser pitched back-to-back shutouts the next two nights, but Seattle won on Saturday and the teams split the Sunday double-header, so the Beavers left Seattle with a two and one-half game lead over the Rainiers. Catcher Eddie Adams was able to play on Sunday, which helped.

At this point, Portland had not lost a series on the road, winning 27 and losing 11 away from home. But this was about to change as Portland embarked on the most trying part of its schedule. The Beavers had to go from Seattle to Los Angeles for one week and then return home to play Seattle again. The Beavers had to play the Angels series without Frank Demaree and Frank Shone, so Spencer Harris, Frank Lucchesi and even utility infielder Curt Schmidt played in the outfield. Portland won three of the first four games only to see the Angels come back and take the last three and cop the series, four games to three.

Because of the long rail trip from LA, the Beavers could not start the second crucial Seattle series until Wednesday night, June 13. Injuries were taking their toll on Portland. In addition to Demaree and Shone, Spencer Harris injured his leg, Larry Barton hurt the other leg — not the one that caused him to stop at Boyes Springs — and pitcher Jake Mooty had a poor pitching shoulder. Charley English could now pinch-hit but had to come out for a runner. Things got so bad that pitcher Clarence Federmeyer had to play in the outfield. Seattle opened this series with a win, cutting Portland's lead to half a game again. But that was as close as Seattle would get to the league lead again in 1945. The Beavers won on Thursday night and both games on Friday night to increase the lead to three and one-half games. Seattle won Saturday, but Portland won the Sunday double-header to take the series, five games to two, and increase its lead to four and one-half games. Baseball players are superstitious and since Portland wore all white stockings and white caps for this series, they stayed with them for all the rest of their home games in 1945.

After this series, the Beavers had a split week with Sacramento and San Diego at home. They lost two of three to the Solons but won three of four from the Padres to end the homestand with nine wins and five losses. Frank Lucchesi played center field all this week but Adams was able to catch most of the games. Mel Nunes played almost all the games at second base.

On June 26, the Beavers had reached the halfway point in the 1945 season, leading Seattle by four and one-half games. They had 52 wins and 32 losses, a .619 pace. Seven pitchers accounted for all but two of Portland's wins and losses: Don Pulford, Syd Cohen, Roy Helser, Jake Mooty, Ad Liska, Jack Tising and Wandel Mosser. Clarence Federmeyer, with a 1–1 record, accounted for the other two games.

Portland next went to Sacramento and to Oakland before returning home. In Sacramento, the heat reached 106 degrees, which hit Marvin Owen quite hard. He had to sit out some games with Charley English able to fill in for him at third. The heat probably hurt Larry Barton too, because he was in a five for 52 slump. But the Beavers were able to win this series from the Solons, four games to three, to keep their lead at five and one-half games.

The series at Oakland was an eight-game affair over the Fourth of July week. After leaving Sacramento, the Beavers pulled a trade with the Solons, sending Curt Schmidt to the Sacs for the versatile Roy Younker, who could catch, play first, second or the outfield. He caught the second game of the Fourth of July double-header at Oakland, while Schmidt immediately played for Sacramento. Eddie Adams sprained his wrist, so the acquisition of Younker paid immediate dividends as he moved in behind the plate for the Beavers. But outfielder Frank Demaree had to be hospitalized in Oakland with the flu, and his wife rushed down from Portland to be with him. He was able to get back into the lineup on Saturday. The Beavers won five of the eight games at Oakland but their league lead was cut to three and one-half games as Seattle won seven of eight from LA.

Before the Beavers returned home to start a series with San Francisco, the Pacific Coast League announced a doubling of the prize money for postseason play. The pennant winner would now get $5,000, the playoff winner $10,000, the final-round loser $5,000 and each first-round loser $2,500. This was an incentive for the teams to make the first division. But the Beavers were also hit with news of another kind. Catcher Hank Souza and utility infielder Mel Nunes both had to report for their draft physicals this week Souza was rejected but Nunes was accepted even though he had one leg shorter than the other. He was able to play until September before reporting.

The Beavers played eight games with the Seals; the extra game was because of the postponed games when Portland was in San Francisco when Roosevelt died. The Beavers won six of the eight games from the Seals, who were using Charley Petersen in right field. The Beavers got hot and won the last five games of the Seals series and kept on winning with last-place Hollywood following the Seals into Vaughn Street Park. Larry Barton broke out of his slump against the Stars and the whole team seemed to respond. Portland won all six games from Hollywood, with the Saturday night game being rained out. At this point, Portland had won 11 games in a row, its longest winning streak of the season. Marvin Owen now had to treat his team to steak dinners again. They were now seven games ahead of Seattle and heading up to Sick's Stadium for a seven-game series.

Frank Shone set a team record by hitting safely in 39 straight games, beating the old record of Nino Bongiovanni of 34. Shone was stopped on July 26 at Seattle. Seattle won this series from Portland, but by only a margin of four games to three, so Portland's lead on July 30 was six games. This series in Seattle was a very rough one with a lot of mean words exchanged between the clubs. Bill Skiff was notably feisty and his team followed their manager. Jack Tising, who was ejected earlier in the season for throwing a spit ball, came in one game to relieve, pulled out a big chew of tobacco, pretended to spit on the ball, and Skiff roared out of the dugout only to be shown a perfectly clean ball. Marvin Owen said this series, which drew a total of 68,381 fans, was more antagonistic than the 1934 World Series he played in for Detroit against the Gas House Gang of St. Louis.

The 1945 schedule may have been drawn up by someone connected with the Seals but it was not kind to Portland. Once before they had to travel from Seattle to Los Angeles and then back to Portland, and now they had to travel from Seattle to Hollywood and then back home again. The Beavers could not get to Hollywood in time to play on Tuesday, so they began the series with a double-header on Wednesday. A second double-header was scheduled for Friday night to make up for the rained-out game when Hollywood was at Portland. The first-place Beavers had no trouble with the last-place Stars, taking seven of the eight games. They finished that series, leading Seattle by eight games. So Portland was able to win 13 of 14 games with Hollywood over a three-week period, and ended the season's play with them, winning 24 and losing only four. Younker was mainly being used in the outfield now with English at third, Nunes at second and Owen at first because Barton hurt his foot and Ted Gullic did not make the trip to Hollywood.

The series from Wednesday, August 8, through Monday, August 13, was the final regular season meeting of the two top clubs. Seattle won this series, five games to two, cutting Portland's lead to five games. Barton was able to return to first in this series but Younker was still playing in the outfield for the injured Ted Gullic. A total crowd of 52,217 saw these games, with the teams playing on Monday night, rather than a Friday night double-header to get more attendance.

After this series, Portland released Spencer Harris and Clarence Federmeyer and purchased shortstop Glenn Crawford from the Phillies and outfielder Nick Rhabe from the Angels. Rhabe started this season in the International League and was traded to LA for Hal Douglas, so he was now with his third club in 1945. Both acquisitions were left-handed batters.

Oakland followed Seattle into Vaughn Street Park and on August 15 it was announced that Japan surrendered. The game was played but some fans were unruly. Oakland allowed catcher Ed Kearse, a veteran, to take the night off to celebrate the war's end. The series with the Oaks called for eight games because of the rain out when Oakland first visited Portland. At the end of Saturday's games, the Beavers had a six and one-half game lead over Seattle and a four to two series lead over Oakland, but Oakland won the Sunday double-header, as Seattle also won two, so Portland's lead was cut to four and one-half games. Rhabe played quite a bit in right field while Crawford played second and short in this series.

The Angels followed Oakland into Vaughn Street Park, also for an eight-game series, making up for a previous rain out. During this series, Portland switched the starting times of its night games from 8:30 to 8:15 because the sun was setting later in late August. But on Tuesday night, the Angels won the first game of this series 5–4 as Portland outfielders lost two fly balls in the twilight, so the starting times were immediately put back to 8:30. After this opening game loss, the Beavers won four in a row over LA, only to have the Angels win on Saturday and both games on Sunday to tie the series at four games apiece. Mel Nunes, filling in at short for Johnny O'Neil, made two costly errors in each game on Sunday. Los Angeles was the only team in the league to have a winning record over Portland at this point, which saw its league lead cut to three games.

Portland was now embarking on its last road trip of 1945, to San Diego for seven games, to LA over Labor Day for just five games and then to San Francisco for six games in three days, with double-headers each day. The 1945 Beavers were up to the challenge.

4—The 1945 Season

The Beavers won the first game at San Diego but lost the second one, to see their lead cut to a game and a half. But then Portland won four of the remaining five games of the San Diego series to increase the lead over Seattle to five games. Ted Gullic was now able to play, joining Luchessi and Rhabe in the outfield. The Beavers next moved up to Wrigley Field to play the Angels. This time, the Beavers were not going to let the Angels beat them. Portland won the Labor Day double-header, then again 2–1 on Tuesday night, and split the Wednesday double-header, taking the short series four games to one. By doing so, they ended their season play with the Angels at 13–13, which was the only team they did not have a winning record against. When they left LA, they had a seven-game lead over Seattle.

There was no game on Thursday, September 6, but the Beavers had to play three straight double-headers at Seals Stadium on Friday, Saturday and Sunday. All three double-headers were split, but Portland left San Francisco with a six-game lead, down only one game from what it had been when the team left Los Angeles. But most important of all, Portland's magic number was now nine. Any combination of Portland wins or Seattle losses totaling nine, and the Beavers would win the pennant.

The final two weeks of the season called for Portland to be home facing San Diego and Sacramento, while Seattle was at home playing the same two clubs. League president Clarence Rowland announced that Portland and Seattle would face each other in the first round of the playoffs and that San Francisco and Sacramento would also meet in the opening round, to cut down on travel. Even though the war had ended, there was still a large military demand for rail cars. Even the 1945 World Series between the Cubs and Detroit was a one-trip series.

A former Beaver outfielder, Danny Escobar, returned from military duty and joined his team. He pinch-hit and played some outfield. Returning servicemen were allowed to play in the postseason regardless of when they rejoined their team.

Portland won five of the seven games from San Diego, and with their double-header win on Sunday, September 16, they clinched the 1945 pennant. All week long the Portland fans counted down the magic number as the Beavers won and Seattle lost. It was three going into the Sunday double-header but Seattle split while the Beavers were taking both games, so it was all over.

The final week against Sacramento was anticlimactic. Three of that week's games were rained out and not made up. The Beavers won that

Vaughn Street Park in Portland, the oldest park in the league. Note the "buy war bonds" sign in right center field. The fire department was concerned about the narrow aisles in the center field bleachers. Courtesy of Dave Eskenazi.

shortened series, three games to one. On Wednesday night, a special night was held at the park to honor manager Marvin Owen. He received quite a few gifts from the fans that night. Sportswriter L. H. Gregory urged the fans to contribute to a fund to buy engraved watches for the players. He lamented that the 1936 Portland club did not receive any memento for their winning season. But that was during the Depression and it was harder for people to contribute then. On Monday night, September 24, a banquet was held for the team at the Multnomah Hotel and Governor Earl Snell was on hand to present the watches to each player. The ball club also provided each player a special gold and diamond ring.

The Beavers received $5,000 for winning the pennant and voted 22 full shares, giving one to groundskeeper Rocky Benevento and to trainer George Enigh. Half shares were given to Spencer Harris and to Clarence Federmeyer. Quarter shares were given to Nick Rhabe and Glenn Crawford. The playoff money was to be divided among those eligible to play. Marvin Owen wanted to start the playoffs in Seattle and have the last four, if necessary, in Portland. But he was overruled by the owners, who wanted to be guaranteed of at least three home games. Portland won the three home games from Seattle to take a commanding 3–0 lead in the series.

Jake Mooty pitched a 3–0 shutout to win the opener, and Portland rallied from a 3–0 deficit in game two with four runs in the last of the eighth to give Ad Liska a 4–3 victory. Returning navy veteran Danny Escobar hit the game-winning pinch-hit two-run homer that inning, and the fans were so delighted they showered the field with coins, totaling $81 for their returning hero. The third game was an 11–0 rout for Roy Helser.

So the Beavers felt rather confident as they went up to Seattle for a Sunday double-header on September 30. The Beavers brought very little in the way of changes of clothing with them, figuring they would end the series quickly. But Seattle won both games on Sunday, and then on Monday night, Portland scored three runs in the first inning before anyone was out. But they scored no more that night, and Seattle rallied to win 4–3. Then on Tuesday, Seattle pulled off the greatest comeback in playoff history, by winning the final game, 3–1. The Portland players said they felt more like chumps than champs. Losing the opening round of the playoffs, as the Angels did in 1943, can take the joy out of winning the pennant.

Portland was not to win any more pennants nor any more playoff series. They never won another playoff series after winning the opening round back in 1937.

2. Seattle. The Rainiers were back in the first division in 1945 after missing the playoffs in 1944 for the first time since 1937. Manager Bill Skiff wanted to get more power in his lineup and not rely on 2–1 type games. But he did overlook one outfielder that might have helped his team catch the Portland Beavers: the very popular Jo Jo White, who was returning to the Pacific Coast League in 1945 after spending the previous two years with the Philadelphia Athletics and Cincinnati Reds. White, although not a power hitter, was a very good Coast League hitter, and when Skiff did not want to deal for him, White went to the Sacramento Solons, where he led the league in batting with a .355 average.

Seattle had six pitchers back from the 1944 club: Joe Demoran, Glen Elliott, 48-year-old Byron Speece, 44-year-old Sylvester Johnson, 42-year-old Hal Turpin and 39-year-old Carl Fischer. Newcomers to the pitching staff were Keith Frazier, who could also play first base and outfield; "Chesty" Chet Johnson; John Orphal; Pat McLaughlin and Alex Palica. Palica, whose name was shortened from Pavliecivich, later had two brothers pitch in the Pacific Coast League.

Returning position players were catcher Hal Sueme, infielders Joe

The 1945 Seattle Rainiers, who finished second to the Portland Beavers. In the post-season playoffs, Seattle lost the first three games to Portland but came back to win four in a row and eliminate the champion Beavers. This was the third time during World War II that Seattle eliminated the league champion in the first round of the playoffs. Courtesy of Dave Eskenazi.

Dobbins, Bill Lyman and Bob Gorbould and outfielders Bill Kats, Paul Carpenter and 42-year-old Roy Johnson. But Seattle got a lot of good baseball out of some their newcomers. Outfielder Ted Norbert was purchased from Los Angeles and led the league in homers, even though his batting average dropped to .258. First baseman George McDonald and outfielder Jack Whipple were obtained in a trade with San Diego for Dick Gyselman and two pitchers. Third baseman Chuck Aleno came from Cincinnati for Al Libke and catcher Bob Finley arrived from the Phillies in exchange for Hal Spindell. In May, Seattle purchased outfielder Johnny Gill from Portland and received centerfielder Hal Patchett in a trade with Oakland for pitcher John Babich, who had a war plant job in Oakland and wanted to play close to his home. Before the Rainiers acquired Patchett, they tried the diminutive Manny Vias in centerfield, but he did not hit any better for Seattle than he did for Sacramento the two previous years and was soon released.

The Rainiers opened the very long 1945 season in San Diego. Their first three series were with the three teams that would finish sixth, seventh and eighth, the Padres, Angels and Stars, so Seattle did very well against these clubs to get off to a good start. They won four of five in San Diego, four of six in LA and four of five in Hollywood, to return home in first place with a 12–4 record. Two games were missed in Hollywood because of FDR's death and funeral. Sportswriters in Los Angeles remembered catcher Bob Finley because he had played in the 1936 Rose Bowl for Southern Methodist against Stanford. They pointed out that while he made a nice 25-yard run, he fumbled on the next play and his team lost 7–0.

Seattle's one-game lead over Portland for the league lead did not last long. The Rainiers returned home to much fanfare to play Oakland and the hapless Hollywood Stars. But things did not go well on this opening homestand. Not only did they lose their home opener to Oakland, but they also lost out to Portland on having the larger opening day crowd. The series had to start on Wednesday because the Rainiers could not get home in time for a Tuesday game. The two clubs made up for it by a playing a double-header on Friday night. One damaging blow to Seattle was the beaning of George McDonald. This put him out of the lineup for about two weeks. He was replaced by pitcher Keith Frazier and second baseman Bob Gorbould. For three days in this series, Seattle and Portland were tied for first place, but when Oakland won the Sunday double-header on April 22, Seattle fell out of first place and never regained it all season. The Oaks won that series, four games to three, and were to win the season series from Seattle, 14 games to 12.

First baseman George McDonald, shown here in 1945 with his new team, Seattle, after playing nine years for San Diego and two years before that with the same club when it played at Hollywood. Courtesy of Dave Eskenazi.

With Hollywood coming to Seattle, the fans assumed their team could catch Portland but the Stars surprised the Rainiers by taking the series, four games to three. This was the only series Seattle lost to

Hollywood in 1945 as it won 16 of 25 games from the Stars. Nevertheless, Seattle came within a half game of Portland a couple of times, but immediately fell further behind the Beavers. Johnny Gill was now in the Seattle outfield, playing alongside Roy Johnson and Ted Norbert.

Seattle next went on the road to Oakland and Sacramento. The Oaks continued giving the Rainiers a bad time, taking five of the seven games from them. At this point, sportswriters were describing Seattle's play as a crack up, since they had lost 13 of their last 20 games after opening with a 12–4 record. They attributed Seattle's slump to the beaning of George McDonald. At the conclusion of the series in Oakland, the two clubs exchanged players: Seattle got 36-year-old centerfielder Hal Patchett for pitcher John Babich, who refused to report to Seattle because he lived in Oakland and had a war job there. When Germany surrendered on V-E Day, no games were called off but all wounded veterans were admitted free to Coast League games.

The week of May 8 to 13 saw the return of George McDonald to first base as the Rainiers went to Sacramento. Seattle did well in this series, taking four of the five games that could be played. The Friday night game was called after 13 innings with a 9–9 tie and the scheduled Saturday double-header was rained out. With Patchett now in center field, Manny Vias was released. The Rainiers returned home for three weeks to play the Seals, Angels and the Portland Beavers in a crucial series.

The series with San Francisco could not start on Tuesday because the Seals could not get to Seattle in time. Because of this delay, all the Seattle players except one voted to fly to or from California on future trips if possible. But it rained on Wednesday and Thursday nights, so the series began with a Friday night double-header. The Rainiers won the opener 1–0 but the second game was called after 10 innings with a 3–3 tie because of a curfew. The Seals won on Saturday but the Rainiers took both games on Sunday to get within four games of first-place Portland. Since the Seals were only going to Portland the next week, the Rainiers and Seals played another double-header on Monday night, May 21, which the two clubs split. The second game was the debut of Chet Johnson, the left-hander, owned by the St. Louis Browns, who allowed him to pitch for the Rainiers since he was stationed nearby while still in the military. Johnson lost to the Seals, but Seattle won the series, four games to two.

The following week, the team the Rainiers loved to beat came to Sick's Stadium. The Los Angeles Angels and Seattle had been on bad terms since the 1938 season when former Angels manager Jack Lellivelt began managing the Rainiers. This animosity continued when the feisty Bill Skiff took over the reins. In this week of May 22 through May 27, the Rainiers wiped out the Angels, six out of seven games, to get to within a half game of Portland. During this series, Skiff was able to use almost all his outfielders, going with Gill, Patchett and Whipple one game and then Norbert, Kats and Johnson in another. When Chuck Aleno was beaned, Joe Dobbins moved from second to third base and Bob Gorbould went in at second. The only game the Angels won was on Saturday, when Don Osborn, who had been with Seattle back in 1936, beat Alex Palica. During this season, Seattle was able to win 21 out of 28 games from Los Angeles.

During this second homestand of 1945, pitcher Pat McLaughlin was still unable to find a place to live. He was so desperate he began looking in Everett, which was over 20 miles north of Seattle. Third baseman Chuck Aleno was also in need of housing and former Seattle third baseman Dick Gyselman would not report to San Diego until the Padres could find him a place to live down there.

On Tuesday, May 29, the two top teams, Portland and Seattle, met for the first time in 1945. Even this early in the season, it looked to be a two-team race because Oakland, in third place, was six games behind Seattle. Even though the Rainiers were now playing good baseball, winning 14 and losing four and tying two in their last 20 games, the Beavers just would not let Seattle catch them.

Had the Rainiers been able to win the opening game of this series, they would have gone into first place, but the visiting Beavers won 4–3 in 12 innings to lead by a game and a half. The two clubs split the Memorial Day double-header before a crowd of 12,446. Portland shut the Rainiers out the next two nights to increase its lead to three and one-half games but Seattle won on Saturday and the teams split the Sunday double-header, so Portland left town with a two and one-half game lead and a series win of five games to three. Some bad blood rose between the two clubs on Sunday June 3, when Larry Barton's throw hit pitcher Joe Demoran on the head while he was standing on second base. Demoran missed only one start because of this incident. Seattle writers were also lamenting that Ted Norbert had cooled off considerably, hitting eight homers in April and only one in May.

After this disappointing series loss to Portland, the Rainiers went on a road trip to San Francisco and then to Portland, for another crucial series. In San Francisco, the two clubs alternated wins through the first five games, with the Seals taking a three to two series lead. George

McDonald got spiked on Saturday, so pitcher Keith Frazier finished the game at first base. But on Sunday, John Gill went to first for both games and Ted Norbert was put back in left field. A Seals Stadium crowd of 15,000 saw their team lose both games and the series to Seattle. Hal Turpin and Chet Johnson each won a game that day and Bob Gorbould was moved to short with Bill Lyman playing second. Hal Sueme and Bob Finley each caught a game that day as the Rainiers pulled to within a game and a half of Portland, which was losing a double-header at Los Angeles.

The second crucial series for the league lead could not start until Wednesday at Vaughn Street Park because the Beavers were coming from LA. The Beavers decided to play a double-header on Friday night, rather than on Wednesday, to allow some injured players time to heal. Seattle also got the disturbing news that outfielders Jack Whipple and Bill Kats and catcher Bob Finley had to report for their army physicals. As things turned out, with the war nearing its end, none of these players had to report for military duty. But while Finley was reporting to his draft board in Texas, Hal Sueme had to catch the first six games of this series, including both games on Friday night. Finley did get back in time to catch the second game on Sunday.

On Wednesday night, June 13, Seattle beat Portland behind Joe Demoran 4–3 to move to within a half game of the first-place Beavers. But as was the case two weeks earlier, that would be as close as Seattle would get to the top of the standings. The Beavers won on Thursday night and both games on Friday evening to go up by three and one-half games. Seattle did win on Saturday but Portland won both games on Sunday before 10,000 fans to increase its lead to four and one-half games, while taking the series five games to two.

Even though none of the Seattle players who had to take their draft physicals were called, Bob Finley was told that he would have to report to nearby Fort Lewis on June 19. Next he was given two more weeks and finally he was not called at all, but this news did cause Bill Skiff to scramble to find another catcher. They did make a deal for one, Phil Gatto, but he refused to report. As it turned out, this did not matter with Finley and Sueme available all season.

The Rainiers moved home for a split week with San Diego and Sacramento. Seattle fans and sportswriters were disappointed that former third baseman Dick Gyselman did not accompany the Padres to the Northwest because he did not want to leave his playground job in San Diego. But the fans did get to see their former hero, Jo Jo White, play for the Solons. Seattle won two of three from the Padres and then won the first two games of the Sacramento series only to lose the Sunday doubleheader to the Solons before a large, disappointed crowd. After this week, Portland still led the Rainiers by four and one-half games.

Seattle now had to go all the way to San Diego, a trip of 1,200 miles, which was made by rail, so the series could not start until Wednesday night. During this series, Seattle made some player changes. It released Roy Johnson who, at 42, was unable to cover much ground, and purchased the speedy 22-year-old outfielder Joe Passero from the Kansas City Blues. They also acquired relief pitcher John Carpenter, who had just been released from the Canadian army. While in San Diego, the Rainiers lost the series to the Padres, four games to three.

But now Seattle moved into Wrigley Field to take on

Pitcher Hal Turpin, known as the Oregon farmer, won 203 games in the Pacific Coast League from 1927 to 1945. He won over 20 games for Seattle four straight years, from 1939 to 1942, but had to leave the club in mid–1943 because he could not get anyone to work his farm. He never played in the majors. Courtesy of Dave Eskenazi.

their "cousins," the struggling Los Angeles Angels. This series was all Rainier fans could hope for, as their team won seven of the eight games from hapless Los Angeles. The eighth game was played because this was Fourth of July week. On Thursday night, July 5, Ted Norbert, who played for the Angels in 1944, hit a homer in the top of the 12th inning to give Seattle a 1–0 victory for Chet Johnson. Angels fans felt especially bad because Norbert was sold to Seattle when the Angels got Lou Novikoff back from the Cubs. While Novikoff had a higher batting average than Norbert, he hit only nine homers compared to Norbert's 23. Joe Passero took over in center field in this series, with Hal Patchett moving to right. Even though the Rainiers had a great series in Los Angeles, they gained only two games on Portland that week and still trailed them by three and one-half games.

The Rainiers returned home on July 10 to play Hollywood, San Francisco and the Portland Beavers. Before this homestand began, Seattle sent pitcher John Orphal to Kansas City for shortstop Dick Briskey. Bill Skiff was still trying to find the best combination at short and second base. He had been rotating Bill Lyman, Joe Dobbins and Bob Gorbould in those spots. Lyman was the best fielder of those three, but the weakest hitter.

Seattle won the first three games of the Hollywood series to extend its winning streak to 10 games, but the Stars won the second game of the Friday night double-header, to stop it. In that double-header, the new outfielder, Joe Passero, playing in his first game before the home crowd, tripped over a base and fractured a bone in his leg. This hurt the outfield defense, causing Patchett to return to center with Bill Kats playing right field. Hollywood also won on Saturday but Seattle won the Sunday double-header to win the series, six games to two. At this point, Seattle trailed Portland by three and one-half games and, while no one knew it at the time, the eight clubs were in the exact positions in the standings where they would finish the season. Third-place Sacramento was about nine games behind Seattle.

The Seals next came to Sick's Stadium for eight games because of a previous rain out, but Saturday's game was rained out, so it could not be made up this week. The Seals won this series over Seattle, four games to three, even beating Chet Johnson on Friday night, stopping his personal six-game winning streak. At the conclusion of this series, the Rainiers trailed Portland by seven games.

At this point in the season, on July 24, things looked dim for Seattle as Portland was coming to Sick's Stadium with an 11-game winning streak. But Seattle gave the Beavers a real fight, winning the series, four games to three, to shave one game off the lead. The series drew 68,381 fans, setting a league attendance record for one series. The fans saw a lot of animosity and trash talk between the two league leaders. There would be one more series between these top two clubs in Portland in just two weeks.

The Rainiers were now going to San Francisco and to Portland. While Joe Passero was still unable to play, the team got the good news that Bill Matheson, an outfielder who had been with Seattle since 1941, was able

4—The 1945 Season 151

to rejoin the team after quitting his war plant job. In his first game back on Thursday night, August 2, Matheson singled in the tying run in the ninth and the winning run in the 11th to help his team win its third straight game over the Seals. Matheson also made a great running catch in the outfield. But San Francisco won the next three games to tie the series before Seattle won the Sunday double-header to take the series, five games to three. Unfortunately for the Rainiers, they did not gain on Portland, which were also winning, so they went into Portland trailing the leaders by eight games.

This was the last regular series between the two Northwest antagonists, and this time the Rainiers beat Portland decisively, five games to two. However, that only cut Portland's lead to five games. The series started on Wednesday and ended up on Monday night, rather than play a weeknight double-header, in order to get a bigger crowd. The teams drew 52,217 for the week, which was not as large as they drew in Seattle, but Vaughn Street Park was smaller than Sick's Stadium. Even though Seattle won this series, Portland won the season's series between the two clubs, 15 games to 14. However, the two would meet in the very exciting playoffs.

Seattle's spirits were buoyed by the fact that the Angels were coming to Seattle for a seven-game series. This was the one team Seattle really had its way with in 1945 up until now. They had won 17 of the last 19 games played with Los Angeles, going back to April. But this time, the Angels played a little better, taking three of the first four games from Seattle. But then things returned to normal, and Seattle won on Saturday and both games on Sunday to cop the series, four games to three. At this point, on August 20, Seattle trailed Portland by four and one-half games. But by this time the four playoff teams were set, with Sacramento and San Francisco safely ahead of fifth-place Oakland. While the Solons and Seals were close to each other in the standings, it did not matter which finished third because the league announced that those two would meet in the opening round of the playoffs, as would Seattle and Portland, to cut travel costs.

The Oaks followed the Angels into Sick's Stadium and Seattle won the first four games of that series to stretch their winning streak to seven games, but gained only a half game on Portland over this period. Ted Norbert was starting to hit homers again and Joe Passero was able to play on a part-time basis. Oakland stopped the winning streak by taking the Saturday game and the clubs split the Sunday double-header, so Seattle won the series, five games to two. Portland's lead was now down to three games. The Rainiers had now won five series in a row and two of them over Portland.

Catcher Bob Finley was injured in the Oakland series, so Seattle signed Dominic Castro as a back-up catcher to Hal Sueme. Castro caught for Portland early in the 1942 season. The Rainiers were now about to embark on a road trip that called for 20 games in 12 days in Sacramento, Oakland and Hollywood. The extra games were because of rain outs and the death of FDR, but these games were going to put a strain on the older players.

The Sacramento series, beginning on Tuesday August 28, was a nine-game set. Seattle won the first three games to cut Portland's lead to a game and a half. Joe Demoran won his 12th straight game and Ted Norbert was hitting the long ball again. Dominic Castro was splitting time behind the plate with Hal Sueme, but Joe Dobbins had to play third because Chuck Aleno was hurt. But this game and a half was as close as Seattle was going to get to Portland for the rest of the season. Sacramento won the next four games of this series, and the teams split the Sunday double-header, giving the Solons the series, five games to four. At the end of this series, Portland moved ahead of Seattle by five games, making Seattle's chances of catching them quite bleak.

The Rainiers next moved into Oakland for a

Slugger Ted Norbert, shown in 1945 when he played with Seattle. He hit a total of 205 homers in the Pacific Coast League from 1935 to 1946, winning the home run title four times, the batting title once and the RBI title once. He previously played with San Francisco, Portland and Los Angeles, but never played in the majors. Courtesy of Dave Eskenazi.

4—The 1945 Season

five-game series over Labor Day, and even though they won the holiday double-header, Portland also won its, to keep the lead at five games. But Seattle was feeling the pressure of these crucial games, and lost the last three to the Oaks, while Portland was winning, so the lead was back up to seven games. The Rainiers now had to play three double-headers in three days in Hollywood, but so did Portland in San Francisco.

Aleno was now back at third and Ted Norbert was still knocking homers, but the Rainiers could only split the first two twin bills at Gilmore Field. Portland also split its first two double-headers, so the lead remained at seven games. Even though Seattle did win both games on Sunday at Gilmore Field, while Portland split again, the Beavers' lead was six games with only two weeks to play. Portland's magic number was down to nine.

The final two weeks called for Seattle to host Sacramento and then San Diego while Portland was hosting the same two teams in reverse order. The magic number went down very quickly. Portland won the first two games of its series while Seattle lost one after being idle the first night. The magic number was now six. On Thursday, Portland lost while Seattle split a double-header, cutting it to five. On Friday, the Beavers won while the Rainiers lost, so it fell to three. Seattle was rained out on Saturday while the Beavers lost, but on Sunday, Portland won both games while Seattle split, giving Portland an eight and one-half-game lead with only seven to play. The magic number was now zero!

The two clubs merely went through the motions while playing out the final week of the regular season, resting their players for the playoffs. Seattle and Portland had known for some time that they would be facing each other in the opening round of the Governors' Cup series. Portland had the option of where the first three games would be played and it chose to open at home, overruling manager Marvin Owen, who wanted to have the final games in Portland.

The Portland fans and the Beaver players were ecstatic as the Beavers rolled over Seattle in the first three games at Vaughn Street Park. The clubs took Saturday off for college football, and perhaps that game was an omen. Washington beat Oregon 20–6 at Husky Stadium in Seattle. Even though Seattle writers were now conceding the series to Portland, the baseball team from Oregon still had to win one game in the state of Washington. They never did! A crowd of 8,500 went to Sick's Stadium on Sunday, September 29, hoping to see a double-header, but this would only be the case if Seattle won the opener. The Rainiers won that game 7–4, as Joe Demoran got the win, while old Sylvester Johnson, the last man to pitch to Babe Ruth in a regular season game back in 1935, saved the game with one and two-thirds innings of shutout ball. Even though the Pacific Coast League used four umpires for playoff games, they still were playing only seven innings in postseason double-headers. The second game that day was also won by Seattle, 4–2, with Carl Fischer getting the win.

On Monday night, October 1, it looked very much like Seattle's goose was cooked. Portland scored three runs in the top of the first with no one out and Jake Mooty was the Portland pitcher. Mooty had shutout the Rainiers in the first game of the series. However, the now 43-year-old Hal Turpin settled down after that and did not allow Portland another run all night. It was still 3–0 when Seattle finally scored a run in the sixth inning when Bill Matheson, who went three for three that night, tripled and scored on George McDonald's fly ball. Then in the last of the seventh, the 6,237 Seattle fans were thrilled as their team rallied for three runs to take the lead. Norbert singled and went to second on a ground out. The next play was the play of the series. Bob Finley hit a smash back through the box for a single, scoring Norbert, but the blow hit Jake Mooty's pitching hand. Mooty insisted in staying in the game, a mistake that may have cost Portland the series. Hal Turpin, who was allowed to bat that late in the game with his team trailing by two runs, drew a walk. Bob Gorbould then doubled off Demaree's glove, scoring Finley and sending Turpin with the lead run to third. At this point, Mooty was relieved by Jack Tising, who purposely walked Hal Patchett to load the bases. Bill Matheson then singled in the run that proved to be the winner and the Oregon farmer, Hal Turpin, shut down the Beavers to allow Seattle to tie the series at three games each.

On Tuesday night, October 2, a crowd of 9,326 came out to Sick's Stadium and saw their Rainiers pull off the greatest comeback in Coast League playoff history. Bill Skiff tricked the Beavers by announcing lefty Chet Johnson as his starter, causing Portland to take batting practice against lefty Carl Gunnarson. However, Skiff gave the ball to Joe Demoran who had pitched seven and one-third innings just two days earlier in Sunday's first game. Demoran pitched a two-hitter. He gave up a solo homer to Ted Gullic in the second but the Rainiers got three unearned runs off submariner Ad Liska in the fourth, and eliminated Portland from the playoffs. After the first two runners were retired, George McDonald tripled and Joe Dobbins walked. Then Ted Norbert hit a routine grounder to short but Johnny O'Neil fumbled it, allowing the tying run to score. Chuck Aleno then singled in Dobbins with the go-ahead

4—The 1945 Season

Air view of Sick's Seattle Stadium, taken on a day they had a packed house. Courtesy of Dave Eskenazi.

run and Bob Finley singled in Norbert for an insurance run. Demoran then shut the door on the champion Beavers.

The final round of the playoffs involved the same two teams that had met in the final round of the 1943 playoffs, Seattle and San Francisco. The results were the same, with the Seals winning the series, four games to two. But this one did have a few more twists and turns. Since the two opening playoff series both went seven games and finished on October 2, each team had the same lack of rest. Seattle had its choice, and wanted to have the first three games at Sick's Stadium. The plan was to play on Wednesday, Thursday and Friday nights, and then move to Seals Stadium for a Sunday double-header and for any additional games that were needed. The Seals planned to fly to Seattle on Wednesday and play that evening but they could not get a flight because it was difficult to charter an airplane, even though the war had ended, because there were still heavy demands by the government. So the Seals took the train north to Seattle on Wednesday morning, arriving on Thursday afternoon, October 4. The Rainiers decided to play a double-header that night and a single game on Friday, so the two clubs could still play the double-header in Seals Stadium on Sunday, October 7. A crowd of over 8,000 was on hand to root for Seattle to knock off the Seals. Both teams were there also but the Seals' equipment was not. The railroad had misplaced it. The Rainiers offered to let Seattle wear their road uniforms and use their gloves, but no sporting goods store could come up with 25 pairs of baseball shoes, so the crowd was sent home.

This completely changed the plans for the rest of the series. The Seals had sold a lot of tickets to the Sunday double-header and had to tell fans to exchange them for a later game. Some fans that could come out on Sunday may not have been able to attend at night. Meanwhile, the Rainiers had already leased Sick's Stadium for an exhibition game between Bob Feller's All Stars and Satchel Paige's Negro League All Stars on Sunday afternoon. So the two teams decided to play single games on Friday, Saturday and even on Sunday night, the latter being a first for the Pacific Coast League. In addition, the Seals had leased their ballpark to the same two All Star teams for a Tuesday night game, so the games in San Francisco could not start until Wednesday night, October 10.

Therefore, the final series began on Friday night, October 5, in Seattle and the Rainiers got off to a good start, winning 3–2. Carl Fischer gave up a run in each of the first two innings, but settled down after that. In the seventh, Fischer was lifted for pinch hitter John Gill, who doubled home Bob Finley, who reached third on a misjudged fly ball. Gill scored the tying run on Hal Patchett's single. Keith Frazier, a former Seal, pitched shutout ball the last two innings, to get the win. Ted Norbert homered in the eighth for the winning blow.

On Saturday night, Hal Turpin was staked to a 2–0 lead in the first but could not hold it. He gave up three runs in the fifth and another in the sixth as the Seals tied the series.

On the first Sunday night game, a crowd of 6,501 turned out but a larger crowd was there that afternoon to see Bob Feller and Satchel Paige. Joe Demoran went seven and two-thirds innings for the win, relieved by Sylvester Johnson. The Seals had a 2–1 lead going into the last of the fourth, when Seattle struck for six runs. The key blows were a bases-loaded double by Chuck Aleno, and after three walks, which forced in a run, a two-run single by Bill Matheson. So after three games, the Rainiers went to San Francisco with a two-games-to-one lead.

Seattle felt confident even though it was going on the road because it had won 16 and lost 12 from the Seals during the season and had won nine and lost six in San Francisco. The teams left by train on Monday morning and arrived in Oakland on Tuesday afternoon, but could not play until Wednesday night because of the exhibition game scheduled for Tuesday night. The Seals won the series by taking all three games from Seattle, 6–1 on Wednesday, 7–4 on Thursday after Seattle led 4–0 going into the last of the seventh, and 6–5 on Friday, after Seattle had taken a 5–4 lead in the top of the ninth in the sixth, and last, game. The last two were tough losses to take but Portland probably felt worse, after blowing a three-games-to-none lead in the opening round.

Outfielder Johnny Gill, shown here in 1945, after being sold to the Rainiers after playing five years with Portland, thus missing out on the Beavers' pennant winning season. Courtesy of Dave Eskenazi.

3. Sacramento. The last war year turned out to be a big improvement for the Solons both on the field and at the box office. After two dismal years finishing deep in the second division, Sacramento moved up to third place and set a new attendance mark: 310,741. Manager Earl Sheely was back for his second of three years at the helm and had some good additions to his team which helped them make the playoffs.

The most important new player was outfielder Jo Jo White, who had been a star with Seattle from 1939 to 1942 and had played with the Philadelphia Athletics and the Cincinnati Reds the next two seasons. White led the league in batting with a .355 average. Other new players that helped the Solons were shortstop Jack Calvey from San Diego, catcher Norm Schlueter, outfielders George Manish and Jesse Landrum, third baseman/outfielder Jim Grant and the versatile Roy Younker from Hollywood.

While Sacramento did have some new pitchers in 1945, it was the greatly improved years of two returning hurlers that made the biggest impact. Guy Fletcher improved his record from 12 and 19 in 1944 to 24 and 14 in 1945. Bud Beasley, who could join the team only in June after teaching school in Reno, improved from 5 and 6 to 12 and 4. Unfortunately, he got a sore arm late in the season and could not help much at the end.

Other returning pitchers were 49-year-old Herman Pillette, who was also the pitching coach, John Pintar, Gene Babbitt, Dick Powers, Earl Porter, Steve LeGault and 19-year-old Lou Penrose. Newcomers to the pitching staff were Joe Wood Jr., son of the famed Red Sox pitcher who won 34 games in 1912; Jim Antanazio; Jim McCarthy, just out of the Coast Guard; and three youngsters who pitched occasionally, Le Roy Stevens, age 17; Jo Vivalda, age 20; and Don Kornahrens, age 16.

The position players who returned were second baseman Gene Handley, catcher Lilio Marcucci, who also played third, and outfielders Ted Greenhalgh and Al McElreath.

First base was a problem for the Solons until the end of May when they acquired Ed Zipay from Louisville. Zipay had been out of baseball in 1944 but had received a trophy for the highest minor league batting average (.419) in 1936 when playing in the Ohio State League. He hit .311 for the Sacs in 1945. The Solons tried left-handed Roy Wetmore at first to start the season but he broke the webbing in his glove in the second game and had to be replaced by Roy Younker because there was no other left-handed first baseman's mitt. With wartime shortages, it took several days for the sporting goods stores to find him one, and when he got one, the Solons found out he could not hit very well.

Earl Sheely was able to acquire Bill Prout in late April. Prout had played first for Sacramento back in 1937 when it had finished in first place. Prout belonged to Chattanooga in the Southern Association but refused to report, preferring to stay with his war plant job in Los Angeles. The deal was made while Sacramento was in San Francisco but Prout remained in Los Angeles for another week until the Solons came there. Prout had a bad ankle, so Sheely tried to get one of the Angels' two first basemen, Reggie Otero or Mel Hicks, but when that failed he got Ed Zipay from Louisville. Then both Bill Prout and Roy Wetmore were dealt to San Diego.

4—The 1945 Season

The Solons as usual, opened the season at home with two scheduled short series, and a third that was shortened by President Roosevelt's funeral. The Sacs won three of five from Hollywood, the team that was going to finish last, lost four of six to Portland, the team that was going to finish on top, and then took four of the five games that could be played with Los Angeles. The two teams that were to finish seventh and eighth, LA and Hollywood, were easy marks for the Solons in 1945. Sacramento won 18 and lost 10 to the Angels and won 15 and lost 9 to the Stars.

However, Sacramento did have trouble with San Diego, losing 17 of 29 games with them and also with Portland, losing 12 of 20 with the Beavers. After late July, there was no chance for the Solons to rise above third place, nor any danger they would fall out of the first division.

Baseball at all levels has always been opposed to gambling ever since the 1919 Black Sox scandal. When it became apparent that some professional gamblers were sitting in the front-row seats at Doubleday Park and luring fans into betting, the Solons' business manager, Lubi Separovich, hired extra police to stamp out betting. Announcements were made over the public address system warning gamblers that they would be evicted from the ballpark. Similar announcements were also made in other Pacific Coast League parks.

Jim Grant was one of the new players that Earl Sheely had counted on to help the club. But he had bad knees, so they moved him from third base to right field to keep his bat in the lineup. However, while playing the outfield against Oakland on June 10, he dove for a ball and broke his shoulder. He was in the hospital for over a week and his season was at an end. He was hitting .310 at the time.

The Solons picked up another infielder with an interesting background, Barney Bridges, after the season had started. Bridges had been with Sacramento very briefly in 1940, but had gone into the navy when the war started. He was torpedoed off the coast of Africa and was in a life raft for four and a half hours before he was rescued. Bridges filled in at short when Jack Calvey got hurt, and even had to start some playoff games because Calvey got his hand caught in a taxicab door in Portland and had to have 24 stitches in it.

The San Diego Padres were now managed by the man who had led the Solons to their 1942 pennant, Pepper Martin. When the Padres first came to Sacramento in June, both managers agreed to start 17-year-old pitchers on Saturday night, the 16th. The Solons started Le Roy Stevens, born in November 1927, and the Padres started Jerry Womak, born in October 1927. The Solons knocked out young Womak in the fifth on their way to an 11–3 win, with Stevens going the distance. The two pitchers had a rematch on July 28 and this time the Padres won 10–8 in 11 innings, but Stevens was not the loser. He was relieved by another youngster, Joe Vivalda, who took the loss. Ex-Solon Bill Prout was now playing first base for San Diego.

It was in July that the announcement was made that the military would not allow the use of Pullman cars for any civilian travel under 450 miles. This affected travel within the state of California but not trips to Portland and Seattle. The Solons, as did the other California clubs, spent Sunday night in a hotel if on the road, and then took the day train on Monday morning, which could get them to their destination in time for a Tuesday night game.

One thing that helped stir up fan interest in the 1945 Solons was the return of radio broadcasting of Sacramento's games. According to John Spalding in his *Sacramento Senators and Solons* announcer Tony Koester returned to station KFBK for the first time since before the war. However, he could not get air time until 9:30 P.M., over an hour after the game had started, so he had to spend time reviewing what had happened. He also came on late on Sundays, sometimes after the first game of the double-header was over. He also recreated the road games. At night, station KFBK could be heard up and down the West Coast, so fans in other league cities could listen to Tony Koester if they wanted to.

In late May, when pitcher Bud Beasley joined the team when his school year in Reno was over, the Solons sold two pitchers to Hollywood: "Smokestack" Steve LeGault and Earl Porter. But in July, the Sacs made a poor trade. They let sentiment rule when they traded the versatile, and very valuable, Roy Younker to Portland for the 26-year-old Curt Schmidt, an infielder, who was born and raised in Sacramento. But Schmidt played very little for the Sacs, and hit only .185.

As part of the war effort, the Solons held a special bond drive at Doubleday Park on Wednesday June 6, the one-year anniversary of D-Day. Actor George Murphy, who was to become a U.S. senator 20 years later, entertained the crowd of 8,982 who could enter the park only by buying a war bond. A total of $1,957,575 worth of bonds were sold that night as the Solons pleased the crowd with an 11–1 win over Oakland.

On July 20, a very sad event occurred for Sacramento sports fans. Dick Edmonds, sports editor of the *Sacramento Union*, died of viral pneumonia at the age of 31. His last column appeared in the paper on June 14, and everyone expected him to return. Almost immediately, fans started a petition to rename the ballpark for him because he was the leader in the effort to save the Solons for the city of Sacramento during the winter of 1943-1944. The club had almost been moved to Tacoma. The renaming took place on Sunday September 9, which was the last regular season home game for Sacramento in 1945.

When Japan surrendered on August 15, there was no off day while the Solons were in Hollywood, but the crowds at most of the games were small because many folks were out celebrating. But back in Sacramento, many citizens went hungry because all the restaurants and grocery stores were closed while the celebration was taking place.

Late in the season, around Labor Day, most clubs, including Sacramento, were faced with a lot of make-up games that called for many double-headers. But by this time, the Solons were seven and one-half games ahead of fifth-place Oakland and about eight games behind second-place Seattle. The only question was would Sacramento or San Francisco finish third, but it did not matter because the playoffs called for those two teams to meet in the first round to save on travel costs. One small difference would be that the team that finished higher had its choice of playing the first three games at home or on the road, and Sacramento won out, and chose to open at home.

The last two weeks of the season were spent up in Seattle and Portland. The Solons, by winning the series in Seattle four games to three, helped clinch the pennant for Portland. One especially disappointing game for Seattle occurred on Friday night, September 14. The Rainiers were leading the Solons 3–1 going into the ninth inning and Sacramento struck for 10 runs to win 11–3. George Mandish was used as a pinch hitter in that inning, got a single, came around to score a run, and went in the clubhouse to take a shower. As the Solons kept rattling their bats, a teammate had to run in and tell him to get dressed because he was going to have to bat again. This time he hit a homer.

The Solons chose to open the playoffs against San Francisco at home because they had won 11 and lost four to the Seals at home but had won only four and lost 10 at Seals Stadium. But what happens during the regular season does not always hold true for the postseason, and this year it did not. The Sacramento fans were very enthusiastic for these playoffs because their team had been so poor the previous two years. All reserved seats for the three games at Edmonds Field were snapped up, but the fans went home disappointed. The Solons lost all three games at home. In the first game, Barney Bridges played short for the injured Jack Calvey and he was trapped off third base to kill what could have been a big inning.

The Sacramento ball park was renamed Edmonds Field at the end of the 1945 season to honor the memory of sports writer Dick Edmonds, whose effort helped save the club from moving to Tacoma in 1944. This is the rebuilt park shown in 1949 after it burned down during the 1948 season. Courtesy of Dave Eskenazi.

The Solons blew a 4–0 lead and lost 6–5, with the Seals getting the winning run in the ninth.

The next night, Bridges was benched with Gene Handley moving over to short from second, and Jess Landrum moved from right field to second base. Al McElreath replaced Landrum in the outfield but the Solons lost 3–1. On the third night, the Seals won with the help of a crucial error on Gene Handley, who was not used to playing shortstop. This let in two unearned runs, and the Seals won 4–3. But when a Sacramento runner was called out on a close play at first, two fans ran out onto the field to attack umpire Al Floresi. This earned them a night in jail.

The teams moved to San Francisco to finish the series, with a double-header scheduled for Sunday, September 30, if Sacramento won the opener. Otherwise, the series would be over. Jack Calvey was now able to play short and the Solons, behind Joe Wood Jr., won the opener, 4–1. Unlike the situation in Seattle, the second game of the double-header in San Francisco was scheduled for nine innings. "Grumpy" Guy Fletcher went the distance and beat the Seals 5–2, to require a sixth game. That game was played on Monday night, October 1, and the teams were scoreless through eight innings. John Pintar allowed 10 hits but no runs. The Solons got a run in the top of the ninth on two singles and a ground out. Then in the last of the ninth, Earl Sheely made a defensive move in the outfield that paid off. Ted Greenhalgh was put in center field, which moved Jo Jo White to right. Greenhalgh made a sensational catch of a drive that could have been a triple. Then with two outs and a runner on second base, White was able to throw that runner out at the plate on a single. So the Solons, just like Seattle, had come from three games down to tie the series.

But Sacramento was not able to pull off the four-game sweep as Seattle was. The Solons started Jim McCarthy but sent in Guy Fletcher in the third inning when the Seals scored two runs to close the Sacramento lead to 4–2. The Sacs added a run in the top of the fifth to go up 5–2, but the roof fell in on Fletcher in the last half of that inning as the Seals scored six runs. The final score was 9–6, and the Seals advanced to the final round. But Sacramento accomplished a great deal in 1945 after the two previous losing seasons. The players received an extra week's salary by being in the playoffs and split $2,500, which was the amount given to the first-round losers.

4. San Francisco. The Seals had their greatest success in the postseason again as they won their third of four straight playoff series in 1945. But the club got off to a slow start and floundered in the second division until mid–May before firmly establishing itself as a first-division club in June. By mid–July, the eight teams were in the exact order in which they were to finish. By early August, there was no more suspense because even fifth-place Oakland was no longer a threat to overtake the Seals or Sacramento for a first-division spot.

The Seals had only a few personnel changes from the 1944 season. Roy Nicely began his first of several seasons as the team's shortstop, but Joe Futernick was still with the club. The New York Giants sent out three pitchers, Ken Brodnell, Ken "Whitey" Miller and Frank Seward in exchange for "Cowboy" Ray Harrell. Ray Perry, who had been on the team in 1942, returned to play third. The Seals also picked up Battle Malone "Bones" Sanders, a left-handed hitter, to alternate at first base with Gus Suhr. Suhr loved to ride trains and kept railroad timetables in his pocket. Emil Mailho came over from Oakland to play in the outfield. Other new pitchers were Elmer Orella, Floyd Ehrman and Bob Barthelson.

The 1945 Seals had winning seasonal records against only three teams, Oakland, Hollywood and Los Angeles, while San Francisco lost four more games than it won from Seattle and three more to the champion Portland Beavers and to San Diego. The Sacramento Solons won just one more game from the Seals than they lost. Before the season began, O'Doul was informed that his young pitcher, Larry Jansen, would not be released by his Oregon draft board to leave his farm in order to play baseball. But when the war ended in August, Jansen did join the club in September, but was not eligible for the playoffs.

The Seals opened the season against one club they could beat fairly easily, Los Angeles at Wrigley Field. The Seals did win the opener after watching the Angels hoist their 1944 pennant flag, but lost the short series, three games to two. In addition, the Seals suffered a couple of injuries in that opening series. There were no warning tracks in Coast League parks and outfielder Ben Guintini ran into the red brick wall at Wrigley Field. He was out of the lineup for a few days and replaced with Frenchy Uhalt. Then 42-year-old catcher Joe Sprinz had to be taken to the hospital after being struck on the head by Jim Tyack's knee in a home-plate collision. There was a worry that the injury could be in the same place where Sprinz was struck in the face by a baseball dropped from a blimp at the 1939 World's Fair, but he was able to rejoin this club in their next series at San Diego. The Seals were slumping in April, losing that six-game series at San Diego, four games to two, before returning home for three weeks. Just as they got home they got the bad news that their long-time trainer, Bobby Johnson, died at age 60. He had been sent home from Los Angeles when he took ill.

The Seals won their home opener over the eventual pennant winner, Portland, by a 6–3 score, with pitcher Bob Joyce going four for four at the plate. This was the year that Joyce was to win 31 games, the first time the league had had a 30-game winner since the Angels' Buck Newsome in 1933. This series was shortened to five games because of FDR's death and funeral, with the Beavers winning three of the five games. A large crowd of 19,000 came out for the Sunday double-header, as the 1945 season was to break the record attendance achieved in 1944.

Before the next series with Sacramento began, the Seals and Oakland played an exhibition game at Oaks Park for the benefit of the widow of Ernie Raimondi, an infielder who had played for the Seals and the Oaks before the war. Raimondi, who was the brother of Oaks catcher Billy Raimondi, was killed in action in France. A crowd of 3,000 came out for the benefit.

4—*The 1945 Season* 165

The Sacramento series was the one series in the first six that the Seals were able to win, taking five of seven from the Sacs. Another nice crowd of 18,300 came out on Sunday to see the Seals win the doubleheader.

The San Diego Padres next came to Seals Stadium not just to play there but also to bunk there in the clubhouse. The conference to establish the United Nations began that week with the delegates meeting in the San Francisco Opera House, making hotel space very scarce. But these poor living quarters did not keep the visitors from taking five of the seven games from the Seals. The Padres won both games on Sunday before 15,500 disappointed fans, even beating Bob Joyce.

Front of San Francisco scorecard, 1945. Courtesy of Doug McWilliams.

The slump continued as the Seals went to Sacramento the first week of May. New pitcher Ken Brondell was losing consistently and needed relief each time he pitched. He was finally traded in mid–June. The Solons won five of the seven games from San Francisco, including the Sunday double-header by lopsided scores of 15–7 and 11–1. Things were so bad in the second game that Lefty O'Doul sent infielder Johnny Cavalli in as a mop-up pitcher. The one highlight for the Seals in this series occurred on Saturday when Joe Futernick got his only homer of the season, an inside-the-park grand slam, to lead the Seals to an 8–5 victory. On the negative side that day, pitcher Whitey Miller set a Pacific Coast League record by hitting five batters in the seven innings he pitched. On Monday, May 7, the Seals were in seventh place, 10½ games out of first place.

The following week, the Seals returned home and finally found a team they could beat. The last-place Hollywood Stars came to Seals Stadium and were able to win only one of the six games that could be played. There was one rainout. The opening game was played for the UN delegates, which were admitted free but no attendance was announced.

The next two weeks called for the Seals to visit Seattle and Portland. Both the Seals and the Rainiers went north on the same train and arrived there in time to play on Tuesday night, but decided to play a doubleheader on Wednesday night instead. But rain washed out both Wednesday's and Thursday's games. So the series began with two games Friday night, but the second game had to be called when tied 3–3 because of a curfew. So two games had to be played on Saturday, Sunday and even on Monday, which was normally an off day. The Seals lost four of the six games played.

The Seals did better the following week in Portland, but were still hampered by rain. One game had to be called after seven innings and only one game could be played on Sunday because of wet grounds. But the Seals did win four of the six games played to break even on this Northwest trip.

After the Seals left Portland, Lefty O'Doul was able to purchase the contract of Charlie Petersen from the Beavers. Petersen, a very versatile player, had been with the Seals in 1943 but played with his hometown Portland team in 1944 in order to keep his war plant job there. But when the War Manpower Commission stated at the beginning of the 1945 season that players could quit those jobs and play full time, the Seals wanted Petersen back. He had played mostly just at home for Portland in 1944.

The Seals returned home to face their cross-bay rivals, the Oakland Oaks, for an eight-game series over Memorial Day. Catcher Brusie Ogrodowski cracked his rib in Portland and could not swing a bat or throw to second base. This meant that 42-year-old Joe Sprinz would have to do all the catching, including the Memorial Day double-header. Ogrodowski did, however, make it back into the lineup before the week was out. The Seals won five of the eight games from Oakland, sweeping the holiday twin bill before 11,000 and splitting the Sunday double-header that was witnessed by 15,042 fans.

The following week, June 5–10, Seattle came to Seals Stadium. The Friday night game was devoted to the American Women's Voluntary Services, an organization that was spending over $2,000 a month for free food and drinks for servicemen in the Bay Area. The Seals helped this patriotic cause by donating the evening's receipts to this organization.

4—The 1945 Season

About 5,400 attended, but Seattle won the game. On Sunday, the Seals came out in new home uniforms with "Seals" printed in brown instead of blue. But the Rainiers took both games that day before 14,244 fans. Seattle won the series, four games to three, and at this juncture the Seals were in sixth place, eight games off Portland's pace.

The Seals then crossed the bridge to Oakland for a seven-game series, which they managed to win by a 4–3 margin. But this was very well attended, a total of 47,289 jamming their way into that small park in Emeryville. The Sunday crowd drew 12,149 fans, which was Oakland's largest for a single day since 1924.

After the Oakland series, the Seals traded the ineffective Ken Brondell to Jersey City for pitcher Jack Swope. Swope got quite a writeup because he was a veteran of 44 bombing missions over Germany, but he played practically no role for the Seals while Brondell improved quite a bit when he got to Jersey City.

The last full week of June was a split week in which the Seals played four games at home against Hollywood and then went to Gilmore Field for four more. The extra game was a makeup for a previous rainout. The Seals won five of eight from the last-place Stars, ending the week in third place, eight and one-half behind Portland.

But the next series was a one good for San Francisco. The Angels came to Seals Stadium and lost the first six games, winning only the seven-inning second game on Sunday. At this point, on July 2, the Seals were still third, but now only one game behind second-place Seattle and six and one-half behind Portland. But that was as close to Seattle as the Seals were to get in 1945.

In the heat at Sacramento, the Seals melted. They won only two of eight games over the Fourth of July week, but Bob Joyce did win his 19th of the season. But things were to get worse. O'Doul's club headed up to the Northwest to take on the two top clubs in the league. The first-place Beavers won six of eight from San Francisco. On July 16, the Seals were in fourth place, 13 games behind Portland and no longer a threat to Seattle. The following week, the Seals went to Seattle, where they won the series, four games to three, but were now 16 games off the pace, and a half game behind third-place Sacramento. The eight clubs were now in the same spots where they would finish the season.

The Seals returned home to face the Oakland Oaks, who were now a game and a half behind them in fifth place. This series drew big crowds because it was a battle for the first division. Bob Joyce won his 23rd game in this series. By winning the series, four games to three, the Seals increased their lead over fifth-place Oakland to two and one-half games. It was not important that the Seals overtake Sacramento for third place, but it was vitally important that they stay ahead of Oakland for the first division, which they did. But there were still some dramatic moments left, which kept up fan interest.

The Seattle Rainiers followed the Oaks into Seals Stadium and were able to avenge the series loss they suffered to the Seals in Seattle. The Seals had a lead in this series, three games to two, going into the Sunday double-header. Lefty O'Doul started Frank Seward in both games and he lost them both. He pitched only a third of an inning in the opener in which Seattle demolished the Seals 17–4, so he was able to start the second game, but lost 6–3 before 12,000 unhappy fans.

While the Seals were losing this series, Oakland was pounding San Diego down at Lane Field, so on Monday, August 6, the two clubs were tied for fourth place. As luck would have it, they were to meet at Oaks Park for the final time in 1945. This was the series that finally settled the battle for a playoff spot. The Seals won five of the seven games, including the Sunday double-header before an overflow crowd of 12,000. Bob Joyce won his 25th game this week, and on Monday, August 13, the Seals were three games ahead of Oakland, and two behind third-place Sacramento.

Before the San Diego Padres could begin their series at Seals Stadium, World War II ended with the surrender of Japan. The next two days were declared to be holidays but the fans wanted to celebrate, so only 500 showed up at spacious Seals Stadium to see the opening game on Tuesday, August 14. A better crowd of 5,000 came out on Wednesday night as Bob Joyce won his 26th game. The Seals won the odd game in this series to win it four games to three, with Joyce getting his 27th win on Sunday.

The following week, the Seals hosted Sacramento, a team they could beat at home but not in the capital city. After taking this series, five game to two, the Seals were six games ahead of Oakland, and 14 off Portland's pace. There was no longer any suspense about finishing in the first division.

The Seals next headed to Los Angeles, with the excitement of Bob Joyce having a chance to win his 30th game this week. He had won number 28 at home against the Solons, and on Wednesday, August 29, he won his 29th against the Angels. Then on Friday night, with the score tied, Lefty O'Doul sent Joyce in to relieve late in the game but the Angels beat him, preventing him from reaching that magic number. But on Sunday,

4—The 1945 Season

September 2, in the first game of the double-header, Bob Joyce outpitched the Angels' Red Adams to win 4–1, and become the first 30-game winner the league had had since 1933.

The month of September was just one of marking time for the start of the playoffs for the Seals. They had a split week with San Diego and Portland at home, with several double-headers because of earlier rain-outs and the postponed games in April when FDR died. The last two weeks they lost the odd game at Hollywood and won the odd game at home against the Angels to finish the season in fourth place, 17½ games behind Portland and just a half game behind Sacramento. The Solons had three games rained out the last week that were not made up, so the Seals actually won one more game than Sacramento, but lost two more.

For four straight years, from 1943 through 1946, San Francisco won the Governors' Cup playoffs and ended up with the most prize money of any club, including the pennant winner. In 1945, the Seals earned an extra $10,000 compared to Portland's $7,500 and Seattle's $5,000. In addition, the players got two extra weeks of salary.

Even though the Seals won only four games at Sacramento during the season while losing 11, they opened the playoffs in Sacramento by winning all three games there. Bob Joyce won the first game, Frank Seward the second and Bob Barthelson the third in relief of Elmer Orella. The clubs then moved on to San Francisco to finish the series, where the Seals had won 10 and lost only four to the Solons. But here is where things got tough. The Sacs beat Floyd Ehrman and Joyce in the Sunday double-header before 11,000 disappointed fans, to cut the Seals' lead to three games to two. Then on Monday night, the Seals got 10 hits but no runs as Frank Seward lost by yielding a run in the ninth, 1–0, and the Sacs had tied the series. On Tuesday night, October 2, before 8,795 fans, Joyce was pounded out of the game in the fifth inning, as the Solons led the Seals, 5–2. But in the last of the fifth, the Seals struck for six runs to ice the game and the series. Elmer Orella, who pitched only a third of an inning, was the beneficiary of that onslaught, and got credited with the win, while Bob Barthelson pitched the final four innings of one-run ball to save the game.

The final series was against second-place Seattle, a club that had won 16 and lost 12 from the Seals during the season. Seattle chose to open at home, as the Solons did in the opening round, by virtue of finishing higher in the standings. Because of a railroad mishandling of the Seals' equipment, the series could not start until Friday night, October 5. Frank Seward let a 2–0 lead get away, and Seattle rallied for a 3–2 win, the loss going to reliever Floyd Ehrman. But on Saturday night, it was the Seals that overcame a 2–0 deficit to give Bob Joyce the victory, 4–2. Then in the first Sunday night game in league history, necessitated by Sick's Stadium being rented for an exhibition game between Bob Feller's All Stars and Satchel Paige's All Stars that afternoon, the Rainiers chased Bob Barthelson with six runs in the fourth, to give Seattle a 7–5 win, and a two-games-to-one series lead.

The final games at Seals Stadium could not start until Wednesday night, October 10, because Seals Stadium had been rented to Feller's and Paige's players on Tuesday night. The 1945 World Series between Detroit and the Cubs had just finished that afternoon. The Pacific Coast League started before any other league and was the last one to end play in 1945. Frank Seward won game four, 6–1, to tie the series. Then on Thursday night, a crowd of 5,600 saw the Seals pull one out for their ace, Bob Joyce. Trailing 4–0, going into the last of the seventh, the Seals struck for two runs to cut Seattle's lead in half. Then in the eighth, the Seals tied the game with two more runs. With the score tied in the last of the ninth, Neil Sheridan, who had been hitless up until then, hit a three-run homer to win it for San Francisco, 7–4. Joyce went the route and got two hits in four at-bats.

On Friday night, October 12, the Seals blew the lead twice but still won the game and the series. Their 3–0 lead was erased when Seattle got three runs in the fourth, and one in the fifth, to take a 4–3 lead. San Francisco tied it in the seventh, and Lefty O'Doul sent his ace, Bob Joyce, in to preserve the tie in the ninth. But Joyce gave up a run and would have been the losing pitcher if his team had not come back in the last of the ninth. Frenchy Uhalt, Ben Guintini and Gus Suhr singled to tie the game. Guintini got trapped between second and third, but stayed in the rundown long enough for Suhr to take second. Then Neil Sheridan became the hero for the second night in a row with a single that scored Suhr with the run that won the series.

5. Oakland. After finishing in a tie with San Francisco for third place in 1944, the Oaks were optimistic that the 1945 season would be even better, but it was not to be. The Oaks were never a threat to the two top teams, Portland and Seattle, but did manage to stay in the race for the first division until mid–August. But they then lost a crucial series to the Seals and never challenged them again for fourth place.

Dolph Camilli was starting his second season as playing manager of Oakland but he wanted the young Bay Area star, Vic Picetti, to play

The 1945 Oakland Oaks, who finished fifth. Courtesy of Doug McWilliams.

first base, so he did most of his managing from the bench. Picetti did not turn 18 until July 1945, but he showed great promise. Unfortunately, this young man's career was cut short by his untimely death in June 1946.

Oakland had a big turnover in its pitching staff for this season with only Jack Lotz, Floyd Stromme, Italo Chelini, Al Raimondi and Damon Hayes returning. Hayes had a war plant job in the Los Angeles area and could pitch only on weekends for Oakland because his draft board would not defer him if he quit that job even though the War Manpower Commission did allow players to leave their jobs and play baseball full time. Hayes would could pitch only twice a week for the Oaks when they were visiting Hollywood or Los Angeles. Elsewhere in California, he would fly to that city and pitch on Sunday for them, but in June, he was bumped off a flight at the Burbank airport and missed a crucial start against the Seals.

New pitchers for Oakland in 1945 were Leonard "Meow" Gilmore, Mitch Chetkovich, 45-year-old "Sad" Sam Gibson from the Seals, Garth "Red" Mann from Dallas of the Texas League, Maury Ayala, Carl "Snuffy" Monzo and John Babich. Babich, who pitched for Seattle in 1944, had a war plant job in nearby Richmond and refused to report to the Rainiers in 1945, so in May, Oakland traded outfielder Hal Patchett to Seattle for Babich.

Position players returning were Chet Rosenlund at third, Jake Caulfield at short, Frank Hawkins in the outfield, Billy Raimondi and Sam Fenech at catcher, plus utility men James Herrera and Lin Storti, and the aforementioned Vic Picetti and Dolph Camilli. Les Scarsella, the 1944 batting champion, was slow to leave his war plant job, and did not report until May 4. Newcomers were Glenn "Gabby" Stewart at second, outfielders Norm DeWeese from Portland, Don Smith, and Tom Hafey, who could also pitch and play third or first. As the season wore on, several players made brief appearances with the Oaks, such as Matt Zidlich, Charles Bates, Frank Silvanic, Clarence Jay Difani, Ed Kirby, Billy Dunn, Andy Ivaldi and Charley Metro, whose real name was Moreskonich.

Front of Oakland scorecard, 1945. Courtesy of Doug McWilliams.

Oakland got DeWeese in a trade for Charley English and Hal Patchett in a trade for John Kreevich, but then traded Patchett to get Babich. They got Stewart and Chetkovich from the Phillies for Les Scarsella, but were able to keep them even though Scarsella refused to report to Philadelphia. Gilmore came from Pittsburgh in exchange for Ken Gables and Hafey was purchased from the St. Louis Browns.

The Oaks opened the 1945 season at home against the Portland Beavers on Saturday, March 31. A crowd of 11,000 saw a military pageant that would have rivaled anything the East-West Shrine game would have had. There was a salute to the United Nations with 120 flags displayed. Governor Earl Warren threw out the first pitch left-handed to manager Dolph Camilli, who relayed it to starting pitcher Floyd Stromme. The Oaks lost their opener but split the Sunday double-header the next day before 9,500 fans. That day, which was both Easter and April Fool's Day, was one of the worst conditions players and fans had to endure, with

4—The 1945 Season

Oaks Park in Emeryville, as players warm up before a game. Courtesy of Dave Eskenazi.

wind gusts up to 50 mph, causing paper wrappers to fly in the faces of players while dust swirled about them.

The Oaks lost four of five to the eventual 1945 champions, but fared much better against the team that was to finish last, the Hollywood Stars. This split week called for just six games and Oakland won five of them, losing only the one Damon Hayes pitched on Sunday, after flying up from Burbank.

That Saturday night, April 7, the Oaks tried a night game but when only 3,100 showed up to see the Stars and Oaks, they announced that they would play all the rest of the Saturday games in the daytime.

The Oaks then traveled to San Diego and played only five of the seven games because of the death and funeral of FDR. Again, Damon Hayes was able to pitch on Sunday and he lost again. Oakland lost that series, three games to two.

After leaving San Diego, the Oaks had to make the longest trip possible in the Coast League, a 1,200 mile journey to Seattle. They could not start this series until Wednesday, April 18, because they stopped off in Oakland to play a benefit game for the widow of Ernie Raimondi. Raimondi, brother of the Oaks' catcher Billy and relief pitcher Al, was killed in action in France. The Seals provided the opposition because Ernie Raimondi had played for them as well as for the Oaks. The Oaks and

Seattle played a double-header on Friday night. Since this was the first home series for Seattle, attendance was very good, with crowds of over 12,000 on opening day and again on Sunday. The Oaks won this bitter series, four games to three, but league president Clarence "Pants" Rowland warned Camilli and the Oaks about their loud profanity in that series. Camilli countered that Bill Skiff and his Seattle players were obnoxiously rude in their harassment of 17-year-old Vic Picetti. During the following week in Portland, the Oaks were able to get in only six games, but ended up tying the series at three games each after winning the Sunday double-header.

When they returned home the first week of May, the Oaks had to play Seattle again. The Oaks were still upset with Skiff's team and happily won five of the seven games that week. This was the week that Les Scarsella finally played for the first time. Damon Hayes won his Sunday start after flying up from Burbank. One of Oakland's relief pitchers, Carl Monzo, worked daytime as a troubleshooter for an electric supply company.

Just as the Seattle–Oakland series was over, the two clubs pulled a trade. Outfielder Hal Patchett was sent to the Rainiers for pitcher John Babich, who was working in a Richmond, California, steel mill.

The following week was the beginning of some real trouble between manager Dolph Camilli and the Oaks' front office. Shortstop Jake Caulfield was sold to the Phillies without the prior knowledge of either Caulfield or Camilli. As it turned out, Caulfield, just as Scarsella did over the winter, refused to report to the Phils, and stayed with Oakland the rest of the year. But then the Oaks released infielder Lin Storti along with two little-used pitchers. This upset Camilli because he had praised Storti as an extremely valuable player, who was like a coach to the younger players. This week in Los Angeles, Damon Hayes was able to pitch twice, winning on Wednesday and losing on Sunday, because he worked there. The Oaks lost this series, four games to three, and more trouble erupted when pitcher Floyd Stromme got mad at Camilli for taking him out of the game on Sunday.

When the Oaks returned home to play Sacramento, the Wednesday night game on May 16 was designated war bond night, with the purchase of a bond required for admission. A crowd of 6,000 was on hand and $4,977,000 worth of bonds were sold. The Oaks had a three-games-to-two lead in this series until they lost the Sunday double-header before 11,267 unhappy fans. Hayes flew up and lost one of those games.

The San Diego Padres followed Sacramento into Oaks Park and lost five of seven to the Oaks. It was in this series that many were remarking what a strong arm Tom Hafey had for a third baseman. This led to his eventually moving to the mound, where he won four and lost only one for Oakland later in the season. Damon Hayes won his game on Sunday that week.

The following week was Memorial Day week, which called for an eight-game series with the Seals at Seals Stadium. Vic Picetti, who had missed a few games of the San Diego series, returned in midweek of this series after attending the funeral of his father. Frank Hawkins was kicked out of a game and suspended for four games for abusive language to an umpire. The Oaks lost this series, five games to three, but Hayes won his game on Sunday.

The next series was not a good one for the Oaks in very hot Sacramento. Frank Hawkins did not show up at all this week even though his suspension was over. He missed almost all of the following week too, saying he was going to quit the game and open a tavern. However, he relented and played in one game on June 17. The Oaks lost five of the seven games to the Sacs and then returned home to face the Seals.

The Oaks would face the Seals at home without manager Dolph Camilli, who was fired before this series began. Camilli was upset about the sale and reappearance of Jake Caulfield, the release of Lin Storti and surprised by the suspension of Frank Hawkins. But the Oaks' front office was upset with Camilli for not playing because he was a drawing card, having had a good career in the National League. But Camilli wanted young Picetti to play and used himself mainly as a pinch hitter. The front office also did not like Camilli's refusal to travel with the team. He would fly out of a town on Sunday night while the club was on the train. The new manager was long-time catcher Billy Raimondi, who guided the Oaks the rest of the 1945 season but said he never wanted to manage again.

The Oaks won their first game for the new manager as Red Mann beat the Seals, 3–2. This series set an attendance record for Oaks Park when 42,289 saw these two Bay Area rivals. The Sunday crowd of 12,149 was the largest day crowd since 1924. But the Oaks lost the series to the Seals, four games to three. Frank Hawkins returned to the team to play in the second game on Sunday. This was the week that Damon Hayes was bumped off his plane in Burbank and could not pitch.

At this point in the season, June 19, the Oaks were in fourth place, 19½ games behind front-runner Portland. However, they were in a fourth-place tie with San Diego, Los Angeles and Sacramento.

The next week was a split week with the Oaks in Los Angeles for three games and the Angels coming up to Oakland for the final three. Damon Hayes lost his game on Thursday in Los Angeles and did not travel up to Oakland for Sunday's game. The Oaks and Angels each won three games that week. The Oaks acquired a new catcher at this time, Ed Kearse, who had been with Seattle in 1940. Kearse was a returning war veteran who had seen quite a bit of action. Unfortunately, he got spiked in his first game and had to sit out a few days.

The next week was a very disappointing one for the Oaks as they went back to the Southland to play Hollywood, the eighth-place club. The Oaks won the first three games of that series only to lose the final four. Damon Hayes won the first game and lost on Sunday. Ed Kearse was back behind the plate on Sunday.

After playing the last-place club, the Oaks had to tackle the first-place Beavers at Oaks Park over the Fourth of July week. The Oaks lost the holiday and the Sunday double-header to the league leaders, as well as Saturday's game. The Beavers won five of the eight games with Oakland, with Hayes losing on Sunday.

The following week the Sacramento Solons moved into Oaks Park and this time the Oaks were able to win four of the seven games. Hayes did not make it up to Oakland to pitch in this series. At the end of this week, on July 16, the Oaks were in fifth place, one game behind the Seals. The Padres followed the Solons into Oaks Park and Oakland lost this series, four games to three, but were only a game and a half behind fourth-place San Francisco.

It was the Seals the Oaks were to play next, this time in San Francisco. The Seals again won the series, four games to three, to go up two and one-half games on fifth-place Oakland. The following week was the first week in August, and the one that gave the Oakland fans hope that their team could finish in the first division. The Oaks went down to San Diego, a team they beat 16 times while losing only 12 in 1945. In this series, the Oaks won six of the eight games played, one game being a make up for one of the two missed when FDR died. Damon Hayes pitched twice in this series and won both times. Since the Seals were losing their series this week, the two Bay Area clubs were tied for fourth place, 19 games behind Portland.

A crucial seven-game series was to open at Oakland with the Seals, but before that could start the Oaks had to play an exhibition game with the Treasure Island Navy team. The Oaks also made some roster changes. Jake Caulfield was sold to the other Philadelphia team, the Athletics, for

4—The 1945 Season

delivery in 1946, but the A's sent outfielder Charley Metro to Oakland immediately, so one player had to be dropped. The player dropped was 22-year-old Andy Ivaldi, a seldom-used outfielder who had played semi-pro ball in the Oakland area while working at a printing company. When released, Ivaldi went back to the printing company full time.

This was the series that did in Oakland for 1945. The Oaks now trailed the Seals by three games and were never able to catch them again. The Seals now led Oakland by three games and were never again able to catch them.

The next two weeks the Oaks went to Portland and Seattle. While in Portland, on August 15, Japan surrendered, ending the war. While the Oaks and Beavers did play that night, Mitch Chetkovich and Ed Kearse were given the night off to celebrate because they were veterans who had seen a lot of action. The Oaks and Beavers each won four of the eight games played, the extra one being a make up for an earlier rainout. The following week in Seattle, Damon Hayes announced he could play full time now that the war was over, but he immediately hurt his arm, which required a season-ending operation. Seattle took five of the seven games from the Oaks.

It was now the last few days of August, and it was very apparent that the Oaks had no chance of catching either San Francisco or Sacramento for fourth place. Even though the Oaks won seven of the eight games played at home against the last-place Stars, they were five and one-half games behind the Seals. In the Hollywood series. Tom Hafey made his first start as a pitcher in the second game on Sunday and won it, 7–1.

From this point on, the Oaks were merely playing out the string. They won a short series over Labor Day from Seattle, three games to two, but lost four of five in the next short series to the Solons in Sacramento. In that series, Frank Hawkins was beaned and was sent to the hospital.

The following week, against Los Angeles at home, pitcher Mitch Chetkovich had some fainting spells as a result of his combat experiences. He was very wild on Wednesday night as the Oaks lost to the Angels 12–11. He had to be relieved by Lotz. But he did come back to win on Saturday, 4–3. Hawkins was able to pinch-hit on Sunday against the Angels. The Oaks won that series, five games to three.

The last week of the season saw the Oaks in Hollywood, where they lost the series four games to three, as they did in June, but their losses were dispersed throughout the week, and not all at the end of the series. The Oaks ended the 1945 season in fifth place, with 90 wins and 93 losses. They were 23½ games behind first-place Portland and six games behind fourth-place San Francisco.

6. San Diego. The Padres in 1945 hired as their new manager the popular John "Pepper" Martin, who had managed Sacramento in 1941 and 1942. The St. Louis Cardinals transferred Martin to Rochester to manage that club in 1943 and then kept him as a reserve outfielder on their world championship club of 1944, but he played very little that season. Martin was replacing the former Padre catcher George Detore as San Diego manager, but he did not have anywhere near the talent he had when he managed those two Sacramento teams. The Padres were in their third of six straight years of finishing in the second division and had a revolving door of players in 1945. They had winning seasonal records against only San Francisco and Sacramento. They even had losing records against the two teams that finished below them in the standings, Los Angeles and Hollywood.

Before the season started, the Padres and Seattle pulled off a big trade. San Diego sent long-time first baseman George McDonald and outfielder Jack Whipple to the Rainiers for third baseman "Tricky" Dick Gyselman and pitchers Frank Tincup and Jack McClure. Tincup lost three games with no wins and McClure was in only one game but Gyselman had a good year, hitting .321. But Gyselman was slow to report to the Padres because he wanted to be assured of a place to live in that tight housing market with all the navy personnel. Gyselman also held down a playground job with the San Diego Parks Commission and was reluctant to go on long road trips for fear of losing this job. The fans and sportswriters in Seattle were very disappointed when he did not travel with his new team to Seattle for a series in June.

The rest of Pepper Martin's infield was not set, with many players coming and going and playing at different spots. Marvin Gudat, now 42 years old and normally an outfielder, began the year at first base, but later the Padres acquired two Sacramento castoffs to fill in there. They were Ray Wetmore and Len Prout, with the latter playing much more than the former. At second base, the Padres had an incredible number of players including Bob Boken; Vern Reynolds, who was sold to Hollywood in midseason; Jack Dunphy; Frank Gira; Hank Sciarra; Frank Pacheco; Claudio Solano; Jerry Womack, who also had a one and three record as a pitcher; William Justice; Frank Cirimele; and even Pepper Martin. Gira and Dunphy played the most games at short but Bob McNamara, Womack, Sciarra and Justice also filled in at that key position.

4—The 1945 Season

SAN DIEGO PADRES 1945
PACIFIC COAST LEAGUE

Wm. Starr — PRESIDENT

'Pepper' Martin — MANAGER

Eaves — Dumler — Brillheart — Ferguson — Knowles — Womack — Trahd — Les Cook (TRAINER)

Nelson — Harshman — Prout — Boken — Gyselman — Ballinger — Grigg

Dunphy — Gira — Abbott — Thompson — Vezelich — Sciarra — Criscola — Gudat

The 1945 San Diego Padres, managed by Pepper Martin, finished in sixth place. Courtesy of Dave Eskenazi.

San Diego's outfield was much more stable with Tony Criscola, Rupert "Tommy" Thompson and Lou Vezlich starting most of the games. The two reserves were Mike Kreevich and Morry Abbott, who also caught some games. The regular catcher did yeoman work in 1945: Del Ballinger, who caught 171 of the Padres' 183 games. Two seldom-used backups were Herman Bey and Dick Willis.

The Padres had two 21-game winners on the mound in 1945, Vallie Eaves and Carl Dumler, while also having a 21-game loser in Bob Ferguson. Other starters were 42-year-old Jim Brillheart and Victor Trahd. In midseason, the Padres picked up Giles Knowles from Sacramento and Carl Monzo from Oakland. Besides Frank Tincup, other relievers were Jerry Nelson, Don Campbell, Earl Jones and Robert Bailey.

Before the 1945 season began, Padre fans and players were saddened to hear that Manny Hernandez, a part-time outfielder with their 1944 club, was killed in action in Germany in March, just a few weeks before Germany was to surrender.

The Padres, as usual, opened the season at home. The season began on Saturday, March 31, with a short series with Seattle. The Padres lost four of five to the Rainiers, who were going to finish second in 1945. They then were able to win four of six from the Seals at home before the Oaks came to Lane Field. This was the week that FDR died so only five games could be played, with San Diego winning three of them.

When the Padres went to San Francisco the week of April 24–30, they were forced to sleep in the Seals Stadium clubhouse because all the hotels were taken up with the United Nations conference. Later, teams were able to get space in Oakland or other East Bay cities.

The Padres began to unravel in May when the Portland Beavers, the team that was to win the pennant in 1945, came to Lane Field. After winning the first two games, the Padres lost the last five. They were also unable to win against the league's two poorest teams, the Angels and the Stars, winning only 11 of 25 from Los Angeles and only 12 of 29 from Hollywood.

The Padres spent Memorial Day week playing Sacramento at home. The Padres and Solons split that series at four games each. But Pepper Martin's first appearance in Sacramento since he led the Solons to victory in 1942 did not occur until the week of June 12–17. The Padres did their new manager a big favor by taking five of the seven games up there. The highlight of the series occurred on Saturday night, the 16th, when each team started a 17-year-old pitcher. Jerry Womack, who also played in the infield, started for the Padres but got knocked out of the box in the fifth inning, as the Solons won 11–3. Young LeRoy Stevens of Sacramento went the distance for the win. These two youngsters were matched up again in San Diego on another Saturday night, July 28, and this time the Padres won 10–8, in 10 innings. Neither starter was involved in the decision.

It became apparent after late July that the Padres were doomed to the second division. There was very little chance of them catching fifth-place Oakland and not much chance of seventh-place Los Angeles catching them.

The 1945 Padres had some good hitters but very little power. Lou Vezelich led the club in homers with just six. But several players had high batting averages: Rupert Thompson hit .346, Bob Boken .330, Dick Gyselman .321, Tony Criscola .311, Lou Vezlich .307, Del Ballinger .299 and Len Prout .292. But the 1945 season was clearly a forgettable one for San Diego fans.

7. Los Angeles. The Angels were the only team in the league that had a drop in attendance over the 1944 season as the Pacific Coast League was setting its record attendance for the second of four straight years. The reason for this decrease was obvious: the Angels fans were used to their team winning the pennant or being very close to the top. The 1945 season was disastrous. The Chicago Cubs won the pennant that year and therefore sent very little talent to Los Angeles. What angered Angels fans was that even some of the players the Cubs did not keep all season were sent elsewhere, such as Johnny Ostrowski and Red Lynn.

The one former Angels hero that was sent to Los Angeles was "The Mad Russian," Lou Novikoff, who won the triple crown while playing for LA in 1940. Even though Novikoff had won four batting titles in four minor leagues in consecutive seasons (the Three I League in 1938, the Texas League in 1939, the Pacific Coast League in 1940 and the International League in 1941), Novikoff in 1945 was not the player he had been in 1940. He hit only .310 for the Angels this time with just nine homers, a far cry from his .363 average and 41 homers in 1940. But the Angels fans gave him a big cheer the first week of the season when the Wrigley Field public address announcer told the crowd that the Russians had just entered Berlin, as the war in Europe was nearing its end.

The 1945 season was so dismal for the Angels that they won the season's series from only one team, San Diego. They even lost the city series to the cellar-dwelling Hollywood Stars, and with it went Sheriff Gene Biscaluz's trophy. The one bright spot was their breaking even with the champion Portland Beavers. The Angels actually had a 12–9 games lead on Portland until the last five-game series over Labor Day weekend, when the visiting Beavers won four of five games to end the season with the Angels at 13 wins each. No other club played Portland that closely in the regular season.

Only a few Angels players returned from the championship club in 1944. Glenn "Rip" Russell moved to the outfield in 1945 after playing first and second in 1944. Guy Miller returned to play short and third, Reggie Otero was back at first, Johnny Moore as a pinch hitter and Red Adams, Don Osborn and "Pancho" Jorge Comellas were back as moundsmen.

New position players were Mel Hicks at first and outfield, Pete Elko at third, Ray Viers at second, Jim Tyack in center field, Hal Douglas in the outfield and three new catchers, Roy Easterwood, Mickey Kreitner and Leonard "Doc" Greene. Later Charlie Brewster and Roy Paton joined the club to play short and the outfield, respectively. New pitchers included

Charley Cuellar, Warren "Bud" Merkle from San Diego, George Woodend, 16-year-old Richie Colombo, Joe Slotter, 20-year-old Paul Lammers and 18-year-old Ken Hicks.

Only Red Adams and Don Osborn had good years on the mound, with Adams winning 21 games and becoming the team's most valuable player. Osborn won 18 but the pitcher with next highest wins was Charley Cuellar, who won 13 and lost 17. The biggest disappointment of the year turned out to be Jorge Comellas, who won only six and lost 16 after going 18–14 in 1944.

The highlight of the 1945 season may have occurred on opening day, Saturday March 31, when the Angels raised their 1944 pennant flag. Each Angels player was introduced, but only a few of the players from 1944 were still on the club. The visiting team was the San Francisco Seals and manager Lefty O'Doul was miffed that only the Angels players were introduced to the crowd. Even though the Angels won that short series, three games to two, the Seals were one of the teams that gave the Angels the most trouble in 1945, winning 17 and losing only nine to LA.

The team that hurt the Angels the most in 1945 was the next one to appear in Wrigley Field, the Seattle Rainiers. Seattle won every one of the four series from LA, taking 21 of the 28 games the two teams played against one another. In fact, it was losing two series to the Seals and the Rainiers back to back in late June and early July that absolutely ended any possibility that the Angels could make the first division. The Angels lost six out of seven at San Francisco and then came home and lost seven of eight to Seattle.

It was about this time that the Angels made a poor trade. They sent the popular 20-year-old Hal Douglas, who was hitting .303 and playing well in the outfield, to an International League club, for Nick Rhabe, who never became a favorite with the fans. Later, they sold Rhabe to the champion Portland Beavers, so they ended up with only cash to show for the loss of the popular Douglas.

Surprisingly, the Angels played rather well against Portland, winning the first two series from them before tying them at four games apiece the third time they met in late August. The Portland sportswriters and manager Marvin Owen said they feared LA more than any other team, probably because they thought the Cubs would send them some help. But instead, the Cubs took players from LA, calling up Reggie Otero and 43-year-old pinch hitter Johnny Moore in September. Another blow to the Angels occurred when Lou Novikoff was called for military duty in August.

One thing the Angels fans liked to brag about was beating their crosstown rival, the Hollywood Stars. Even though Hollywood finished last in 1945, the Angels could not even win the city trophy from them. The Stars won 16 and lost 13 to the Angels. As previously mentioned, the Angels were the only 1945 club to draw fewer fans than they did in 1944, but the drop was only about 12,000, from 362,000 to slightly less than 350,000.

8. *Hollywood.* When the Stars failed to make the first division in 1944, the owners fired manger Charlie Root and made third baseman Buck Faucett their new manager. But things got much worse in 1945. The military took several players from the 1944 team, including their top star, Frankie Kelleher. Others taken were shortstop Tod Davis, infielder Ray Olsen and pitchers Clint Hufford and Earl Escalante.

Besides Faucett at third, Kenny Richardson was back at second and Butch Moran returned to play first. But shortstop was a big problem. They started the season with Jack Smith, and then tried several others in that spot. Some of these given a trial there were Al Gonzales, not to be confused with Joe Gonzales, who was with the club in 1944; Vern Reynolds from San Diego; Hugh Willingham, who had been with the Angels in 1944; Ralph Watson from Sacramento; and Johnny Cavalli from San Francisco.

Brooks Holder was the one returning regular outfielder. Newcomers were Ben Cantrell, Ed Stewart, who had been with San Diego in the late 1930s, and Mel Steiner, who had been with the Padres, Sacramento and Oakland in 1944. Les Powers, who could play when Loyola University was not in session, returned as a part-time player, as he had in 1944. He had played full time for the Seals and Sacramento in the mid–1930s. Stewart was hitting .323 when he went into the navy in June.

The popular Babe Herman, deluxe pinch hitter in 1944, chose not to return, but in mid–1945, the Brooklyn Dodgers coaxed him out of retirement and his contract was purchased from the Stars.

Jim Hill was back at catcher and backed up by Harry "Moose" Krause, who hit .309 in 63 games. The returning pitchers were Newt Kimball, who won 19 games while losing 21; Ron Smith, who won 15 and lost 20; Joe Mishasek, who won 17 and lost 16; John Intlekofer, who was one and eight; and Jim Sharp, who was one and seven. The Stars picked up two pitchers from Sacramento, "Smokestack" Steve LeGault and Earl Porter. They got John Marshall from Oakland and lefty Bob Williams from a lower minor league. None of these distinguished themselves.

The Stars opened the season at Sacramento, losing that short series three games to two. By April 8, the Stars landed in last place and never were able to get out of the cellar. The pennant-winning Portland Beavers gave them the most trouble, winning 24 of the 28 games played. They also did very poorly with Seattle, Sacramento, Oakland and San Francisco. But they did have a winning record against San Diego and Los Angeles. Hollywood won 16 and lost 13 to the Angels, winning Sheriff Gene Biscaluz's trophy for the first time since 1941.

The Stars were home hosting Seattle in April when FDR died so two games were missed that week. Sacramento was at Hollywood when Japan surrendered in August, but the game was played that night before a sparse crowd. Most people were celebrating and watching a last-place ball club was not high on their agenda that evening. But when the Stars entertained the Angels, the crowds packed Gilmore Field, even though both clubs were way down in the standings. About one-fifth of the season's attendance came when Los Angeles visited Gilmore Field. Not only did Hollywood win the season's series from the Angels, they outdrew them by about 12,000 fans.

Appendix A: Records of Individual Players

Players are listed by club and by year.

The 1942 Sacramento Solons—First Place

Pitching Records

	G	W	L	IP	K	BB	ERA
Clarence Beers	39	16	12	210	72	56	3.81
Sylvester Blix Donnelly	42	21	10	270	165	128	2.83
Tony Freitas	44	24	13	295	93	36	2.93
Larry Kempe	7	2	2	30	10	17	unk
Hershel Lyons	32	10	10	164	76	68	3.62
Frank Nelson	16	3	4	60	26	29	6.45
John Pintar	30	3	0	72	27	22	3.63
Bill Schmidt	37	10	8	140	36	27	3.09
Kemp Wicker	52	16	12	250	83	63	3.24

Position Players

	G	AB	H	HR	RBI	AVE	POSITION
Elvin "Buster" Adams	178	647	200	27	107	.309	OF
Debs Garms	160	606	190	7	96	.314	OF

	G	AB	H	HR	RBI	AVE	POSITION
Gene Handley	89	312	80	0	34	.256	2B
Eddie Lake	176	633	176	19	69	.278	SS-2B
Gene Lillard	29	97	33	3	20	.340	3B-1B-P
Charley Marshall	76	188	43	1	19	.229	2B-C
John "Pepper" Martin	130	223	55	0	24	.247	INF-OF
Steve Mesner	178	680	205	1	74	.301	3B-SS-2B
Ray Mueller	166	565	168	16	102	.297	C
Mel Serafini	47	104	21	2	10	.202	3B-2B-1B
Bill Shewey	44	154	46	0	14	.299	OF
Guy "Jack" Sturdy	169	587	176	1	57	.300	1B
Averett Thompson	153	553	175	1	54	.316	OF

The 1942 Los Angeles Angels—Second Place

Pitchers

	G	W	L	IP	K	BB	ERA
Charles "Red" Adams	11	6	4	67	21	31	4.16
Ray "Peaches" Davis	28	6	2	61	10	16	4.13
Jess Dobernic	36	5	5	98	64	51	4.96
Jesse Flores	37	14	5	185	100	63	2.63
Paul Gehrman	46	11	6	196	81	60	2.57
Japhet "Red" Lynn	43	12	13	211	108	67	3.11
Garman "Pete" Mallory	44	10	8	154	47	48	3.21
Ray Prim	39	21	10	277	121	39	2.47
Ken Raffensberger	51	17	18	242	138	51	3.46

Position Players

	G	AB	H	HR	RBI	AVE	POS
Fern Bell*	128	427	105	5	43	.246	OF
Gilly Campbell	97	249	50	1	19	.201	C
Jack Hanson	28	76	14	0	0	.184	INF
Roy Hughes	166	630	188	1	61	.298	2B
Harry "Peanuts" Lowrey	96	393	101	5	39	.257	OF
Eddie Mayo	171	635	195	12	110	.307	3B
Johnny Moore	134	487	169	7	85	.347	OF
Barney Olsen	174	645	195	15	87	.302	OF
Bill Schuster	179	640	191	6	78	.298	SS
Arnold "Jigger" Statz	100	263	60	2	22	.228	OF

*Also with Hollywood and Oakland.

Appendix A: Records of Individual Players 187

	G	AB	H	HR	RBI	AVE	POS
Glen "Gabby" Stewart	49	71	20	1	11	.282	INF
Bill Sweeney	17	16	3	0	1	.188	PH
Al Todd	122	375	96	5	44	.256	C
Eddie Waitkus	175	699	235	9	81	.336	1B

The 1942 Seattle Rainiers—Third Place

Pitchers

	G	W	L	IP	K	BB	ERA
"Kewpie" Dick Barrett	40	27	13	330	178	101	1.72
Bill Bevens*	31	4	11	126	65	84	4.43
Mike Budnick	28	7	6	123	49	62	2.78
Ed Carnett	22	4	6	84	26	37	3.54
Carl Fischer	34	10	15	190	81	63	2.61
Larry Guay	26	9	5	138	40	53	3.39
Al Libke	25	6	10	109	34	55	4.21
Dewey Soriano	22	5	7	116	60	73	3.18
Hal Turpin	36	23	9	321	67	44	2.07

Position Players

	G	AB	H	HR	RBI	AVE	POS
Bill Beard	70	172	40	0	10	.233	C
Ed Carnett	42	62	16	0	4	.258	OF-P
Bob Collins	109	332	86	3	42	.259	C
Dick Gyselman	178	647	181	2	64	.280	3B
Spencer Harris	96	261	72	2	26	.276	OF-1B
Ed Kearse	45	123	32	0	18	.260	C
Lynn King	145	470	132	0	43	.281	OF
Bill Lawrence	40	142	44	0	13	.310	OF
Bill Matheson	169	627	196	5	87	.313	OF-INF
Al Niemiec	174	612	163	1	67	.266	2B
Les Scarsella**	167	640	171	7	97	.267	1B
Ned Stickle	180	669	174	1	37	.260	SS
Earl Torgeson	147	523	163	4	52	.312	1B-OF
Joyner "Jo-Jo" White	166	590	175	2	69	.297	OF

*Also with Hollywood.
**Also with Oakland.

The 1942 San Diego Padres—Fourth Place

Pitchers

	G	W	L	IP	K	BB	ERA
Norm Brown	41	13	12	197	76	80	3.56
Frankie Dasso	42	15	18	284	155	127	2.88
Rex Dilbeck	30	11	6	123	48	23	3.29
Wally Hebert	40	22	15	319	125	78	2.37
Al Olsen	45	18	16	293	94	93	2.76
Herman Pillette	11	1	1	24	7	9	4.44
Cletus "Boots" Poffenberger	38	9	10	168	40	80	3.86
Bill Thomas*	44	9	13	163	57	35	2.65
Ed Vitalich	10	2	1	34	15	17	unk

*Also with Hollywood.

Position Players

	G	AB	H	HR	RBI	AVE	POS
Del Ballinger	22	44	8	0	5	.182	C
Jack Calvey	149	545	153	4	66	.281	SS-2B
George Detore	106	303	76	2	38	.251	C-1B-2B
Art Garibaldi	100	298	67	0	25	.225	3B-SS-OF
Johnny Hill	146	544	154	2	62	.283	3B-2B
John "Swede" Jensen	164	578	159	11	64	.275	OF
Mel Mazzera	158	575	177	14	90	.308	OF-1B
George Mc Donald	70	272	73	0	19	.268	1B
Hal Patchett	172	663	191	0	43	.288	OF
Bill Salkeld	121	354	101	7	60	.285	C
Mel Skelley	148	489	123	2	49	.252	2B-1B-SS
Stan Sperry	36	96	28	0	1	.292	2B
Frank Stinson	78	259	68	1	18	.263	1B
Jack Whipple	85	259	65	3	20	.251	2B

The 1942 San Francisco Seals—Fifth Place

Pitchers

	G	W	L	IP	K	BB	ERA
Al Epperly	34	7	10	130	38	42	4.22
"Sad" Sam Gibson	34	20	12	249	87	41	2.78
"Cowboy" Ray Harrell	36	4	8	137	39	50	3.74
Larry Jansen	32	11	14	173	46	39	4.32

Appendix A: Records of Individual Players

	G	W	L	IP	K	BB	ERA
Bob Joyce	38	22	10	234	59	41	3.19
Al Lien	19	6	8	120	49	25	2.78
Tommy Seats	38	10	18	250	89	56	3.67
Ed Stutz	40	8	10	179	42	40	4.17

POSITION PLAYERS

	G	AB	H	HR	RBI	AVE	POS
Ollie Bejma	105	344	94	1	32	.273	2B
Joe Brovia	24	36	6	0	4	.167	OF
Ferris Fain	162	519	112	4	53	.216	1B-OF
Frank Hawkins*	72	124	32	2	11	.258	OF-3B
Chuck Henson	61	130	23	0	16	.177	OF-1B
Ralph Hodgin	173	675	216	4	112	.320	OF
Brooks Holder	179	652	194	6	51	.298	OF-2B
Ted Jennings	122	376	110	3	60	.293	3B-SS-OF
Kermit Lewis	175	628	196	20	115	.312	OF
Bill Lillard	21	62	12	0	3	.194	SS-2B
Ambrose "Brusie" Ogrodowski	104	297	89	1	23	.300	C
Ray Perry	167	536	137	12	75	.256	2B-SS
Joe Sprinz	106	302	73	0	33	.242	C
Don Trower	165	607	153	1	35	.252	SS-2B-3B
Don White	13	54	25	0	13	.463	OF-3B

*Also with Portland.

The 1942 Oakland Oaks—Sixth Place

PITCHERS

	G	W	L	IP	K	BB	ERA
Ralph Buxton	33	13	16	204	74	65	3.50
Italo Chelini	40	9	13	188	38	44	2.59
Stan Corbett	37	8	11	181	49	54	4.48
Vince DiBiasi	40	10	13	181	74	73	3.43
Norbert "Nubs" Kleinke	11	6	2	64	17	26	4.36
Henry "Cotton" Pippen	38	11	17	211	51	66	4.18
Jack Salveson	39	24	12	310	93	60	2.58
John Yellovic	39	4	7	112	68	56	3.05

Position Players

	G	AB	H	HR	RBI	AVE	POS
Fern Bell*	128	427	105	5	43	.246	OF
Mike Christoff	37	107	19	1	8	.178	OF
Mel Duezabou	50	173	52	1	17	.301	OF
Joe Glenn	78	232	57	1	22	.246	OF
Marvin Gudat	112	360	100	0	41	.278	OF-1B
Hugh Luby	177	667	207	3	75	.310	2B-3B
Bill Lyman	33	104	13	0	7	.125	3B-SS-2B
Emil Mailho	155	599	178	1	42	.297	OF
Billy Raimondi	128	415	102	0	33	.246	C-OF-3B
Bill Rigney	177	638	184	1	57	.288	SS-3B
Les Scarsella**	167	640	171	7	97	.267	1B
Herman "Ham" Schulte***	156	547	142	1	45	.260	2B-3B
Fred Tauby	64	194	57	1	30	.294	OF-3B
Johnny Vergez	107	335	88	3	31	.263	3B-1B
Wally Westlake	169	593	159	7	74	.268	OF

*Also with Los Angeles and Hollywood.
**Also with Seattle.
***Also with Hollywood.

The 1942 Hollywood Stars—Seventh Place

Pitchers

	G	W	L	IP	K	BB	ERA
Bill Bevens*	31	4	11	126	65	84	4.43
John Bittner	28	13	8	174	70	59	2.48
Eddie Erautt	7	0	4	17	5	9	9.18
Fred Gay	36	8	19	229	76	82	3.69
Walter "Whitey" Hilcher**	38	7	16	220	59	63	3.60
"Pappy" Roy Joiner	37	12	18	234	80	38	3.85
Wayne Osborne**	34	10	14	175	46	64	5.40
Manny Perez	41	14	15	227	95	87	3.33
Charlie Root	30	11	14	215	103	39	3.18
Bill Thomas***	44	9	13	163	57	35	2.65

*Also with Seattle.
**Also with Portland.
***Also with San Diego.

Appendix A: Records of Individual Players 191

Position Players

	G	AB	H	HR	RBI	AVE	POS
Bill Atwood	106	300	76	4	26	.253	C-1B
Bill Barisoff	21	25	6	0	1	.240	OF
Fern Bell*	128	427	105	5	43	.246	OF
Bill Brenzel	98	287	65	1	20	.226	C
Bill Carney**	65	183	51	0	12	.279	OF
Jack Devincenzi	35	92	25	4	16	.272	OF
Johnny Dickshot	175	623	189	11	87	.303	OF
Bill Garbe	112	355	94	2	36	.265	1B-OF
Floyd "Babe" Herman	85	149	48	5	42	.322	1B
Joe Hoover	149	590	193	11	62	.327	SS-OF
Bob Kahle	161	634	167	0	62	.263	3B
Frank Kalin	127	450	137	13	79	.304	OF
Herman "Ham" Schulte***	156	547	142	1	45	.260	2B-3B
Charlie Sylvester	75	250	58	0	27	.232	1B-OF
Bernard "Frenchy" Uhalt	173	669	184	1	40	.275	OF
Del Young	133	425	106	2	37	.249	2B-SS-3B
Roy Younker	35	85	19	3	7	.224	C-2B-OF

*Also with Los Angeles and Oakland.
**Also with Portland.
***Also with Oakland.

The 1942 Portland Beavers—Eighth Place

Pitchers

	G	W	L	IP	K	BB	ERA
Syd Cohen	37	10	14	224	48	56	3.90
Bob Fitzke	23	1	4	71	7	28	5.70
Roy Helser	5	1	2	33	13	22	1.95
Walter "Whitey" Hilcher*	38	7	16	220	59	63	3.60
Ad Liska	43	15	21	322	164	73	3.63
Forest Joe Orrell	39	11	22	280	121	94	4.02
Wayne Osborne*	34	10	14	175	46	64	5.40
Walt Schafer	11	0	6	18	11	20	unk
William Schubel	32	8	8	141	43	51	4.98
Elmer Singleton	6	1	2	14	4	7	3.77
Byron Speece	19	9	6	124	48	36	3.92
Lee Stine	12	0	4	19	2	12	13.03

*Also with Hollywood.

Appendix A: Records of Individual Players

Position Players

	G	AB	H	HR	RBI	AVE	POS
Danny Amaral	79	250	77	2	27	.308	3B-OF
Larry Barton	155	564	172	10	74	.305	1B
Bob Bergstrom	62	160	38	0	14	.238	3B-2B-OF
Lindsey Brown	134	492	108	0	31	.220	SS
Dominic Castro	37	97	19	0	9	.196	C
Johnny Gill	124	387	117	11	57	.302	OF
Frankie Hawkins*	72	124	32	2	11	.258	INF-OF
John Leovich	117	337	64	1	31	.190	C-SS
Henry Martinez	85	284	69	3	26	.243	INF-OF
Ted Mayer	47	127	27	0	9	.213	C
Ted Norbert	149	481	182	28	99	.378	OF
Marvin Owen	147	535	162	3	66	.303	3B-SS-1B
Lee Stine	100	281	78	2	40	.278	OF-INF-P
Rupert Thompson	175	650	200	11	49	.308	OF-2B-3B
Al "A-1" Wright	110	395	90	0	18	.228	2B-SS

Also with San Francisco.

The 1943 Los Angeles Angels—First Place

Pitchers

	G	W	L	IP	K	BB	ERA
Oren Baker	33	10	3	111	34	18	2.84
Paul Gehrman	35	20	7	226	80	49	2.43
Japhet "Red" Lynn	36	21	8	248	110	64	2.47
Garman "Pete" Mallory	34	11	8	192	81	47	3.09
Jake Mooty	5	2	2	18	4	6	3.93
Don Osborn	30	10	1	102	30	29	2.65
Jodie Phipps	33	17	5	202	80	69	3.03
Ken Raffensberger	35	19	11	244	134	53	2.14

Position Players

	G	AB	H	HR	RBI	AVE	POS
Charley English	157	591	191	16	98	.323	3B
Eddie Fernandes	30	53	10	0	4	.189	C
Cecil Garriott	98	286	73	10	47	.255	OF
Billy Holm	97	271	79	2	28	.292	C-2B
Roy Hughes	121	461	149	0	41	.323	2B-SS
Harry Land	27	92	22	0	9	.239	C

	G	AB	H	HR	RBI	AVE	POS
Elmer Mallory	47	159	55	3	18	.346	2B-SS
Johnny Moore	81	217	63	1	31	.290	OF
Johnny Ostrowski	143	472	133	21	82	.282	OF
Andy Pafko	157	604	215	18	118	.356	OF
Wellington "Wimpy" Quinn	157	572	135	11	80	.236	OF-1B
Glenn "Rip" Russell	53	153	49	7	26	.320	OF-1B
Bill Sarni	33	83	19	1	9	.229	C
Bill Schuster	157	618	170	5	67	.275	SS

The 1943 San Francisco Seals—Second Place

Pitchers

	G	W	L	IP	K	BB	ERA
Win Ballou	16	1	1	16	2	8	6.06
Tony Buzolich	21	1	1	42	7	17	unk
Al Epperly	26	16	5	166	60	45	3.47
"Sad" Sam Gibson	20	6	5	125	34	27	2.45
Ray Harrell	37	17	16	241	106	74	3.17
Bob Joyce	34	20	12	259	75	37	2.43
Al Lien	34	13	12	222	76	39	2.55
Tommy Seats	32	14	11	229	75	41	2.48
Bill Werle	9	1	2	27	9	13	4.73

Position Players

	G	AB	H	HR	RBI	AVE	POS
Jimmy Adair	94	301	72	0	36	.239	2B-SS
Bill Enos	82	223	68	6	38	.305	INF-OF
Logan Hooper	76	188	45	1	16	.239	OF-2B
George Metkovich	71	268	87	3	38	.325	OF-1B
Ambrose "Brusie" Ogrodowski	80	248	65	0	22	.262	C
Erwin "Babe" Paul	64	173	43	0	11	.249	2B-3B-SS
Charlie Petersen	139	510	146	0	49	.286	2B-3B-OF
Harry Rosenberg	26	94	34	0	18	.362	OF
Joe Sprinz	92	298	63	0	22	.211	C
Henry Steinbacher	156	569	181	2	105	.318	OF
Gus Suhr	149	527	130	1	65	.247	1B-3B
Don Trower	64	263	58	2	18	.221	SS
Bernard "Frenchy" Uhalt	136	512	160	1	47	.313	OF
Al "A-1" Wright	18	59	13	0	5	.220	2B-3B
Del Young	150	549	135	4	56	.246	2B-SS

Appendix A: Records of Individual Players

The 1943 Seattle Rainiers — Third Place

Pitchers

	G	W	L	IP	K	BB	ERA
John Babich	8	3	2	40	9	20	4.50
Ed Carnett	11	4	4	63	18	22	3.14
Joe Demoran	33	16	15	256	66	73	2.57
Glenn Elliott	24	6	7	136	36	41	3.84
Carl Fischer	15	10	3	103	36	36	2.71
Sylvester Johnson	21	8	7	104	38	7	2.51
Wilfred "Pete" Jonas	31	12	14	193	78	78	2.98
Byron Speece	27	13	9	175	54	41	2.83
Frank Tincup	6	4	2	48	14	10	3.38
Hal Turpin	14	7	6	106	25	17	2.89
John Yelovic	20	2	1	42	13	18	unk

Position Players

	G	AB	H	HR	RBI	AVE	POS
Nick Buonarigo	39	69	7	0	2	.101	C
Ed Carnett	121	403	121	2	28	.300	OF-1B
Loyd Christopher	49	137	38	4	15	.277	OF
Joe Coscarart	19	59	9	0	5	.153	2B-SS
Joe Dobbins*	115	412	130	0	54	.316	2B-SS
Len Gabrielson	130	421	129	0	54	.306	1B
Stan Gray	52	130	32	0	12	.246	2B-SS-3B
Dick Gyselman	149	518	154	0	49	.297	3B
Hal Hoffmann**	27	50	10	0	5	.200	C
Jim Jewell	70	197	45	1	12	.228	1B-INF
Bill Kats	80	227	54	0	22	.238	OF
Lynn King	73	263	67	0	14	.255	OF
Bill Lawrence	80	256	62	0	17	.242	OF
Bill Matheson	152	548	145	6	67	.265	OF-2B
Ford Mullen	110	426	116	0	31	.272	2B-SS
Hal Sueme	134	398	112	2	49	.281	C

*Also with Hollywood.
**Also with Portland.

Appendix A: Records of Individual Players

The 1943 Portland Beavers—Fourth Place

Pitchers

	G	W	L	IP	K	BB	ERA
Syd Cohen	22	10	8	154	40	31	3.16
Earl Cook	38	5	12	148	42	51	3.83
Earl Escalante*	28	5	8	106	29	44	3.57
Roy Helser	3	2	1	23	12	5	5.48
Bill Herring	24	8	5	121	44	41	2.90
Ad Liska	32	17	11	254	122	31	1.98
Forrest Joe Orrell	22	8	11	170	90	61	2.33
Wayne Osborne	16	9	5	127	35	39	2.48
Marino Pieretti	37	8	11	135	55	50	3.07
Frank Shone	6	2	0	13	3	15	unk
Fay Thomas*	5	0	3	20	3	8	5.40
Jack Wilson	27	8	10	183	76	52	2.75

*Also with Hollywood.

Position Players

	G	AB	H	HR	RBI	AVE	POS
Eddie Adams	98	299	74	3	34	.247	C
Carl Anderson	12	20	5	0	2	.250	1B
Larry Barton	145	499	142	11	72	.285	1B
Roy Easterwood	21	77	20	1	9	.260	C
Les "Bubba" Floyd	116	440	116	0	32	.264	2B-SS
Johnny Gill	121	393	127	2	60	.323	OF
Tedd Gullic	142	513	138	17	82	.269	OF-3B-1B
Spencer Harris	117	366	101	6	44	.276	OF-1B
Hal Hoffmann**	27	50	10	0	5	.200	C
Johnny O'Neil	124	453	115	0	49	.254	SS-2B
Marvin Owen	73	260	80	0	32	.308	3B
Stan "Packy" Rogers	150	551	136	3	52	.247	2B-SS-3B
Bill Krueger	36	66	11	0	2	.167	3B-SS
Merv Shea	41	86	19	0	9	.221	C
Frank Shone	24	57	12	0	7	.211	OF
Rupert Thompson	148	524	147	2	35	.281	OF

**Also with Seattle.

The 1943 Hollywood Stars—Tied for Fifth Place

Pitchers

	G	W	L	IP	K	BB	ERA
Cy Blanton	24	9	9	150	70	43	2.70
Eddie Erautt	20	5	9	115	33	40	3.29
Earl Escalante*	28	5	8	106	29	44	3.57
"Pappy" Roy Joiner	32	11	11	174	50	56	5.28
Pat McLaughlin	47	4	5	113	23	49	4.22
Don Pulford	7	2	0	24	6	6	unk
Charlie Root	25	15	5	166	70	28	3.09
Ron Smith	44	12	9	168	68	62	3.91
Fay Thomas*	5	0	3	20	3	8	5.40
Bill Thomas	52	11	21	249	78	66	3.90

Also with Portland.

Position Players

	G	AB	H	HR	RBI	AVE	POS
Bill Brenzel	88	271	67	2	26	.247	C
Harry Clements	156	612	187	0	51	.306	3B
Connie Creeden	23	70	16	1	8	.229	OF
Thomas Tod Davis	103	362	80	2	37	.221	SS
Johnny Dickshot	158	583	205	13	99	.352	OF
Joe Dobbins**	115	412	130	0	54	.316	SS-2B
Marvin Gudat***	128	407	104	0	26	.256	OF
Floyd "Babe" Herman	81	147	52	4	22	.354	OF-1B
Jim Hill	62	157	36	1	9	.229	C
Brooks Holder	149	543	148	6	62	.273	OF
Art Lilly	65	189	38	0	10	.201	2B-3B
Bill Knickerbocker	68	236	67	0	26	.284	2B-SS
Butch Moran	156	592	168	4	64	.284	1B
Kenny Richardson	111	310	80	6	43	.258	INF-OF
Hank Robinson	17	20	2	0	1	.100	OF
Roy Younker	132	414	116	13	67	.280	OF-C-2B

**Also with Seattle.
***Also with San Diego.

Appendix A: Records of Individual Players 197

The 1943 Oakland Oaks—Tied for Fifth Place

Pitchers

	G	W	L	IP	K	BB	ERA
Ralph Buxton	29	11	11	183	92	51	2.75
Italo Chelini	31	12	7	147	26	30	3.67
Vince DiBiasi	29	7	11	154	70	73	4.15
Earl Jones	13	5	6	91	39	47	2.18
Hubert "Hub" Kittle	14	2	1	59	30	22	2.75
Norbert "Nubs" Kleinke	33	1	10	106	34	45	4.42
John Lotz	33	11	16	216	42	73	3.75
Henry "Cotton" Pippen	36	20	15	270	56	69	3.03
Floyd Stromme	18	2	2	73	31	37	4.44

Position Players

	G	AB	H	HR	RBI	AVE	POS
Fern Bell*	147	529	139	3	72	.263	OF
Jake Caufield	152	537	132	0	42	.246	SS
Jack Devincenzi	129	426	96	5	54	.225	OF
Joe Gonzales	84	202	37	0	21	.183	OF-1B
Will Leonard	55	119	20	0	8	.168	C
Hugh Luby	157	587	184	3	69	.313	2B-1B
Emil Mailho	155	598	188	2	46	.314	OF-1B
Billy Raimondi	132	430	119	1	41	.277	C-INF
Walt Raimondi	11	27	8	0	3	.296	3B-2B
Chet Rosenlund**	103	374	91	0	34	.243	3B-2B
Les Scarsella	157	589	192	3	85	.326	1B
Johnny Vergez	75	244	46	0	16	.189	3B-SS

*Also with Los Angeles and Hollywood.
**Also with San Francisco.

The 1943 San Diego Padres—Seventh Place

Pitchers

	G	W	L	IP	K	BB	ERA
Jim Brillheart	33	9	14	213	53	99	3.51
Rex Cecil	20	8	10	137	81	51	2.89
Earl Chapple	14	0	3	42	19	37	unk
Frankie Dasso	27	12	8	177	154	93	2.75
Rex Dilbeck	21	7	9	118	37	24	3.51

198   Appendix A: Records of Individual Players

	G	W	L	IP	K	BB	ERA
Chet Johnson	35	14	16	242	106	97	3.27
Warren "Bud" Merkle	23	0	2	49	16	19	6.06
Al Olsen	9	2	4	50	7	8	4.14
Charley Schanz	44	17	18	276	137	130	3.23

POSITION PLAYERS

	G	AB	H	HR	RBI	AVE	POS
Morrison "Morry" Abbott	85	247	60	1	27	.243	OF-C
Del Ballinger	59	135	38	2	15	.281	C-OF
Al Cailteaux	67	185	42	0	13	.227	3B-SS-2B
Jack Calvey	149	534	145	0	54	.272	SS
George Detore	73	187	60	1	29	.321	C-INF
Lou Estes	53	115	24	0	11	.209	3B-2B-SS
Marvin Gudat*	128	407	104	0	26	.256	OF
John "Swede" Jensen	49	153	39	3	21	.255	OF
Walter Lowe	144	499	132	2	55	.265	1B-3B-OF
George McDonald	112	391	129	0	50	.330	1B
George Morgan	71	152	41	0	16	.270	INF-OF
Hal Patchett	141	522	148	1	49	.284	OF
Bill Salkeld	111	309	85	2	47	.275	C
Mel Steiner	36	90	18	0	10	.200	OF
Ed Wheeler	133	493	150	3	32	.304	2B-3B-SS
Jack Whipple	64	225	49	1	25	.218	OF

*Also with Hollywood.

The 1943 Sacramento Solons—Eighth Place

PITCHERS

	G	W	L	IP	K	BB	ERA
Alpha "Al" Brazle	22	11	8	160	69	60	1.69
Eldred "Bud" Byerly	34	9	21	246	98	91	2.49
Clem Dreisewerd	42	9	20	236	65	37	3.89
Clyde Fischer	13	0	1	30	7	18	unk
Bob Fitzke	23	0	8	70	9	26	5.53
Steve LeGault	12	3	6	69	20	29	2.22
Herman Pillette	28	2	3	41	7	13	5.71
John Pintar	42	5	27	221	63	57	4.68
Henry Polly	10	1	7	58	21	22	4.50
Jean-Pierre Roy	12	1	8	73	29	44	4.81

Appendix A: Records of Individual Players

Position Players

	G	AB	H	HR	RBI	AVE	POS
Jack Angle	148	512	115	3	48	.225	1B-2B-OF
Ora "Mickey" Burnett	145	552	152	6	43	.275	SS-2B-OF
Dick Cole	26	76	17	0	0	.224	SS-2B-3B
Fred Hensley	133	434	119	1	44	.274	INF-OF
Vernal "Nippy" Jones	129	477	145	4	37	.304	2B
George Jumonville	75	241	50	3	27	.207	3B-SS
Gene Kavanaugh	141	485	129	1	40	.266	OF-3B
Eddie Malone	117	359	94	1	28	.262	C-2B-3B
Joe Molina	75	211	47	1	12	.223	OF
Earl Petersen	98	278	75	5	34	.270	C-OF-1B
Bill Ramsey	110	379	89	0	21	.235	OF
Jake Suytar	56	168	37	0	10	.220	1B
Manny Vias	108	346	84	0	24	.243	OF

The 1944 Los Angeles Angels — First Place

Pitchers

	G	W	L	IP	K	BB	ERA
Charles "Red" Adams	44	10	7	186	87	56	3.58
"Pancho" Jorge Comellas	41	18	14	276	128	94	2.61
Dick Conger	26	13	7	169	65	35	2.88
Claude Horton	18	9	4	91	26	31	3.38
Garman "Pete" Mallory	12	6	3	73	46	17	2.59
Don Osborn	42	15	13	216	47	44	3.25
Jodie Phipps	18	2	4	31	8	19	unk
Ray Prim	41	22	10	286	139	40	1.70
Irvin Stein	25	1	4	67	21	13	4.70
Boyd Tepler	11	3	4	48	51	52	2.81

Position Players

	G	AB	H	HR	RBI	AVE	POS
Pete Elko	16	42	13	0	4	.310	3B
Charlie English*	124	447	131	2	59	.293	3B
Eddie Fernandes	130	400	112	5	57	.280	OF-C
Cecil Garriott	170	619	177	13	70	.286	OF
Stan Gray**	62	149	43	0	12	.289	2B-SS-3B
Don Grigg	20	29	7	0	1	.241	C-OF
Guy Miller	156	519	121	0	47	.233	SS-2B-3B
Johnny Moore	85	120	39	3	30	.325	OF

Appendix A: Records of Individual Players

	G	AB	H	HR	RBI	AVE	POS
Ted Norbert	111	363	105	10	57	.289	OF
George O'Gorek	50	188	46	0	14	.245	2B
Johnny Ostrowski	124	475	134	10	67	.282	OF-3B
Reggie Otero	129	421	129	0	54	.306	1B
Glen "Rip" Russell	155	585	184	17	89	.315	1B-2B
Manuel Salvatierra	45	122	30	1	14	.246	OF
Bill Sarni	87	229	52	5	24	.227	C
Eddie Sauer	108	392	115	5	52	.293	OF-1B
Tufeck "Tom" Skaff***	39	55	8	0	1	.145	C-OF
Roy Smalley	61	160	30	1	11	.188	SS-3B

*Also with Oakland.
**Also with Seattle.
***Also with San Francisco.

The 1944 Portland Beavers—Second Place

PITCHERS

	G	W	L	IP	K	BB	ERA
Syd Cohen	27	10	13	150	44	56	3.54
Clarence Federmeyer	38	6	6	144	59	109	4.19
Roy Helser	37	20	16	280	156	120	2.41
Ad Liska	32	18	9	236	124	40	2.48
Wandel Mossor	11	0	1	30	23	19	unk
Al Ott	14	0	2	28	5	10	unk
Marino Pieretti	48	26	13	322	139	125	2.46
Don Pulford	21	3	10	121	48	43	3.72
Joe Sullivan*	27	3	14	134	41	58	4.23
Jack Wilson	7	1	1	41	9	13	unk
George Windsor	17	1	1	30	14	16	unk

*Also with Oakland.

POSITION PLAYERS

	G	AB	H	HR	RBI	AVE	POS
Eddie Adams	113	310	92	0	37	.297	C
Carl Anderson	25	67	8	0	7	.119	OF-1B
Larry Barton	128	462	117	4	53	.253	1B
Gilly Campbell*	74	193	43	0	12	.223	C
John Ciccimarro	30	87	18	0	7	.207	2B
Don Cook	8	10	2	0	2	.200	C

Appendix A: Records of Individual Players 201

	G	AB	H	HR	RBI	AVE	POS
Norm DeWeese	106	332	84	2	33	.253	OF-2B
Johnny Gill	127	425	122	3	49	.287	OF
Tedd Gullic	103	358	93	8	54	.260	OF-1B-3B
Spencer Harris	124	373	102	5	45	.273	OF-1B
Robert Hedington	34	61	15	0	6	.246	INF
Earl Norager	48	96	17	0	4	.177	C
Mel Nunes	105	302	66	1	21	.219	2B-SS-3B
Johnny O'Neil	159	631	149	0	43	.236	SS
Marvin Owen	131	449	130	1	63	.290	3B
Charley Petersen	91	355	97	0	28	.273	2B-3B-OF
Frank Shone	145	509	140	0	48	.275	OF

*Also with Oakland.

The 1944 Oakland Oaks—Tied for Third Place

Pitchers

	G	W	L	IP	K	BB	ERA
Archie Campbell	13	3	2	33	9	7	2.97
Italo Chelini	4	1	1	8	3	5	4.70
Ken "Coral" Gables	16	5	6	74	51	45	4.99
Damon Hayes	16	7	6	110	56	38	2.62
Norb "Nubs" Kleinke**	30	5	10	138	45	57	3.91
John Lotz	37	18	13	254	68	78	3.22
Elmer Phillips	16	3	1	33	9	14	unk
Henry "Cotton" Pippen	23	8	11	176	77	31	3.17
Al Raimondi	21	2	4	63	22	28	2.86
Manny Salvo	27	18	7	210	58	38	2.14
Les Scarsella	9	3	1	67	18	26	1.75
Floyd Stromme	29	11	11	182	55	78	2.57
Joe Sullivan*	27	3	14	134	41	58	4.23

*Also with Portland.
**Also with San Diego.

Position Players

	G	AB	H	HR	RBI	AVE	POS
Dolf Camilli	113	357	103	14	60	.289	OF-1B
Gilly Campbell*	74	193	43	0	12	.223	C
Jake Caufield	150	605	156	2	45	.258	SS
Jack Devincenzi	74	134	28	2	13	.209	OF

	G	AB	H	HR	RBI	AVE	POS
Charley English**	124	447	131	2	59	.293	2B-3B
Sam Fenech	24	46	11	0	3	.239	C-OF
Frankie Hawkins	94	334	104	3	45	.311	OF
James Herrera	71	220	55	0	27	.250	2B-SS
John Kreevich	143	501	134	2	50	.267	OF-3B
Louis Lorenz	23	61	18	0	11	.295	C
Emil Mailho	123	465	129	0	27	.277	OF
Vic Picetti	14	48	10	0	1	.208	1B
Billy Raimondi	143	452	131	0	45	.290	C
Chet Rosenlund	158	592	149	1	59	.252	3B
Les Scarsella	156	596	196	6	96	.329	OF-1B-P
Mel Steiner***	110	345	92	1	36	.267	OF
Lin Storti	53	135	26	0	12	.193	1B-2B-3B
Al "A-1" Wright	79	256	55	0	26	.215	1B-2B

*Also with Portland.
**Also with Los Angeles.
***Also with San Diego and Sacramento.

The 1944 San Francisco Seals—Tied for Third Place

PITCHERS

	G	W	L	IP	K	BB	ERA
Win Ballou	13	1	2	14	5	7	4.50
"Sad" Sam Gibson	18	4	8	114	27	26	3.95
"Cowboy" Ray Harrell	44	20	18	300	168	91	2.61
Bob Joyce	41	21	20	324	105	73	2.81
Knowles Piercey	15	0	2	49	16	15	2.94
Tommy Seats	39	25	13	320	129	51	2.36
Bill Werle	36	14	19	289	129	84	4.05

POSITION PLAYERS

	G	AB	H	HR	RBI	AVE	POS
Wally Carroll	31	74	33	0	9	.446	OF
John Cavalli	109	387	83	2	44	.214	SS-2B-3B
Will Enos	82	241	68	1	31	.282	OF-INF
Joe Futerick	120	398	116	0	28	.291	SS-2B
Ben Guintini	117	408	100	2	59	.245	OF-3B
Logan Hooper	71	159	46	0	13	.289	OF
Ambrose "Brusie" Ogrodowski	90	266	72	0	29	.271	C
Dino Restelli	38	137	47	1	19	.343	OF-1B-3B

Appendix A: Records of Individual Players

	G	AB	H	HR	RBI	AVE	POS
Jim Ripple*	21	43	13	0	2	.302	OF
Neill Sheridan	42	150	44	4	21	.293	OF
Tuteck "Tom" Skaff**	39	55	8	0	1	.145	OF-C-INF
Joe Sprinz	92	272	75	0	28	.276	C
Henry Steinbacher	137	492	122	1	86	.248	OF
Gus Suhr	164	588	164	0	75	.279	1B
John Trutta	79	241	63	0	28	.261	3B-2B
Bernard "Frenchy" Uhalt	154	612	169	0	52	.276	OF
Del Young	149	541	125	0	53	.231	2B-SS-3B

*Also with Seattle.
**Also with Los Angeles.

The 1944 Seattle Rainiers—Fifth Place

Pitchers

	G	W	L	IP	K	BB	ERA
Johnny Babich	22	8	8	134	38	66	3.16
Joe Demoran	38	18	16	264	64	79	2.42
Glenn Elliott	25	6	6	131	58	42	3.44
Carl Fischer	32	16	13	234	144	47	1.85
Sylvester Johnson	13	2	1	36	13	2	unk
Jack McClure	13	1	0	31	8	23	unk
Byron Speece	31	10	13	180	67	30	2.80
Frank Tincup	32	8	10	164	78	72	2.80
Hal Turpin	31	13	15	229	52	33	3.10
John Yellovic	4	0	1	8	4	2	unk

Position Players

	G	AB	H	HR	RBI	AVE	POS
Nick Buonarigo*	32	67	15	1	8	.224	C
Paul Carpenter	110	333	75	3	39	.225	OF
Loyd Christopher	126	398	113	6	35	.284	OF
Connie Creeden	59	207	58	2	24	.280	OF-1B
Bill Derflinger	5	7	1	0	0	.143	OF
Joe Dobbins	132	445	99	1	49	.222	INF-OF
Bobby Gorbould	87	327	81	0	23	.248	2B-SS
Stan Gray**	62	149	43	0	12	.289	INF
Dick Gyselman	160	607	185	0	49	.305	3B
Hal Hoffmann	9	14	2	0	3	.143	C
Roy Johnson	115	369	96	2	35	.260	OF-3B

Appendix A: Records of Individual Players

	G	AB	H	HR	RBI	AVE	POS
Bill Kats (Katsilometes)	49	155	31	1	10	.200	OF
Jim Keesey	18	50	12	0	5	.240	1B
Bill Krueger***	36	107	22	0	4	.206	1B-2B-OF
Al Libke	117	397	122	5	51	.307	1B-OF
Bill Lyman	118	375	84	0	31	.224	SS-2B-3B
Bill Matheson	153	567	156	2	52	.275	OF-1B-3B
John Penso	22	58	10	0	5	.172	2B-3B
Jim Ripple****	21	43	13	0	2	.302	OF
Hal Spindell	65	211	75	0	32	.355	C
Hal Sueme	106	314	71	1	29	.226	C-1B

*Also with Hollywood.
**Also with Los Angeles.
***Also with Sacramento.
****Also with San Francisco.

The 1944 Hollywood Stars—Sixth Place

Pitchers

	G	W	L	IP	K	BB	ERA
Darrell "Cy" Blanton	14	4	5	68	44	23	3.18
Earl Escalante	41	10	14	200	89	96	4.10
Don Hanski*	15	2	7	73	21	22	4.07
Clint Hufford	36	7	6	137	32	70	3.61
Johnny Intlekoffer	40	11	6	145	46	45	2.92
Joe Mishasek	39	16	10	209	73	74	3.79
Charlie Root	21	3	5	87	58	28	3.21
Jim Sharp	29	6	10	134	60	103	4.90
Ron Smith	46	16	12	213	64	79	3.63
Alex Weldon	34	6	8	125	47	53	3.89

*Also with San Diego.

Position Players

	G	AB	H	HR	RBI	AVE	POS
Nick Buonarigo**	32	67	15	1	8	.224	C
Harry Clements	37	148	36	1	15	.243	3B
Thomas "Tod" Davis	169	604	150	4	77	.248	SS
Robert "Buck" Faucett	94	381	120	0	35	.315	3B
Joe Gonzales	52	119	35	1	15	.294	OF
Floyd "Babe" Herman	78	107	37	0	23	.346	1B-OF

Appendix A: Records of Individual Players 205

	G	AB	H	HR	RBI	AVE	POS
Jim Hill	112	375	95	2	35	.253	C-OF
Brooks Holder	161	583	163	6	54	.280	OF
Del Jones	110	367	103	0	20	.281	OF
Frank Kelleher	130	487	160	29	121	.329	OF
Otto Meyers***	100	284	69	0	23	.243	OF
Cyril "Butch" Moran	141	521	164	2	65	.315	1B
Ray Olsen	92	302	70	5	35	.232	2B-3B
Les Powers	83	239	67	3	32	.280	OF-1B
Ernest Potocar	14	29	3	0	0	.103	C-OF
Kenny Richardson	159	536	135	7	62	.252	INF-OF
Roy Younker	106	299	71	3	27	.237	C-OF

**Also with Seattle.
***Also with Sacramento.

The 1944 Sacramento Solons—Seventh Place

PITCHERS

	G	W	L	IP	K	BB	ERA
Gene Babbitt	32	8	15	203	42	73	3.24
Andrew "Bud" Beasley	15	5	6	105	21	32	3.00
Clem Dreiswerd	31	20	9	252	137	21	1.61
Guy Fletcher	38	12	19	268	126	94	2.82
Larry Kempe	9	1	2	31	8	19	unk
Steve LeGault	30	9	16	218	86	65	3.84
Herman Pillette	20	3	2	37	9	8	2.45
Earl Porter	30	10	13	190	68	62	3.65
Dick Powers	40	7	9	136	37	56	2.98

POSITION PLAYERS

	G	AB	H	HR	RBI	AVE	POS
Jack Angle	96	351	98	1	25	.279	INF
Jack Balesteri	7	18	1	0	0	.056	OF
Paul Bowa	72	145	32	0	8	.221	3B-SS-2B
William Cox	46	140	36	0	17	.257	OF-INF
Tony Governor	12	27	8	0	3	.296	OF
Ted Greenhalgh	52	115	30	0	13	.261	OF
Gene Handley	134	499	129	0	44	.259	2B-SS-3B
Jim Jewel	8	27	7	0	1	.259	3B-2B
Bill Kreuger*	36	107	22	0	4	.206	2B-OF-3B
Lilo "Mark" Marcucci	72	156	42	1	17	.269	C-OF

	G	AB	H	HR	RBI	AVE	POS
Al McElreath	114	425	123	2	42	.289	OF
Otto Meyers**	100	284	69	0	23	.243	OF
Joe Molina	12	28	5	0	3	.179	OF
Bill Ramsey	166	687	191	2	70	.278	OF
Forest Rogers	94	328	80	0	20	.244	INF-OF
Joe Rossi	45	154	33	1	17	.214	C
Mel Serafini	96	308	73	6	29	.237	3B
Mel Steiner***	110	345	92	1	36	.267	OF
Jim "Red" Steiner	95	314	98	0	34	.312	C
Charles "Jake" Suytar	127	466	102	2	45	.219	1B
Manny Vias	22	58	11	0	1	.190	OF-SS
Ralph Watson	112	369	80	0	23	.217	SS
Eddie Weigandt	43	112	26	0	5	.232	OF

*Also with Seattle.
**Also with Hollywood.
***Also with San Diego and Oakland.

The 1944 San Diego Padres—Eighth Place

Pitchers

	G	W	L	IP	K	BB	ERA
Jim Brillheart	27	8	14	190	43	65	3.08
Rex Cecil	36	19	11	246	186	103	2.16
Frankie Dasso	40	20	19	298	253	131	2.81
Rex Dilbeck	9	1	2	24	7	10	unk
Carl Dumler	22	3	6	74	32	45	3.28
Don Hanski*	15	2	7	73	21	22	4.07
Chet Johnson	29	12	11	186	138	94	3.53
Lou Lucier	8	1	5	46	19	7	4.50
Warren "Bud" Merkle	15	1	2	38	17	29	unk
Joe Valenzuela	36	3	10	137	58	98	4.66
Joe Wood Jr.	10	5	4	79	35	37	2.51

*Also with Hollywood.

Position Players

	G	AB	H	HR	RBI	AVE	POS
Morrison "Morry" Abbott	87	197	50	5	25	.254	OF-C
Del Ballinger	99	278	67	0	26	.241	C
Al Cailteaux	46	119	21	0	7	.176	2B-SS-3B

Appendix A: Records of Individual Players

	G	AB	H	HR	RBI	AVE	POS
Jack Calvey	138	514	128	1	44	.249	SS
George Detore	32	48	14	0	4	.292	C-INF
Lou Estes	5	10	3	0	2	.300	3B
Marvin Gudat	113	369	104	0	31	.282	OF-1B
Manny Hernandez	30	82	17	0	5	.207	OF
John Lazor	35	124	38	1	7	.306	OF
Walter Lowe	46	148	41	0	27	.277	OF-1B
Mel Mazzera	15	43	8	0	4	.186	OF-1B
George McDonald	85	313	97	0	34	.310	1B
George Morgan	86	224	52	0	15	.232	2B-SS-3B
Hal Patchett	128	426	117	1	56	.275	OF
Vern Reynolds	120	371	99	0	39	.267	2B-SS-3B
Bill Salkeld	115	340	82	3	49	.241	C
Hank Sciarra	16	19	3	0	0	.158	2B-SS
Mel Steiner**	110	345	92	1	36	.267	OF
Rupert Thompson	39	127	27	0	8	.213	OF-3B
Lou Vezlich	79	265	73	1	31	.275	OF-1B
Ed Wheeler	163	655	175	2	56	.267	2B-SS-3B
Jack Whipple	43	152	37	0	12	.243	OF

**Also with Sacramento and Oakland.

The 1945 Portland Beavers—First Place

Pitchers

	G	W	L	IP	K	BB	ERA
Sydney Cohen	30	14	8	199	67	56	3.26
Clarence Federmeyer	10	1	1	20	8	22	unk
Carl Gunnarson	12	2	0	24	5	16	unk
Roy Helser	37	20	14	270	136	99	3.37
Adolph Liska	35	20	12	273	127	59	2.34
Jacob "Jake" Mooty	27	11	5	156	72	63	3.12
Wandel Mossor	27	13	7	157	138	71	2.92
Burton Don Pulford	37	20	11	274	152	84	2.36
Jack Tising	30	11	10	145	52	38	2.92

Position Players

	G	AB	H	HR	RBI	AVE	POS
Eddie Adams	119	344	81	2	39	.235	C
Larry Barton	144	509	162	6	76	.318	1B
Glenn Crawford	22	69	22	1	8	.319	SS-3B-2B

Appendix A: Records of Individual Players

	G	AB	H	HR	RBI	AVE	POS
Frank Demaree	136	514	156	3	78	.304	OF
Charlie English	129	449	127	4	52	.283	2B-3B
Danny Escobar	6	12	3	0	2	.250	OF-1B
Johnny Gill*	99	241	64	2	32	.266	OF-1B
Tedd Gulic	145	517	134	9	81	.259	OF-1B-3B
Charles Hansen**	17	43	8	0	3	.186	C
Spencer Harris**	114	316	79	3	46	.250	OF-1B
Frank Lucchesi	60	118	29	0	16	.246	OF-INF
Mel Nunes	97	311	85	0	38	.273	2B-SS
Johnny O'Neil	164	585	184	0	88	.315	SS
Marvin Owen	163	566	176	1	83	.311	3B-1B
Charley Petersen***	95	325	84	0	43	.258	3B-C-OF-2B
Nick Rhabe****	74	228	65	0	19	.285	OF
Curt Schmidt*****	38	81	15	3	8	.185	3B-OF
Frank Shone	158	642	195	5	63	.304	OF
Frank "Hank" Souza	61	138	28	0	7	.203	C
Roy Younker*****	118	366	92	5	53	.251	C-1B-OF

*Also with Seattle.
**Also with Hollywood.
***Also with San Francisco.
****Also with Los Angeles.
*****Also with Sacramento.

The 1945 Seattle Rainiers—Second Place

PITCHERS

	G	W	L	IP	K	BB	ERA
John Carpenter	19	1	1	52	16	20	2.08
Joe Demoran	38	20	10	262	77	72	2.85
Glenn Elliott	34	14	12	196	86	67	3.81
Carl Fischer	35	17	14	253	108	60	2.63
Keith Frazier	21	2	4	66	22	32	3.27
Chet Johnson	27	14	12	178	117	82	3.44
Sylvester Johnson	23	6	3	65	24	8	3.05
Pat McLaughlin	9	0	1	22	5	9	unk
John Orphal	8	0	1	13	7	8	unk
Alex Palica	31	10	9	164	55	82	4.39
Byron Speece	17	3	3	54	17	17	4.33
Hal Turpin	31	18	8	229	29	26	2.40

Position Players

	G	AB	H	HR	RBI	AVE	POS
Chuck Aleno	159	536	155	9	84	.289	3B
Dick Briskey	12	15	4	1	2	.267	3B-SS-2B
Paul Carpenter	13	40	9	0	3	.225	OF
Dominic Castro	15	36	10	0	3	.278	C
Joe Dobbins	147	477	154	1	63	.323	INF
Bob Finley	87	261	80	4	48	.307	C-1B
Johnny Gill*	99	241	64	2	32	.266	OF-1B
Bobby Gorbould	165	594	168	1	54	.283	INF-OF
Roy Johnson	69	214	58	1	29	.271	OF
Bill Kats (Katsilometes)	92	221	64	0	21	.290	OF
Bill Lyman	134	385	110	0	38	.286	SS-2B-3B
Bill Matheson	47	152	44	0	17	.289	OF-1B-3B
George McDonald	151	552	183	1	69	.332	1B
Ted Norbert	169	527	136	23	109	.258	OF
Joe Passero	26	53	12	0	3	.226	OF
Hal Patchett**	157	580	178	0	47	.307	OF
Hal Sueme	105	340	91	0	38	.268	C
Manny Vias	15	18	4	0	0	.222	OF
Jack Whipple	93	229	60	1	22	.262	OF

*Also with Portland.
**Also with Oakland.

The 1945 Sacramento Solons—Third Place

Pitchers

	G	W	L	IP	K	BB	ERA
Jim Atanazio	23	5	3	80	27	40	5.06
Gene Babbitt	31	6	13	140	37	53	3.99
Andrew "Bud" Beasley	17	12	4	132	22	30	3.14
Guy Fletcher	45	24	14	335	144	92	2.34
Giles Knowles**	26	8	7	153	43	83	4.29
Steve LeGault*	33	5	8	136	32	49	3.84
Jim McCarthy	29	10	10	159	50	51	4.13
Lou Penrose	16	4	2	77	21	34	5.03
Herman Pillette	7	1	1	12	3	1	3.75
John Pintar	17	6	5	60	27	29	5.25
Earl Porter*	31	6	7	134	34	48	5.10
Dick Powers	25	5	6	108	22	35	4.67

210   Appendix A: Records of Individual Players

	G	W	L	IP	K	BB	ERA
Joe Vivalda	10	4	4	67	20	47	4.16
Joe Wood Jr.	28	9	14	205	64	89	5.22

*Also with Hollywood.
**Also with San Diego.

POSITION PLAYERS

	G	AB	H	HR	RBI	AVE	POS
Barney Bridges	29	34	8	0	4	.235	SS-3B-2B
Jack Calvey	153	553	150	6	80	.271	SS
Jimmy Grant	45	126	39	1	22	.310	3B-OF
Perry Ted Greenhalgh	94	224	66	0	26	.295	OF
Gene Handley	176	700	215	1	44	.307	2B-SS
Jesse Landrum	158	618	184	2	99	.298	OF-INF
George Mandish	140	471	157	4	92	.333	OF
Lilo "Mark" Marcucci	157	523	150	7	93	.287	3B-C
Marion "Al" McElreath	128	406	118	0	69	.291	OF
Len Prout**	110	356	104	0	59	.292	1B
Curt Schmidt***	38	81	15	3	8	.185	3B-OF
Norm Schleuter	134	427	105	2	44	.246	C
Ray Wetmore**	17	42	12	0	3	.286	1B
Joyner "Jo-Jo" White	177	688	244	1	87	.355	OF
Roy Younker***	118	366	92	5	53	.251	C-1B-OF
Ed Zipay	109	427	133	0	83	.311	1B

**Also with San Diego.
***Also with Portland.

The 1945 San Francisco Seals—Fourth Place

PITCHERS

	G	W	L	IP	K	BB	ERA
Bob Barthelson	39	12	14	233	50	97	4.29
Ken Brondell	18	4	10	110	33	55	4.25
Tony Buzolich	37	4	10	96	11	60	4.97
Floyd Ehrman	25	8	4	96	27	44	2.63
Larry Jansen	7	4	1	55	34	12	4.09
Bob Joyce	46	31	11	344	100	55	2.17
Kenneth "Whitey" Miller	16	2	6	58	15	50	6.36
Douglas Oliver	9	0	1	27	9	26	unk
Elmer Orella	30	11	11	187	46	72	3.37
Knowles Piercey	26	2	4	80	15	21	5.29
Frank Seward	37	18	13	257	113	106	3.85

Appendix A: Records of Individual Players

Position Players

	G	AB	H	HR	RBI	AVR	POS
John Cavalli*	109	356	92	1	47	.258	SS-2B-3B
Will Enos	96	286	99	5	57	.346	OF
Joe Futernick	57	144	36	1	14	.250	SS
Ben Guintini	109	304	86	2	35	.283	OF
Emil Mailho	149	484	148	1	69	.306	OF
Roy Nicely	143	484	121	1	44	.250	SS-3B-2B
Ambrose "Brusie" Ogrodowski	99	282	70	0	28	.248	C
Ray Perry	135	469	127	5	67	.271	3B-2B
Charlie Petersen**	95	325	84	0	43	.258	OF-C-2B-3B
Battle "Bones" Sanders	107	287	89	1	60	.310	1B
Neil Sheridan	148	527	153	3	68	.290	OF
Joe Sprinz	106	307	93	0	33	.303	C
Henry Steinbacher	19	46	14	0	10	.304	OF
Gus Suhr	138	399	124	0	56	.311	1B
John Trutta	48	154	42	2	22	.273	3B-C
Bernard "Frenchy" Uhalt	145	508	153	0	41	.301	OF
Del Young	125	456	124	0	47	.272	2B-SS

*Also with Hollywood.
**Also with Portland.

The 1945 Oakland Oaks—Fifth Place

Pitchers

	G	W	L	IP	K	BB	ERA
Maurice Ayala	15	1	0	21	6	11	unk
John Babich	28	4	9	129	36	62	4.40
Italo Chelini	17	5	10	101	28	24	3.74
Mitchell Chetkovich	33	10	11	168	65	72	3.32
"Sad" Sam Gibson	18	2	3	65	17	14	3.18
Leonard Gilmore	38	14	13	220	91	90	4.66
Tom Hafey	5	4	1	35	16	5	3.38
Damon Hayes	18	9	9	130	45	52	4.57
John Lotz	38	5	9	125	38	48	6.12
Garth "Red" Mann	33	15	9	222	131	95	2.88
John Marshall*	35	5	12	148	63	103	5.41
Carl Monzo**	21	3	3	48	25	29	5.06
Elmer Phillips	5	0	1	7	3	3	unk

Appendix A: Records of Individual Players

	G	W	L	IP	K	BB	ERA
Al Raimondi	24	3	2	56	13	19	3.21
Floyd Stromme	37	16	13	218	93	94	3.92

*Also with Hollywood.
**Also with San Diego.

Position Players

	G	AB	H	HR	RBI	AVE	POS
Charles Bates	31	63	19	0	6	.302	1B-OF
Adolph Camilli	11	17	6	1	4	.353	OF
John "Jake" Caufield	172	676	200	3	72	.296	SS-2B
Norman DeWeese	99	361	116	4	56	.321	OF
Clarence Jay Difani	51	187	55	0	19	.294	3B-2B
Sam Fenech	61	165	44	0	18	.267	C-OF
Tom Hafey	129	429	104	9	67	.242	OF-3B
Frank Hawkins	114	399	136	5	66	.341	OF
James Herrera	20	47	14	0	4	.298	INF-OF
Paul Edward Kearse	43	133	30	0	13	.226	C
Ed Kirby	10	35	7	0	1	.200	SS
Charles Metro (Moreshorich)	49	186	45	2	19	.242	OF-3B
Hal Patchett*	157	580	178	0	47	.307	OF
Vic Picetti	152	546	154	1	86	.282	1B
Billy Raimondi	117	341	91	2	40	.267	C-OF
Chester Rosenlund	128	470	119	0	35	.253	3B
Les Scarsella	139	508	165	10	77	.325	OF-1B
Frank Silvanic	18	21	4	0	3	.190	OF
Don Smith	38	151	57	2	20	.377	OF
Glen "Gabby" Stewart	176	608	201	1	86	.331	2B-3B
Lindo Storti**	13	28	2	0	0	.071	2B-3B
Matthew Zidich	42	114	32	0	20	.281	OF

*Also with Seattle.
**Also with Hollywood.

The 1945 San Diego Padres—Sixth Place

Pitchers

	G	W	L	IP	K	BB	ERA
Robert Bailey	6	0	2	18	3	11	unk
Jim Brillheart	45	15	13	236	87	101	4.50
Carl Dumler	42	21	16	282	143	104	2.43
Vallie Eaves	52	21	15	312	187	127	3.00
Bob Ferguson	39	5	21	211	108	114	3.54

Appendix A: Records of Individual Players

	G	W	L	IP	K	BB	ERA
Giles Knowles*	26	8	7	153	43	83	4.29
Carl Monzo**	21	3	3	48	25	29	5.06
William Morales	7	1	0	14	3	11	unk
Jerry Nelson	12	1	2	42	9	24	unk
Frank Tincup	16	0	3	46	18	36	7.83
Victor Trahd	39	5	10	121	41	75	5.21
Joe Valenzuela	9	0	4	17	10	17	unk
Charles "Butch" Wensloff	10	3	4	73	40	24	3.82
Jerry Womack	10	1	3	36	12	27	unk

*Also with Sacramento.
**Also with Oakland.

Position Players

	G	AB	H	HR	RBI	AVE	POS
Morrison "Morry" Abbott	111	268	75	5	42	.280	OF-C
Jesus Amaro	6	10	1	0	0	.100	SS-2B
Del Ballinger	171	562	168	2	82	.299	C
Bob Boken	68	233	77	8	57	.330	2B-1B-SS
Frank Cirimele	23	37	5	0	2	.135	2B-3B
Tony Criscola	180	689	214	1	58	.311	OF
Jack Dunphy	98	283	61	0	12	.216	INF
Frank Gira	77	225	46	0	16	.204	SS-2B-3B
Don Grigg*	43	81	12	0	5	.148	C-2B
Marvin Gudat	102	238	63	0	25	.265	1B
"Tricky" Dick Gyselman	154	576	185	2	74	.321	3B
John Kreevich	71	294	74	1	25	.252	OF-2B
Louis Kubiak	16	52	8	0	6	.154	SS
John "Pepper" Martin	53	97	30	1	15	.309	INF-OF
Bob McNamara	14	42	9	0	1	.214	SS
George Pacheco	24	35	8	0	2	.229	2B-SS
Leonard Prout**	110	356	104	0	59	.292	1B
Vernon Reynolds***	143	473	110	0	42	.233	INF-OF
Henry Sweeney	26	91	19	2	8	.209	1B
Rupert Thompson	126	344	119	1	26	.346	OF-1B-3B
Louis Vezlich	175	628	193	6	110	.307	OF
Jerry Womack	13	20	5	0	1	.250	2B-SS
Ralph Watson****	23	42	12	0	4	.286	SS-2B
Ray Wetmore**	17	42	12	0	3	.286	1B

*Also with Los Angeles.
**Also with Sacramento.
***Also with Hollywood.
****Also with San Francisco and Hollywood.

Appendix A: Records of Individual Players

The 1945 Los Angeles Angels—Seventh Place

Pitchers

	G	W	L	IP	K	BB	ERA
Charles "Red" Adams	41	21	15	298	160	90	2.72
Richie Colombo	6	0	2	10	3	5	unk
Jorge "Pancho" Comellas	26	6	16	156	79	55	4.44
Jesus "Charlie" Cuellar	38	13	17	225	121	83	4.40
Henry "Hank" Glor	9	1	2	37	14	23	unk
Ken Hicks	35	6	10	134	40	109	5.24
Paul Lammers	42	4	11	119	38	83	5.45
Ralph Marshall	10	0	2	19	5	11	unk
Warren "Bud" Merkle	36	2	4	88	25	39	5.63
Don Osborn	41	18	13	269	41	38	2.68
Jodie Phipps	14	1	2	39	24	12	unk
Joe Slotter	10	1	0	25	11	24	unk
George Woodend	20	3	11	90	28	57	7.50

Position Players

	G	AB	H	HR	RBI	AVE	POS
Bill Brenner	22	64	15	1	10	.234	C
Charles Brewster	65	261	74	1	28	.284	SS
Loyd Christopher	9	31	8	0	2	.258	OF
David Hal Douglas	45	142	43	1	9	.303	OF
Roy Easterwood	19	48	11	1	6	.229	C
Pete Elko	174	630	179	4	59	.284	3B-SS
Robert Stan Gray	31	88	15	0	4	.170	SS-2B-1B
Leonard "Doc" Greene	94	223	55	6	32	.247	C-OF-3B
Don Grigg*	43	81	12	0	5	.148	C-2B
Mel Hicks	171	606	181	10	87	.299	1B-OF
Frank Jelincich	14	50	18	0	8	.360	OF
Albert "Mickey" Kreitner	101	328	91	0	36	.277	C
Guy Miller	69	158	32	0	18	.203	SS-3B-2B
Johnny Moore	71	65	23	4	26	.354	OF
Lou Novikoff	101	390	121	9	52	.310	OF
Regino "Reggie" Otero	84	302	104	0	23	.344	1B
Leroy Paton	67	247	61	0	18	.247	OF
Russell Peterson	37	124	28	0	8	.226	2B
Nick Rhabe**	74	228	65	0	19	.285	OF
Glen "Rip" Russell	157	538	184	14	89	.342	1B-2B-OF
Manuel Salvatierra	19	69	19	0	3	.275	OF

Appendix A: Records of Individual Players 215

	G	AB	H	HR	RBI	AVE	POS
Jim Tyack	150	518	169	8	69	.326	OF
Ray Viers	175	606	148	2	53	.244	2B-SS

*Also with San Diego.
**Also with Portland.

The 1945 Hollywood Stars—Eighth Place

Pitchers

	G	W	L	IP	K	BB	ERA
Johnny Intlekofer	34	1	8	100	35	41	5.94
Newell "Newt" Kimball	42	19	21	301	71	57	3.44
Steve LeGault*	33	5	8	136	32	49	3.84
John Marshall**	35	5	12	148	63	103	5.41
John Joe Mishasek	43	16	16	252	84	86	5.14
Earl Porter*	31	6	7	134	34	48	5.10
John Rager	3	0	1	3	2	4	unk
Jim Sharp	18	1	7	59	31	38	8.39
Ronald Smith	44	15	20	281	97	110	4.29
J. Rowe Wallenstein	7	0	0	11	3	7	unk
Alex Weldon	12	2	2	36	11	21	unk
Claude Bob Williams	26	7	10	131	35	100	5.36

*Also with Sacramento.
**Also with Oakland.

Position Players

	G	AB	H	HR	RBI	AVE	POS
Ben Cantrell	148	502	141	3	69	.281	OF
Johnny Cavalli*	109	356	92	1	47	.258	SS-3B-2B
Myer Mike Chozen	37	140	28	0	15	.200	2B
Robert "Buck" Faucett	167	644	203	2	60	.315	3B
Charles Hansen**	17	43	8	0	3	.186	C
Spencer Harris**	114	316	79	3	46	.250	1B-OF
Jim Hill	143	465	132	1	47	.284	C-OF
Richard Brooks Holder	109	312	80	5	41	.256	OF
Harry "Moose" Krause	63	136	42	2	20	.309	C
Butch Moran	169	625	189	6	101	.302	1B
Leslie Powers	118	397	114	4	56	.287	OF-1B
Vernon Reynolds***	143	473	110	0	42	.233	INF-OF
Ken Richardson	157	469	141	14	85	.301	SS-3B-OF

Appendix A: Records of Individual Players

	G	AB	H	HR	RBI	AVE	POS
Hal Schimling	18	38	6	0	1	.158	C
Jack Dempsey Smith	32	73	13	0	9	.178	SS-3B-OF
Mel Steiner	122	339	75	3	27	.221	OF
Ed Stewart	63	251	81	0	34	.323	OF
Lin Storti****	13	28	2	0	0	.071	2B-3B
Ralph Watson*****	23	42	12	0	4	.286	SS-2B
T. Hugh Willingham	121	359	92	10	63	.256	INF-OF

Also with San Francisco.
**Also with Portland.*
***Also with San Diego.*
****Also with Oakland.*
*****Also with San Francisco and San Diego.*

Appendix B: Won-Loss Records of Wartime Pacific Coast League Teams

Clubs are listed in order of finish.

The 1942 Season

CLUB	W	L	PCT	GAMES BEHIND	MANAGER
1. Sacramento	105	73	.590	—	Pepper Martin
2. Los Angeles	104	74	.584	1	Jigger Statz
3. Seattle	96	82	.539	9	Bill Skiff
4. San Diego	91	87	.511	14	Cedric Durst
5. San Francisco	88	90	.494	17	Lefty O'Doul
6. Oakland	85	92	.480	19.5	Johnny Vergez
7. Hollywood	75	103	.421	30	Oscar Vitt
8. Portland	67	110	.379	37.5	Frank Brazill

Appendix B: Won-Loss Records of Teams

The 1943 Season

CLUB	W	L	PCT.	GAMES BEHIND	MANAGER
1. Los Angeles	110	45	.710	—	Bill Sweeney
2. San Francisco	89	66	.574	21	Lefty O'Doul
3. Seattle	85	70	.548	25	Bill Skiff
4. Portland	79	76	.510	31	Merv Shea
5. (tie) Hollywood	73	82	.471	37	Charlie Root
5. (tie) Oakland	73	82	.471	37	Johnny Vergez
7. San Diego	70	85	.452	40	Cedric Durst/ George Detore
8. Sacramento	41	114	.265	69	Ken Penner

The 1944 Season

CLUB	W	L	PCT.	GAMES BEHIND	MANAGER
1. Los Angeles	99	70	.586	—	Bill Sweeney
2. Portland	87	82	.515	12	Marvin Owen
3. (tie) Oakland	86	83	.509	13	Dolph Camilli
3. (tie) San Francisco	86	83	.509	13	Lefty O'Doul
5. Seattle	84	85	.497	15	Bill Skiff
6. Hollywood	83	86	.491	16	Charlie Root
7. Sacramento	76	93	.450	23	Earl Sheely
8. San Diego	75	94	.444	24	George Detore

The 1945 Season

CLUB	W	L	PCT.	GAMES BEHIND	MANAGER
1. Portland	112	68	.622	—	Marvin Owen
2. Seattle	105	78	.574	8.5	Bill Skiff
3. Sacramento	95	85	.528	17	Earl Sheely
4. San Francisco	96	87	.525	17.5	Lefty O'Doul
5. Oakland	90	93	.492	23.5	Dolph Camilli Billy Raimondi
6. San Diego	82	101	.448	31.5	Pepper Martin
7. Los Angeles	76	107	.415	37.5	Bill Sweeney
8. Hollywood	73	110	.399	40.5	Buck Faucett

INDEX

Abbott, Morry 62, 125, 179
Adair, Jimmy 44, 46, 58, 86
Adams, Charles "Red" 18, 69, 169, 182
Adams, Eddie 51, 76, 79, 82, 83, 84, 136, 137, 138
Adams, Elvin "Buster" 12
Aleno, Chuck 144, 147, 152, 153, 154, 156
All Star Games, Pacific Coast League 22, 34
Amaral, Danny 135
American Women's Voluntary Services 166, 167
Anaicz, Tony 29
The Angels: Los Angeles in the Pacific Coast League (Dick Beverage) 2
Angle, Jack 65, 117, 120, 121
Antanazio, Jim 158
Army–Navy Ball Bat Fund 13, 33, 90, 99
Atwood, Bill 32
Ayala, Maury 171

Babbitt, Gene 118, 122, 158
Babich, Johnny 48, 101, 144, 146, 171, 172, 174
Bailey, Robert 179
Baker, Oren 40
Ballinger, Del 62, 124, 179, 180
Ballou, Win 44, 69

Barrett, Dick "Kewpie" 19, 20, 21
Bartelme, Phil 64
Barthelson, Bob 163, 169, 170
Barton, Larry 35, 51, 76, 81, 131, 133, 135, 136, 137, 138, 139, 147
Bates, Charles 172
Bauer, Carlos 3
Bauer, Keith 124
Beard, Bill 19, 22
Beasley, Andrew "Bud" 120, 121, 122, 158, 160
Beers, Clarence 12
Bejma, Ollie 27
Bell, Fern 16, 17, 29, 55
Benevento, Rocky 35, 132, 133, 142
Bevens, Bill 19, 32
Beverage, Dick 2, 33, 41, 60, 70, 111
Bey, Herman 179
Biscaluz, Gene (sheriff) 40, 69, 110, 111, 181, 184
Bittner, John 32, 33
Blackouts in 1942 6
Blanton, Cy 59, 110
Bob Feller's All Stars 156, 170
Boken, Bob 178, 180
Bongiovanni, Nino 139
Boston Red Sox 46, 117, 123, 127
"bottle shower" 13, 93
Bowa, Paul 118, 119
Bowron, Fletcher (mayor) 40, 69, 111

Index

Branham, William G. 10
Brazill, Frank 10, 34
Brazle, Alpha 65
Brenzel, Bill 32, 58
Brewester, Charlie 181
Bricker, John (governor) 69, 111
Bridges, Barney 159, 161, 162
Brillheart, Jim 62, 124, 179
Briskey, Dick 150
Brondell, Ken 163, 165, 167
Brooklyn Dodgers 93, 122, 183
Brougham, Royal 107
Brown, Joe E. 110
Brown, Lindsey 35
Brown, Norm 24
Budnick, Mike 19
Bull, Frank 1, 6, 16
Buonarigo, Nick 101, 103, 106, 116
Burnett, Ora "Mickey" 65, 66
Bus chartering 30, 95, 125
Buxton, Ralph 55, 56, 93
Buzolich, Tony 44
Byerly, Eldred "Bud" 65

Caitreaux, Al "Frenchy" 62, 125
Calvey, Jack 24, 62, 125, 157, 157, 159, 161, 162
Camilli, Dolph 93, 95, 97, 100, 170, 172, 175
Campbell, Archie 94, 97
Campbell, Don 179
Campbell, Gilly 16, 21, 76, 79, 82, 85, 91, 94, 98
Cantrell, Ben 183
Cardinal Field, Sacramento 12, 14, 66, 117
Carnett, Ed 19, 22, 48, 49
Carpenter, John 149
Carpenter, Paul 101, 106, 108, 144
Carroll, Wally 88, 89
Castro, Dominic 36, 152
Caufield, Jake 55, 95, 172, 174, 175
Cavalli, Johnny 86, 165, 183
Cecil, Rex 62, 124, 125, 127
Chelini, Italo 29, 56, 93, 171
Chetkovich, Mitch 171, 177
Chicago Cubs 15, 18, 42, 73, 126, 141, 170, 181
Chicago White Sox 134, 136, 182
Christoff, Mike 29

Christopher, Loyd 43, 48, 49, 101, 103, 108, 109
Ciccimarro, John 76
Cirimele, Frank 178
Clements, Harry 59, 110
Coast League Cyclopedia, 1903–1957 3
Cohen, Sydney 35, 51, 53, 76, 83, 85, 137, 138
Cole, Dick 65
Collins, Bob 19, 22
Colombo, Richie 182
Comellas, Jorge "Pancho" 69, 75, 88, 93, 94, 181, 182
Conger, Dick 69, 72
Cook, A. J. 36
Cook, Don 84
Cook, Earl 51, 54
Corbett, Stan 29
Cox, Billy 122, 123
Crawford, Glenn 140, 142
Creeden, Conie 59, 101, 106, 107
Criscola, Tony 179, 180
Cuellar, Charely 182

D-Day, June 6, 1944 71, 80, 88, 113, 126, 160
Danning, Harry 42
Darrow, George "Lefty" 55
Dasso, Frankie 24, 62, 121, 124, 127
Davis, Ray "Peaches" 16
Davis, Tod 59, 110, 183
Decincenzi, Victor "Cookie" 30, 55, 57, 96
Demaree, Frank 81, 132, 135, 137, 138, 154
Demoran, Joe 49, 101, 143, 147, 148, 152, 153, 154, 155, 156
Depression of the 1930s 5, 46, 66, 142
Derflinger, Bill 108, 115
Detore, George 24, 46, 62, 63, 124, 178
Detroit Tigers 34, 54, 76, 131, 134, 139, 141, 170
Devincenzi, Jack 55, 95
DeWeese, Norm 77, 81, 131, 172,
Dewey, Thomas (governor) 69
DiBiasi, Vince 29, 56, 93–94
Dickshot, Johnny 32, 34, 59
DiFani, Clarence Jay 172
Dilbeck, Rex 24, 62, 124

Index

DiMaggio, Joe 42, 83
Dobbins, Joe 39, 48, 58, 101, 106, 144, 147, 150, 152, 154
Dobernic, Jess 16
Donnelly, Blix 12
Doubleday Park, Sacramento 66, 117, 120, 121, 123, 159, 160
Douglas, Hal 140, 181, 182,
Dreiswerd, Clem 64, 117, 121, 122, 123, 124, 127
Duezabou, Mel 29
Duke University 6
Dumler, Carl 124, 179
Dunphy, Jack 178
Durst, Cedric 14, 46, 62, 63

Easterwood, Roy 51, 181
Eaves, Vallie 179
Edmonds, Dick 65, 66, 116, 117, 122, 160
Edmonds Field, Sacramento 161, 162
Erhman, Floyd 163, 169, 170
Elko, Pete 69, 71, 181
Elliott, Glenn 101, 143
Embree, Earl 110
English, Charlie 40, 69, 70, 71, 72, 73, 75, 91, 93, 95, 99, 131, 135, 136, 137, 138, 172
Enigh, George 142
Enos, Will 44, 86, 146
Epperly, Al 27, 44
Escalante, Earl 51, 53, 59, 110, 112, 183
Escobar, Danny 10, 35, 141, 143
Eskenazi, Dave 11, 14, 16, 20, 21, 24, 25, 43, 47, 49, 50, 77, 102, 104, 105, 125, 132, 134, 142, 145, 149, 152, 155, 157, 162, 173, 179
Estes, Lou 62
Exhibition Games to Benefit Servicemen 17, 22, 42, 57, 74, 82, 83, 89, 90, 99, 107, 115, 130, 157, 164, 176

Fain, Ferris 27, 44
Fanning, Henry 39, 77, 97
Faucett, Robert "Buck" 113, 183
Federmeyer, Clarence 76, 137, 138, 140, 142
Fenech, Sam 95, 172
Ferguson, Bob 179
Fernandes, Eddie 40, 69, 70, 71, 73

Finley, Bob 144, 145, 148, 152, 154, 155
Fischer, Carl 19, 48, 49, 101, 143, 154, 156
Fletcher, Guy "Grumpy" 118, 119, 122, 158, 162, 163
Flores, Jesse 16
Floresi, Al 162
Flowers, Okey 86
Floyd, Leslie "Bubba" 51, 77
Franckovich, Mike 16
Frazier, Keith 143, 145, 148, 156
Freitas, Tony 12, 15, 65
Futernick, Joe 86, 163, 165

Gables, Ken "Coral" 98, 100, 172
Gabrielson, Len 48
Garbe, Bill 32
Garibaldi, Art 24
Garms, Deb 12
Garriott, Cecil 40, 69, 71, 72, 75
Gatto, Phil 148
Gay, Fred 32
Gehrman, Paul 16, 40
Germany, war with 129, 135, 146, 167, 179, 180
Gibson, Sam "Sad" 27, 44, 69, 86, 88, 171
Gill, John 35, 51, 77, 135, 144, 146, 147, 148, 156, 157
Gilmore, Leonard "Meow" 171
Gilmore Field, Hollywood 5, 22, 32, 34, 40, 61, 63, 74, 96, 99, 102, 110, 111, 112, 113, 114, 115, 116, 121, 126, 121, 126, 135, 153, 167, 184
Gira, Frank 172
Glenn, Joe 29
Goldsberry, Gordon 110, 113
Gonzales, Al 183
Gonzales, Joe 55, 110, 114, 183
Gorbould, Bob 103, 104, 108, 144, 145, 147, 148, 150, 154
Governors' Cup Series 92, 101, 138, 143, 151, 169
Graham, Charles 28, 29, 45, 46
Grant, Jim 158, 159
Gray, Stan 75, 93, 101, 107
Greene, Leonard "Doc" 181
Greenhalgh, Ted 118, 158, 163
Gregory, L. H. 53, 81, 136, 142
Grigg, Don 69, 73

Index

Grilk, Jim 13
Guay, Larry 19
Gudat, Marvin 29, 55, 58, 62, 125, 178
Guintini, Ben 75, 86, 92, 93, 164, 170
Gullic, Tedd 51, 52, 80, 81, 135, 139, 140, 141, 154
Gunnarson, Carl 154
Gyselman, Dick "Tricky" 19, 48, 101, 103, 109, 144, 147, 148, 178, 180

Hafey, Tom 172, 175, 177
Handley, Gene 12, 64, 118, 119, 124, 158, 162
Haney, Fred 1
Hanski, Don 110, 124
Hanson, Jack 16
Harrell, Ray "Cowboy" 27, 44, 86, 163
Harris, Spencer 19, 39, 51, 52, 77, 81, 137, 140, 142
Hawkins, Frank 35, 95, 98, 99, 172, 177
Hayes, Damon 94, 97, 171, 173, 174, 175, 176, 177
Hebert, Wally 24
Hedington, Robert 79
Helser, Roy 76, 79, 83, 85, 131, 132, 133, 134, 137, 138, 143,
Hensen, Charley 27
Hensley, Fred 65, 66
Herman, Floyd "Babe" 32, 34, 58, 59, 110, 183
Hernandez, Manny 179–180
Herrera, Jim 95, 172
Herring, Bill 51, 54
Hicks, Ken 182
Hicks, Mel 158, 181
Hilcher, Walter "Whitey" 33, 35
Hill, Jim 58, 110
Hill, Johnny 24
Hodgin, Ralph 27
Hoffman, Hal "Dutch" 53, 101, 103
Holder, Brooks 27, 59, 110, 112, 121, 183
Hollywood Stars 14, 20, 22, 25, 27, 28, 31–34, 35, 38, 39, 40, 44, 53, 56, 57, 58–62, 63, 68, 69, 70, 71, 73, 74, 78, 82, 87, 91, 96, 99, 100, 108, 109–116, 121, 127, 135, 139, 144, 145, 150, 153, 159, 164, 163, 166, 167, 169, 177, 178, 180, 181, 183–184

Hollywood Stars: Baseball in Movieland 1926–1957 (Dick Beverage) 2
Holm, Billy 18, 40
Holt, Gene 108, 115
Hooper, Logan 44, 46, 86, 91
Hoover, Joe 32, 34
Horton, Clause 69, 72
Huffman, Benny 53
Hufford, Clint 110, 111, 183
Hughes, Roy 16, 40, 69

Intelkofer, John 110, 183
Ivaldi, Andy 172, 177

Jansen, Larry 27, 164
Japanese Civilians Interment 7
Japan, war with 5, 6, 82, 129, 130, 140, 161, 168, 177, 184
Jennings, Ted 27
Jensen, John "Swede" 24, 62
Jewel, Jim 48, 118, 119
Johnson, Bobby 164
Johnson, Chet "Chesty" 62, 78, 124, 125, 143, 146, 148, 149, 150, 154
Johnson, Roy 101, 144, 146, 147, 149
Johnson, Sylvester 39, 48, 101, 143, 153, 156
Johnston, Harry 35
Joiner, Roy "Pappy" 32, 59
Jonas, Pete 49
Jones, Del 110, 112
Jones, Earl 56, 124, 179
Jones, Vernal "Nippy" 39, 65, 66
Joyce, Bob 27, 44, 85, 88, 92, 164, 165, 167, 168, 169, 170
Jummonville, George 64
Justice, William 178

Kahle, Bob 32
Kalin, Frank 32, 34
Kats, Bill 39, 48, 101, 104, 108, 143, 147, 148, 150
Kavanaugh, Gene 65
Kearse, Ed 22, 140, 176, 177
Kelleher, Frank 107, 110, 112, 114, 116, 121, 183
Kempe, Larry 64, 118
Kezar Stadium 27
Kimball, Knut 110, 113, 114, 115, 183
King, Lynn 19, 48

Index

Kirby, Ed 172
Kittle, Hub 56
Kleinke, Norbert "Nubs" 29, 56, 94, 99, 124, 125
Klepper, William 36, 51, 53, 134
Knickerbocker, Billy 59
Koester, Tony 119, 160
Kornahrens, Don 158
Krause, Harry "Moose" 183
Kreevich, John 95, 172, 179
Kreitner, Albert "Mickey" 181
Krueger, Bill 51, 118, 121
Krug, Marty 111

Lammers, Paul 182
Land, Harry 40
Landrum, Jesse 158, 162
Lane Field, San Diego 5, 24, 25, 26, 28, 45, 63, 92, 113, 126, 127, 168, 180
Landis, Kenesaw Mountain (commissioner) 5, 37, 38
Lassen, Leo 49
Lawrence, Bill 10, 22, 48
LeGault, Steve "Smokestack" 65, 160, 118, 183
Lellivelt, Jack 19, 146
Leonard, Will 55, 58
Leovich, Johnny 35
Lewis, Kermit 27, 44
Libke, Al 19, 109, 144
Lien, Al 19, 109, 144
Lillard, Gene 15
Lilly, Art 59
Liska, Ad 35, 51, 54, 76, 78, 79, 81, 83, 132, 138, 143, 154
Los Angeles Angels 1, 12, 15–19, 20, 22, 24, 25, 27, 31, 32, 33, 34, 38, 39–43, 45, 47, 49, 50, 51, 52, 54, 56, 57, 58, 59, 62, 65, 66, 68–76, 80, 82, 84, 85, 87, 88, 90, 91, 93, 96, 97, 98, 100, 106, 107, 108, 109, 111, 113, 114, 116, 118, 122, 124, 126, 127, 136, 140, 141, 144, 147, 149, 150, 151, 159, 164, 167, 168, 175, 176, 178, 180, 181–183, 184
Los Angeles Times 1
Lotz, Jack 55, 94, 171, 177
Lowe, Walter 62, 125
Lowrey, Harry "Peanuts" 17
Luby, Hugh 29, 31, 55, 56, 95

Lucchesi, Frank 131, 135, 137, 138, 141
Lucky Lager Brewing Company 36, 81
Lyman, Bill 101, 108, 144, 148, 150
Lynn, Japhet "Red" 18, 40, 42, 181
Lyons, Hershel 12

Maddern, Clarence 18, 19
Mailho, Emil 29, 35, 55, 95, 163
Mallory, Elmer 40
Mallory, Garmen "Pete" 16, 40, 69
Malone, Eddie 65, 66, 124
Mandish, George 158, 161
Mann, Garth "Red" 175
Marcucci, Lilo 118, 158
Marshall, Charlie 12
Marshall, John 94, 183
Martin, John "Pepper" 11, 64, 159, 178, 179, 180
Martinez, Henry 35, 132
Martinez, Ray 94, 98
Mather Field 12
Matheson, Bill 19, 22, 48, 101, 103, 109, 150, 151, 154, 156
Mayer, Ted 35
Mayo, Eddie 16, 18
Mazzera, Mel 24
McArthur, Douglas (general) 27
McCarthy, Jim 158, 163
McClure, Jack 178
McDonald, George 24, 62, 125, 144, 145, 146, 148, 154, 178
McElreath, Al 118, 119, 121, 158, 162
McFadden, Jim 65
McLaughlin, Pat 59, 143, 147
McNamara, Bob 178
McWilliams, Doug 28, 30, 31, 55, 56, 57, 94, 96, 165, 171, 172
Meal Money 6, 7, 130
Merkle, Warren "Bud" 1l82
Mesner, Steve 12
Messerly, Russell 59
Metkovich, George 44, 45, 46
Metro, Charley 172, 177
Meyers, Otto 110, 120
Miles, Dee 46
Miller, Damon 130
Miller, Guy 69, 71, 181
Miller, Ken "Whitey" 163, 165
Mishasek, Joe 110, 183
Molina, Joe 65

224　Index

Monzo, Carl "Snuffy"　171, 174, 179
Moore, Johnny　16, 40, 69, 71, 136, 181, 182
Mooty, Jake　40, 131, 133, 137, 138, 143, 154
Moran, Cyril "Butch"　58, 110, 114, 183
Morgan, George (infielder)　62, 125
Morgan, George (mayor)　52
Mossor, Wandel　76, 131, 138
Mueller, Ray　12, 124
Mullens, Ford "Moon"　48
Mulligan, Bill　10
Multnomah Stadium　84, 133
Murphy, George　160

Nelson, Jerry　179
New York Giants　29, 31, 95, 107, 163
Newson, Buck　164
Nicely, Roy　163
Niemic, Al　19, 20, 21, 22
Night baseball　6, 13, 25, 27, 30, 34, 35, 37, 67, 68, 70, 103, 118
Norager, Earl　82, 84
Norbert, Ted　40, 51, 70, 71, 72, 75, 146, 147, 148, 149, 151, 152, 153, 154, 155, 156
Norworth, Jack　110
Novikoff, Lou　149, 181, 182
Nunes, Mel　51, 53, 76, 79, 83, 135, 138, 139, 140

Oakland Oaks　17, 18, 20, 22, 23, 26, 28, 29–31, 32, 34, 35, 38, 39, 44, 45, 53, 54–58, 68, 69, 72, 81, 85, 91, 93–101, 105, 108, 112, 113, 114, 119, 120, 122, 125, 127, 133, 135, 138, 145, 146, 147, 151, 153, 161, 163, 164, 166, 167, 168, 170–178, 180
Oaks Park Emeryville　55, 56, 60, 62, 65, 87, 89, 91, 92, 95, 96, 98, 164, 167, 168, 173, 174, 176
O'Doul, Frank "Lefty"　2, 10, 13, 26, 27, 29, 35, 41, 44, 45, 63, 83, 85, 87, 88, 89, 90, 92, 93, 101, 134, 136, 164, 165, 166, 167, 168, 170, 182
O'Gorek, George　69, 71
Ogrodowski, Ambrose "Bruisie"　27, 86, 89, 90, 166
Old, John B.　1
Olsen, Al　24, 62

Olsen, Barney　16, 18
Olsen, Ray　110, 112, 116, 183
Olson, Culbert (governor)　32
O'Neil, Johnny　51, 76, 132, 133, 136, 140, 154
Orella, Elmer　163, 169
Orphal, John　143, 150
Orrell, Forest "Joe"　35, 51, 54
Osborn, Don　40, 69, 147, 181, 182
Osborne, Wayne　32, 33, 51, 52, 53
Ostrowski, Johnny　40, 44, 71, 72, 75, 181
Otero, Reggie　69, 70, 158, 181, 182
Ott, Al　76, 81
Owen, Marvin　35, 51, 52, 76, 81, 83, 105, 131, 132, 134, 135, 136, 138, 139, 142, 153, 182

Pacheco, Frank　178
Pacific Coast League: A Statisical History (Dennis Snelling)　2
Pafko, Andy　40
Palica, Alex　143, 147
Parsons, Rudy　44, 86
Passero, Joe　149, 150, 151
Patchett, Hal　24, 62, 125, 144, 146, 147, 150, 156, 171, 172, 174
Paton, Roy　181
Patriotic themes at ball barks　10, 87, 103, 110, 166, 172
Paul, Erwin "Babe"　44
Penner, Ken　13, 64
Penrose, Lou　98, 158
Perez, Manny　32
Perry, Ray　27, 163
Petersen, Charlie　44, 68, 79, 80, 83, 85, 131, 134, 135, 136, 137, 139, 166
Petersen, Earl　65, 66
Philadelphia Athletics　176
Philadelphia Phillies　172, 174
Phipps, Jodie　40
Picetti, Vic　100, 170, 171, 172, 174, 175
Piercey, Joe Knowles　86
Pieretti, Marino　51, 54, 76, 83, 85
Pillette, Herman "Old Folks"　75, 117, 123, 158
Pintar, John　64, 65, 119, 158, 163
Pippen, Henry "Cotton"　29, 56, 57, 94, 98
Pittsburgh Pirates　100, 122, 172

Index

Poffenberger, Cletus "Boots" 24
Pollett, Howard 65
Polly, Henry 64, 65
Porter, Earl 118, 158, 160, 183
Portland Beavers 1, 10, 13, 17, 22, 23, 24, 26, 27, 29, 30, 34–36, 38, 39, 40, 41, 46, 47, 51–54, 56, 58, 61, 68, 71, 72, 73, 74, 75, 76–85, 87, 88, 89, 90, 92, 97, 98, 100, 104, 105, 107, 109, 112, 114, 119, 124, 126, 127, 131–143, 145, 146, 147, 148, 149, 150, 151, 152, 153, 154, 159, 161, 164, 166, 167, 169, 176, 180, 181, 184
Portland Boosters Club 51, 78, 103, 134
Portland Oregonian 2
Potocar, Ernie 110, 112, 113
Powers, Dick 118, 158
Powers, Les 110, 113, 114
Prim, Ray 16, 18, 69
Prout, Bill 158, 160, 178, 180
Pulford, Don 76, 132, 133, 137, 138
Pullman cars 6, 160

Quinn, Wellington "Wimpy" 40

Raffensberger, Ken 16, 40
Rail Travel 6, 23, 52, 74, 75, 79, 82, 83, 95, 108, 117, 136, 141, 156, 160, 166, 169
Raimondi, Al 94, 171, 173
Raimondi, Billy 29, 55, 58, 94, 164, 172, 173, 175
Raimondi, Ernie 164, 173
Raimondi, Walter 55, 56
Ramsey, Bill 64, 65, 117
Rationing of Consumer Goods 9
Redmond, Jack 51
Reich, Herman 10, 35
Reishow, Oscar 74
Restelli 69, 86, 88
Reynolds, Vern 125, 178, 183
Rhabe, Nick 140, 141, 142, 182
Richardson, Kenny 59, 110, 183
Rigney, Bill 29, 31, 55
Ripple, Jimmy 107
Rogers, Forest 118
Rogers, Stan "Packy" 51, 76
Roosevelt, Franklin Delano 5, 129, 134, 139, 145, 159, 164, 169, 176, 180
Root, Charlie 32, 44, 58, 109, 183

Rose Bowl Game 1942 6
Rosenberg, Harry 2, 46, 172
Rosenlund, Chet 55, 95
Rosenthal, Larry 134
Rossi, Jack 122
Rossi, Joe 118, 120
Rowland, Clarence "Pants" 77, 92, 141, 174
Roy, Jean-Pierre 65
Ruffing, Charles "Red" 42
Russell, Glen "Rip" 40, 69, 181
Ruth, Babe 32, 101, 154

Sacramento Air Depot 13
Sacramento Senators and Solons: Baseball in California's Capital (John Spalding) 3
Sacramento Solons 11–15, 17, 19, 23, 25, 27, 32, 34, 38, 41, 46, 56, 58, 60, 62, 63, 64–66, 69, 72, 73, 77, 78, 83, 87, 88, 89, 90, 96, 98, 99, 103, 109, 113, 114, 116–124, 126, 127, 133, 137, 141, 143, 146, 149, 150, 152, 153, 157–163, 164, 165, 168, 169, 174, 175, 176, 177, 178, 180, 184
Sacramento Union 2
St. Louis Browns 95, 103, 146
St. Louis Cardinals 14, 18, 38, 64, 116, 117, 139, 178
Salkeld, Bill 24, 62, 124
Salvatierra, Manuel 69, 71
Salveson, Jack 29, 30
Salvo, Manny 94, 95, 97, 98
San Diego Padres 13, 14, 18, 19, 23, 24–26, 27, 29, 32, 36, 45, 46, 53, 56, 58, 59, 62–64, 66, 70, 71, 72, 78, 84, 88, 89, 95, 98, 99, 103, 108, 109, 113, 114, 120, 121, 123, 124–127, 137, 141, 144, 148, 153, 159, 164, 165, 168, 174, 175, 178–180, 181, 184
San Francisco Chronicle 2
San Francisco Seals 13, 15, 17, 18, 20, 25, 26, 27–29, 30, 38, 39, 41, 43–48, 49, 50, 52, 54, 56, 58, 60, 61, 63, 65, 68, 69, 72, 73, 75, 77, 78, 82, 84, 85–93, 96, 98, 100, 104, 109, 111, 115, 116, 120, 121, 123, 124, 126, 127, 136, 137, 139, 146, 147, 150, 151, 155, 161, 162, 163–170, 175, 176, 177, 178, 180, 182, 184

Index

Sanders, Battle Malone "Bones" 163
Sarni, Bill 2, 39, 40, 43, 69, 71, 73
Satchel Paige's All Stars 156, 170
Sauer, Eddie 71, 72
Scarsella, Les 19, 29, 55, 58, 80, 93, 95, 97, 98, 110, 116, 172, 174
Schaefer, Walter "Tilly" 35
Schanz, Charley 62
Schefter, C. T. 36
Schlueter, Norm 158
Schmidt, Curt 131, 135, 137, 138, 160
Schubel, Bill 35
Schulte, Herman "Ham" 29, 32, 34
Schuster, Bill "Broadway" 16, 20, 21, 32, 69
Sciarra, Hank 178
Scribner, Ira 19
Seals Stadium, San Francisco 5, 27, 28, 30, 44, 45, 46, 51, 54, 68, 72, 75, 83, 86, 89, 92, 93, 100, 104, 120, 121, 126, 130, 134, 148, 155, 156, 161, 165, 166, 167, 168, 170, 175, 180
Seats, Tommy 2, 27, 44, 68, 86, 87, 88, 89, 90, 91, 123
Seattle Boosters Club 103
Seattle Post Intelligencer 2
Seattle Rainiers 2, 10, 15, 17, 18, 19–23, 24, 26, 27, 28, 30, 32, 34, 35, 38, 39, 41, 43, 47, 48–51, 52, 53, 58, 61, 63, 71, 72, 74, 80, 81, 83, 88, 89, 94, 97, 99, 100, 101–109, 110, 112, 114, 119, 120, 123, 124, 126, 127, 134, 135, 137, 138, 139, 140, 141, 142, 143–159, 161, 163, 164, 166, 167, 168, 169, 170, 174, 180, 182, 183
Seattle Rainiers: The Glory Years 1938–1942 (Gary Waddingham) 2, 3
Separovich, Yubi 116, 117, 159
Serafini, Mel 64, 118
Seward, Frank 163, 168, 169, 170
Sharp, Jim 110, 183
Shaughnessy Playoffs 11, 26, 29, 46, 54, 68, 131
Shea, Merv 51, 53
Sheely, Earl 117, 118, 157, 158, 159, 163
Sheridan, Neil 90, 91, 93, 170
Shone, Frank 54, 77, 135, 137, 139
Sick, Emil 36, 50, 109
Sicks Stadium, Seattle 5, 20, 80, 102, 103, 105, 106, 107, 109, 137, 139, 146, 150, 153, 154, 155, 156, 170
Silvanic, Frank 172
Sitek, Steve 111
Skaff, Tom 69
Skelley, Mel 24
Skiff, Bill 19, 22, 47, 48, 51, 74, 102, 104, 105, 106, 108, 109, 139, 143, 147, 150, 154, 174
Slotter, Joe 182
Smalley, Roy 69, 71
Smith, Jack 183
Smith, Don 172
Smith, Ron 59, 110, 115, 183
Snell, Earl (governor) 52, 142
Snelling, Dennis 2
Solano, Claudio 178
Soriano, Dewey 19
Souza, Hank 131, 136, 137, 138
Spalding, John 3, 116
Speece, Byron 35, 39, 51, 101, 104, 143
Spindell, Hal 101, 103, 106, 144
Sporting News 2
Sprinz, Joe 27, 44, 86, 91, 166
Statz, Arnold "Jigger" 15, 16, 19, 39
Steinbacher, Henry 44, 86
Steiner, Jim 118, 120, 124
Steiner, Mel 99, 125, 183
Stevens, LeRoy 158, 159, 160, 180
Stewart, Ed 183
Stewart, Glenn "Gabby" 16, 18, 172
Stickle, Ned 19, 20, 22
Stine, Lee 35
Stinson, Frank 24
Storti, Lin 95, 172, 174, 175
Stromme, Floyd 56, 94, 171, 172, 174
Sturdy, Jack 12
Stutz, Ed 27
Sueme, Hal 48, 101, 103, 104, 106, 108, 143, 148, 152
Suhr, Gus 39, 44, 86, 92, 163, 170
Sullivan, Joe 76, 77, 78, 94, 98
Suytar, Jake 65, 117, 121
Sweeney, Bill 16, 32, 39, 40, 72, 73, 74, 75, 109
Swope, Jack 167
Sylvester, Chuck 33

Tauby, Fred 29
Tepler, Boyd 69

Index

Texas League 30
Thomas, Bill 24, 59
Thomas, Fay 51, 57
Thompson, Averett 12
Thompson, Rupert "Tommie" 35, 51, 76, 84, 125, 179, 180
Tincup, Frank 49, 101, 178, 179
Tising, Jack 131, 133, 138, 139, 154
Todd, Al 16
Torgeson, Earl 19
Trahd, Victor 179
Trower, Don 27, 44, 45, 58
Truitt, Rollie 52
Trutta, John 86
Turpin, Hal 19, 20, 24, 48, 49, 101, 102, 103, 143, 148, 149, 154, 156
Tuttle, W. C. 39, 77
Tyack, Jim 164, 181

Uhalt, Bernard "Frenchy" 59, 86, 164, 170
Umpiring Staff, PCL 10, 25, 27, 39, 42, 77, 92, 93, 97, 101, 154, 162
United Nations Conference, San Francisco 130, 165, 166, 172, 180
"Unplayable Conditions" 6, 19, 26, 52, 53

Valenzuela, Joe 124
Vaughn Street Park, Portland 36, 47, 52, 54, 78, 80, 89, 107, 108, 119, 124, 133, 132, 136, 139, 140, 142, 148, 151, 153
Vergez, Johnny 29, 30, 54, 55, 95
Veteran of Foreign Wars 10
Vezlich, Lou 125, 179, 180
Vias, Manny 65, 117, 119, 120, 144, 146
Viers, Ray 181
Vitalich, Ed 24
Vitt, Oscar 32
Vivalda, Jo 158, 160

Waddingham, Gary 3

Waitkus, Eddie 16, 18
War Bond Sales 44, 59, 89, 121, 160, 174
War Department 6, 95
War Manpower Commission 130, 131, 166, 171
Warren, Earl (governor) 65, 172
Watson, Ralph 118, 119, 122, 183
Weldon, Alex 110
Werle, Bill 86
Westlake, Wally 29
Wetmore, Ray 158, 178
Wheeler, Ed 62, 125
Whipple, Jack 24, 62, 125, 144, 147, 148, 178
White, Don 27
White, Joyner "Jo-Jo" 19, 143, 148, 157, 163
Williams, Bob 183
Willingham, Hugh 183
Willis, Dick 179
Wilson, Jack 51, 54, 76, 81
Wilson, Woodrow 5
Windsor, George 76
Wolf, Al 1
Womak, Jerry 159, 178, 180
Wood, Joe, Jr. 124, 158, 162
World War II 1, 2
Wright, Al "A-1" 35, 95
Wrigley Field, Los Angeles 13, 16, 17, 18, 19, 26, 33, 34, 41, 42, 45, 51, 57, 58, 59, 61, 62, 69, 71, 72, 74, 82, 109, 111, 112, 115, 126, 127, 141, 149, 164

Yellovic, John 29, 101, 103
York, Tony 73
Young, Del 32, 34, 44, 45, 46, 86, 88
Younker, Roy 33, 58, 59, 110, 115, 131, 138, 139, 140, 158, 160

Zidlich, Matt 172
Zipay, Ed 158
"Zoot suitors" 108, 122